THE BLACK PRINCE
OF 1355-1357

THE BLACK PRINCE'S EXPEDITION

OF

1355-1357

H.J.HEWITT

Dear Poppa

Happy Christmas 2009

love from

Bonnie, Paul, Alec and
Fiona x

Pen & Sword

First published in Great Britain in 1958 by Manchester University Press
Published in 2004 in this format by

PEN & SWORD MILITARY
an imprint of
Pen & Sword Books Limited, 47 Church Street
Barnsley, South Yorkshire S70 2AS

Copyright © H.J. Hewitt 1958

ISBN 1 84415 217 0

The right of H.J. Hewitt to be identified as Author of the Work
has been asserted by him in accordance with the Copyright, Designs and
Patents Act 1988.
A CIP catalogue record for this book
is available from the British Library.

Printed and bound in Great Britain by
CPI UK

Pen & Sword Books Ltd incorporates the imprints of
Pen & Sword Aviation, Pen & Sword Maritime, Pen & Sword Military,
Wharncliffe Local History, Pen & Sword Select,
Pen & Sword Military Classics and Leo Cooper.

For a complete list of Pen & Sword titles please contact:
PEN & SWORD BOOKS LIMITED
47 Church Street, Barnsley, South Yorkshire, S70 2AS, England.
E-mail: enquiries@pen-and-sword.co.uk
Website: www.pen-and-sword.co.uk

CONTENTS

CONTENTS

PREFACE

In preparing the following pages, I have not sought to make a contribution to the history of the Art of War. That would have restricted my work to ground already well covered. Nor have I tried to fill gaps in the work of Oman, Longman, Mackinnon, Tout, Belloc, Denifle, Molinier, Delachenal, Lot. For those writers the expedition of 1355-7 was but one episode in the complex history of the fourteenth century and they necessarily chose for treatment only those aspects which were relevant to their themes. Indeed they dealt with little more than campaigning and, in so far as the purpose of the expedition was the advancement of the Plantagenet cause, its means military pressure exerted on the subjects of the French king and its method destruction, a study of the campaigns may appear sufficient to relate the expedition to the course of national history. Yet the expeditionary force included men who had been chosen, armed, clothed, paid, assembled, transported, reinforced—as well as led on the march and in battle. It contained men who were interested in getting loot and prisoners as well as in fighting. It had moreover to be brought back to England with its important captives. To these aspects little or no attention has been given. Nor have writers dealt with the Cheshire archers, the shipping for the two sea journeys, the awards for service, and the fact that statecraft as well as force of arms was to be used.

There is room, therefore, for a more comprehensive account of the expedition than has yet appeared. In attempting to present such an account, I have felt that the purely military and political aspects, though important, need no emphasis; that the best service one could give to the reader was to try to present the expedition 'in the round' so that he might see the body of men sent out, their diverse origins and motives, their experiences and rewards as well as their feats of arms.

Three circumstances have determined the shape of the work here presented. First, of course, come the nature and quantity of the evidence available for study. Next, though I desired to be fairly comprehensive, I have omitted a formal consideration of the financial aspect of the expedition for two reasons: it is inextricably bound up with the general finance of the war; it is also the subject of specialist study now well advanced. But the most important factor has had to be my own judgment of what was necessary to give some kind of unity to the work and proportion to its parts.

So much has been written about the battle of Poitiers that I would have preferred to avoid treating it at all. To have done so, however, would have robbed the expedition of its chief glory and impaired the unity I sought. I have, therefore, followed my general principle: the fighting has its due place, but there are other aspects of the battle and to these also I have given some attention.

I regret that it has not been possible to do justice to two groups of men, namely the Gascons and the Welsh. The former suggested the expedition, sincerely welcomed it, aided it in both campaigns and at the battle of Poitiers; and their leaders were both active and resourceful. An assessment of their importance must, however, rest in part on the number of men they contributed and for that, unfortunately, there is no evidence. As regards the men of North Wales, again the evidence is disappointing. A mere fragment of the Black Prince's Register for that region has survived. If we had the sections for the years 1357 and 1358, it is likely that we should find entries of 'honourable mention' and interesting rewards comparable with those given to the Cheshire men.

I have searched French libraries for the work of learned societies and local historians and have had the privilege of meeting the archivists, departmental and city, at Toulouse, Bordeaux and Poitiers. I have also corresponded with the archivists in several other French towns. Broadly it may be said that French archives, national and local, contain little material relevant to this study; and that Delachenal, Moisant, Molinier and Breuils have utilized most of the matter which is of French origin. A few French studies have cleared up obscurities in the chroniclers' accounts of the prince's route through Languedoc.

However unreliable Froissart may be in points of detail, he is indispensable for his picture of the age. His *Chronicles* have therefore been used—discriminatingly, I hope—and, generally, where it seemed helpful to quote his words, I have felt that the Globe edition of Lord Berners' translation served my purpose better than a rendering into modern English.

It is not possible to do for the campaigns of 1355 and 1356 what Wrottesley did for that of Crécy, but the Nominal Roll (Appendix C) may prove of interest to historians of the fourteenth century. Though for the sake of conciseness, only a single reference is quoted, many of the names may be followed in the indexes of the Black Prince's Register and the Calendar of Patent Rolls and in other parts of Henxteworth's journal.

The attempt to depict a medieval expedition 'in the round' has compelled me to venture into administration, arms, diplomacy, finance, geography, law, shipping, topography and several other fields cultivated by specialists. To have escaped all errors in so wide a study is more than one can expect. Comprehensiveness is not attained without risks.

H. J. HEWITT.

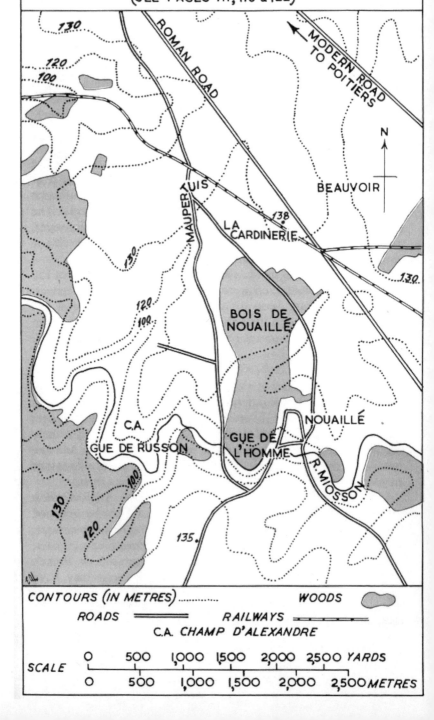

THE BATTLEFIELD AT POITIERS

ANGLO-GASCON FORCES STATIONED AT THE NORTHERN END
OF NOUAILLÉ WOOD FACING N.N.W.
(SEE PAGES III, 116 & 122)

CHAPTER I

THE BACKGROUND

Pᴿɪɴᴄᴇ Eᴅᴡᴀʀᴅ's expedition of 1355 opened a new chapter in the Hundred Years War, in the history of Guienne and in the work of the prince.

In the early phases of the long conflict, both naval and military engagements had on the whole been favourable to the English cause. The victory at Sluys had given Edward III an ascendancy on the sea and cemented an alliance in the north; Crécy had humbled the French king and his nobles; the capture of Calais had given the English a foothold on French soil the importance of which both sides appreciated; the campaign of Henry, Earl (later duke) of Lancaster had shown that English power could be exerted elsewhere than in the north. But the effect of these successes was quite insufficient to shake the Valois monarchy. King Edward could not attain the throne of France without a greater and more sustained effort than had hitherto been attempted.

Three circumstances had prevented the launching of another great campaign. The first was the pestilence which temporarily disorganized social, economic and military activity in western Europe. The second was a condition inherent in the nature of society both in England and in France: neither nation could yet maintain a large army in the field for a long time. The third was the constant policy of the papacy of offering its mediation. Edward, though encouraged by successes, was far from his goal. King Philip, though conscious of the serious blows France had sustained, was in no mood for conceding Edward's claims. Peace was unattainable, but a pause in the fighting might be welcome. A truce was arranged in September 1347 and extended again and again, while representatives of the two nations met and sought to make a peace.

The terms agreed upon had been simple. All the states, belligerent or allied, were included; all sieges in Guienne, Poitou and Brittany were to end immediately; men wishing to pay their ransoms were to have safe-conducts; merchants were to be free to come and go as in time of peace; men were appointed to deal with the breaches of the truce. These terms remained, or were understood to remain, in operation down to the renewal of hostilities in 1355.

The search for a permanent peace filled the years 1348–55 with diplomatic activity. From the palace at Avignon, Clement VI and Innocent VI sent envoys to the courts of the two adversaries and letter after letter was dispatched not only to the envoys, urging the seriousness of their tasks, but also to the kings begging them to dispose themselves to make peace. The letters reveal a gradual hardening of English opinion and growing doubts in English minds about the impartiality of the envoys. Peace was not achieved. The termination of the truce was, however, postponed several times for another year or similar period.

But the skill of diplomats and the good offices of the papacy could not produce a settlement acceptable to both kings. There was as yet scarcely any national sentiment in France. The rule of an English duke in Aquitaine was not repugnant to the people of Gascony. For the most part, it accorded with their inherited sentiments and their commercial interests. Nor was it necessarily at variance with feudal theory: vassals were not obliged to be of the same nation as their overlord. Yet in practice, it was opposed to deep-seated forces operating slowly and imperceptibly towards the union under the French monarchy of all parts of the region known as France. Edward's status was anomalous. As King of England, he was the French king's equal; as Duke of Aquitaine, he was his vassal, obliged in feudal law not only to recognize his suzerainty but also to do him homage for his fief. To this anomalous relationship, Edward had added his claim to the French throne. For purposes of negotiation, he was prepared at times to withdraw this claim in return for formal recognition of the independence of Gascony of the French kingdom. The French, however, could never bind themselves by treaty to such recognition.

An analogous difficulty had existed generations earlier when English kings had been dukes of Normandy. The danger to the kingdom of France arising from that dual status had been removed by Philip Augustus—by force. It remained to remove the danger arising from the inheritance of the duchy of Aquitaine— by force or by other means. Legal process was less expensive and more subtle than open warfare. Gascon subjects of the English king were encouraged to 'appeal' to the highest feudal court. Cases were heard in Paris. At the best, Edward's authority was undermined; at the worst, territory was confiscated. By legal process, the French monarch was nibbling pieces of the English dominions and the gradual diminution of territory could not be arrested. Against legal expropriation Edward had no remedy.

Negotiations, however, appeared at last to be approaching agreement. By April 1354, the plenipotentiaries and two cardinals, assembled at Guines, had formulated a draft treaty by which Edward would renounce his claim to the French throne while John would recognize the independence of the duchy of Aquitaine. That is to say, Edward would be freed for ever from the status of vassal of the French king. As the ratification was to take place in the autumn at Avignon, the Duke of Lancaster, the Bishop of Norwich and the Earl of Arundel were empowered to treat for a final treaty of peace at the papal court. They travelled with an impressive retinue and were given an ostentatious welcome, but no treaty was signed. The French representatives repudiated the terms agreed upon at Guines and the conference had no better result than the prolongation of the truce till midsummer, 1355.

While, however, John, aiming always at the integrity of his kingdom, was determined not to cede a foot of French territory, there were in France particularist forces thwarting his purposes and, at the same time, offering opportunities for English intervention in France. At one time or another, they showed themselves in the coastal areas of Flanders, Artois, Normandy, Brittany, Aquitaine. One such manifestation now occurred in the north where Charles le Mauvais transferred his allegiance and proposed an alliance with the English king. Charles was not only King of Navarre, but also had very extensive possessions in Evreux, Mortain, Port Audemer, Cherbourg, Valognes and Carentan which made him one of the most powerful lords in Normandy. For Edward, wearied of the endless negotiations, Charles's intrigue presented useful support in France against the French king. A treaty was made with him and a promise that troops should be dispatched to help him.

Within a few weeks, another opening for English intervention occurred. A group of barons arrived from Gascony to complain to the king about the policy of Jean d'Armagnac, the lieutenant of the French king in Languedoc, and to ask Edward to allow his son, the Prince of Wales, to go to Gascony.

Satisfied that further negotiations with the French offered little likelihood of a tolerable settlement, and assured of support on French soil for military action, Edward turned his mind towards a renewal of the war. Certain steps taken early in 1355 may perhaps foreshadow a policy not declared till April. In February, three ships were requisitioned to convey victuals for the king's castles in Gascony.[1] The king and the younger Bartholomew de Burghersh received papal permission to defer promised visits to Santiago de Compostella.[2] Early in March, orders were given to requisition ships for the transport of the Earl of Warwick and other magnates to Gascony.[3] John de Chiverston was appointed seneschal of Gascony.[4]

Early in April a clear declaration was made. To the papal nuncios who had come to England with their customary large escort, the king stated that he would not assent to an extension of the truce because the French had used these periods to inflict grievous damage on his overseas possessions. He would confer with his Council and communicate his decision through his own envoy. In short, the two countries would be at war from the following midsummer. In the Council, it was decided that the Prince of Wales should go to Gascony with an army.[5]

Before the end of April, the machinery for assembling ships was in motion and preliminary payments had been made to the magnates who were to accompany the prince.[6] On June 1st, in letters addressed to the archbishops, the king explained that the French envoys to the pope had repudiated the agreement made at Guines and that he was obliged, therefore, to renew the war.[7]

The region to which the Prince of Wales was to go was called in English writings of the fourteenth century Aquitaine, Guienne or Gascony without careful distinction. Aquitaine is of course used to describe the duchy (and later the principality), but in the records, in English chronicles and in Froissart, the name most commonly used is Gascony. French chronicles and modern French historians, on the other hand, usually distinguish Gascony from Guienne and, where precision is unnecessary, they commonly use Guienne. The men drawn from the region between the Pyrenees and Saintonge who joined the prince as allies, used as their battle-cry 'Guienne, St. George' or simply 'Guienne'.

Long before the middle of the fourteenth century, Aquitaine, Guienne and Gascony had ceased to be political units: they had become broad regions divided between the French and English.

The great heritage which Eleanor of Aquitaine had brought to the English crown had been reduced to a strip stretching about two hundred miles along the coast from southern Saintonge (near Rochefort) to the Pyrenees (near Hendaye) and extending inland between thirty and sixty miles. It included however the two bases of English strategy, the Basque country with Bayonne and the lower Garonne with Bordeaux. This was the region which had been suffering losses by French encroachments and bearing the brunt of recent French aggression; the region which had sent to England the call for help; which was to form the base for the prince's operations and to provide him with armed support against the French.

That the inhabitants of this region were anglophile is not surprising. During the two centuries that had elapsed since the marriage which had united the duchy of Guienne with the kingdom of England, the duke-kings had contrived to maintain and strengthen the loyalty of their subjects to their person. Henry II had visited the duchy several times before handing it to his son, Richard Coeur de Lion. Richard in his turn had lived there more than in England. John, it is true, had not paid the duchy a visit, but Henry III and Edward I had spent periods there and at various times royalty had been represented by a member or relative of the reigning family—a Richard of Cornwall, a Simon de Montfort, and a Henry, Earl of Lancaster.

The system of administration under which both the Seneschal of Gascony and the Constable of Bordeaux were appointed by the English king (and were in practice English born) had maintained a steady, political link with England. On the other hand, many secondary posts were held by Gascons; the King's Council in Gascony included the greater barons; in the Three Estates of Gascony the nobles had at least some semblance of consultation over extraordinary taxation. The machinery of government here, as elsewhere, had many imperfections but, in the view of M. Boutruche, 'Guienne (with Normandy) was the best organized of the great fiefs of the period'.[8]

In addition to these political links, there were personal contacts which helped to maintain understanding between England and its distant possessions. Gascon lords attended the English court; Gascon merchants went to England to buy corn; Gascon wine-vendors were constantly dealing with English traders, while English men went to Gascony on royal or private business, and every *chevauchée* brought a crowd of English nobles and men into the country.

But the deepest reason for the continued loyalty of the Gascons to the English king lay in self-interest. For them the Anglo-French conflict was merely a dynastic or feudal quarrel. The ideal of the ultimate union of all the people between the Pyrenees and the Channel in a single state under the king of France, could not yet evoke warm sympathy in the south-west. Their ideal was limited and expressed itself in the battle-cry 'Guienne, St. George' or even 'Guienne'. Its duke was their natural lord; they followed him; the moral grounds of their position were quite clear. The economic grounds were even more evident. Though Gascony enjoyed a considerable trade with northern Europe, her greatest customer was England. In the fourteenth century, she was prosperous and every English *chevauchée* increased her prosperity. The English kings scrupulously respected the municipal and trading rights not only of Bordeaux but also of the smaller towns and, when conflicts of rights arose—and conflicts were frequent— royal policy lay in seeking reconciliation.[9]

At heart, the Gascons were particularist. If complete autonomy was impracticable, they enjoyed under English rule a greater measure of freedom than would be permitted under French rule, and a greater measure of prosperity through their close ties with England than could be attained by a closer tie with France.

But loyalty to the English cause involved exposure to French attack during each fighting period of the war. Between 1337 and 1340, French forces had moved down the valleys of the Garonne and the Dordogne, taking possession of St. Macaire and La Réole, reaching the outskirts of Libourne and St. Emilion and engaging in furious fighting around Bourg and Blaye.[10] During the truce, a deputation of Gascon nobles had gone to England (as another deputation was to go in 1355) to point out to Edward III their need for protection [11] and, when the war was renewed in 1345, the Earl of Derby had turned back the tide, regained the places recently lost and captured also Bergerac, Auberoche, and Aiguillon.

The situation appeared to be saved and, during the suspension (or partial suspension) of hostilities between 1347 and 1355, the Gascon towns which had suffered so seriously during these two episodes were repaired and re-fortified.[12] Actually, however, the situation was quite unstable: no Channel divided the forces of the opposing sides and the frontier was an ill-defined line which moved as pressure was exerted from one direction or the other. Derby's vigorous policy had pressed it eastward but he was withdrawn in 1351. His successor, the Earl of Stafford, was less active. Soon much of Derby's work was undone. Late in 1352, Jean d'Armagnac was appointed lieutenant-general of the French king in Languedoc and the neighbouring provinces. In January 1353, he accepted the return to the French side of certain leaders who had favoured the English side,[13] and in February he began the siege of Saint Antonin in Rouergue.[14] He also sent companies to besiege towns and castles between Agen and Perigueux. Still further measures portended trouble for the Gascons. The consuls of Agen took steps to prevent the exportation of corn to Gascony; the States of Languedoc, assembled by Jean d'Armagnac, voted a large sum which was to be collected immediately, and the Seneschaussée of Carcassonne voted a sum to be collected in three instalments, for the continuance of the struggle; an Ordinance laid down that every man should furnish himself with arms.[15]

The siege of Saint Antonin was raised temporarily in accordance with the terms of a truce but it was renewed in June 1353 when small-scale warfare broke out over a considerable area especially round Beauville. Agen supplied two hundred pioneers 'to go and do damage' to 'enemy lands'. The English resisted. Places changed hands during the fighting but the outcome was that Aiguillon and Praysass fell to the French,[16] the English withdrew and by the end of 1354, Jean d'Armagnac had established an ascendancy which threatened the English possessions in Gascony.

It was in these circumstances that the Gascon lords went to England to lay the situation before King Edward. Their problem was defence. It was imperative that the aggressive policy of Armagnac should be withstood. The help of English forces was needed. Since, however, no English king or heir to the throne had visited Gascony for more than half a century, it would be politically advantageous—it would in fact enhance Gascon loyalty [17]— if the forces were led by one of the king's sons.

Viewed against the wider background of Anglo-French relations the situation presented an opportunity for action on a larger scale. The depredations of Armagnac and his troops had generated sufficient hostility to ensure support for the king if he chose to strike a blow from Gascony to advance his major aim. An

expedition could be sent which would not confine itself to pro-
tective or punitive measures, nor even to counter-attack. It might
demonstrate in southern France the king's determination to press
his claim to the French throne as clearly as other expeditions
demonstrated his will and power in the north. And the appropriate leader would be the heir to the throne.

In June 1355, the prince reached the age of twenty-five. He had
a household of his own at Kennington, a Council which managed
his estates, a revenue which, though great, was insufficient for
the way of life he had chosen. He was not married.

Born heir to the throne, he had been subjected to the influences
which mould the life and character of most of the young men who,
regardless of taste or aptitude, are destined for the highest office.
The nation expects the heir to respect the constitution, to live
with suitable style and to play the part of heir apparent with
dignity, generosity and a certain modesty. It expects him also to
acquit himself worthily in those spheres which are, at his time,
regarded as appropriate for royal interest. Provided the prince
keeps these ends in view and is not conspicuously self-indulgent,
the nation will esteem him highly, note his graces, approve his
virtues and see in him the embodiment of an ideal.

But, as he crosses the threshold of manhood, there comes a
testing time. 'All the world', wrote Bagehot,[18] 'and all the glory
of it, whatever is most attractive, whatever is most seductive, has
always been offered to the Prince of Wales of the day and always
will be. It is not rational to expect the best virtue where temptation
is applied in the most trying form at the frailest time of human
life.' Duty struggles with pleasure. The ideal of the dedicated life
becomes more difficult to maintain. Often the shining youth
passes imperceptibly into an ordinary man. Mediocrity, however,
is not a bar to high esteem. It is sufficient for the princely office
that he should play the princely part.

Now the part a Prince of Wales should play in the middle of the
fourteenth century had been determined while the prince was in
his teens and was clear before he was twenty. Edward III had
been a successful king in the plain sense of the term. He was con-
spicuous for vigour, delight and skill in arms, a brilliant court,
a love of the ceremonial side of chivalry; and he was conducting
a war in France in which knights might gain distinction. These
things the nation approved. And a prince who wished to acquit

himself worthily, could not but strive to fit himself for a role which brought the king personal satisfaction and enjoyed the support of the nobles, the parliament and the people. That such an aim coincided in large measure with Prince Edward's tastes and natural aptitudes is likely. It cannot have failed to mould them.

No heir to the throne had greater opportunities of learning the art of kingship. Born of young parents, brought up at the court, trained by Walter Burley, Sir Walter Manny and Sir Bartholomew de Burghersh, associating with the distinguished men in church and state who visited the court, deputizing for his father in the council during his absences, he must have been familiar since childhood with the machinery and business of government and the principal issues of the period. He had accompanied Edward III in the invasion of Normandy in 1346, had been knighted on French soil, had fought at Crécy, taken part in the operations around Calais and in the sea battle of Les Espagnols sur Mer.

The experience thus gained might be regarded as the normal training for medieval kingship but, by this time, evidence of the prince's own disposition begins to appear. He was the youngest member of the Order of the Garter and seeking to play a part in that distinguished companionship. Familiar with the ideals of chivalry, he was in a favourable position to put them into practice: the court provided one theatre of operations, the tilting ground another. He attended the jousts and participated in some of them.[19] He designed bits for his destriers.[20] He provided the members of the Order with garters, buckles, girdle-tips, bars and ouches.[21] For Audley and Chandos he bought pairs of plates covered with black velvet and for himself plates covered with red velvet.[22] Other presents of armour or horses were given freely to his friends,[23] almost all of them older men, who had had opportunities of gaining knightly distinction before the long truce which had interrupted his own career. It was in terms of achievements in arms that he looked to the future. Twelve years later, he was regarded as the finest living example of knightliness—the 'flower of chivalry'. Froissart endorsed the view [24] and the *Chronique Des Quatre Premiers Valois* described him as 'one of the best knights in the world, in his time renowned above all'.[25]

Subsequent ages have, however, so enlarged the meaning of chivalry that it is necessary to define its scope in the fourteenth century.[26] At that time, Loyalty and Prowess were its chief components. Chivalry accepted the social order as it stood. It refined behaviour at the court and formalized a code for the tournament and even the battlefield, but it stood in no relation to the principles of social equality implied in the question 'Who was then the gentleman?', nor was it expected to show mercy and loving kindness to non-combatants. Chivalry was in fact compatible with stark, ruthless slaughter and the prince was shortly to reveal a streak of cold indifference to human suffering.[27]

But princeliness, as he practised it, was costly and he did not stint his generosity. To his friends he made gifts of money, of horses, of pieces of armour, of jewellery, of mugs of gold, silver or silver-gilt enamelled, while coursers, destriers, sumpter horses, carthorses and palfreys were given not only to friends but to mere acquaintances and even to messengers from important people.[28] He spent large sums at 'play' (probably dice) [29] and he bought for himself elaborate and very costly jewellery.[30] By 1355, his personal expenditure and lavish gifts had loaded his treasury with debt. Messengers hastened to exact revenues at the earliest possible moments and loans were contracted on the security of coming revenue. The reasons for this prodigality must remain a subject for conjecture. It was not a recent tradition. (His father had become king at the age of sixteen. His grandfather had become king nearly half a century earlier at the age of twenty-three without undue princely extravagance.) It may have been calculated policy. It may have been the outcome of uncalculating generosity or simply of weakness.

Though his finances were embarrassed, his zeal to acquit himself worthily in arms remained undiminished. The truce with France had lasted nearly eight years. Its termination afforded a prospect of distinction in campaigning. He was glad that the Captal de Buch made the request for his presence in Gascony [31] and he begged the king to let him be the first to pass beyond the sea.[32] King, Council and Parliament approved both requests.

By the fourteenth century, warfare had come to be regarded as subject in some measure to rules which ought to be observed by both (or all) sides in a conflict. The terms 'laws of war', 'law of arms', 'laws of chivalry' were used by the chroniclers [33] and if, as was inevitable, such laws (having the nature of international conventions) could not be enforced, they nevertheless became

well-established customs the breach of which might be cited as
irregular or even dishonourable. Their origin is twofold. On the
one hand, the general desire for some agreed mode of conduct in
recurrent situations (for example, the surrender of a town) leads
to the recognition of formal relationships between combatants
and between victor and vanquished. This advance has an international quality in that leaders of opposing forces regard it as
binding on one another. On the other hand, chivalry was already
an international institution uniting a fighting class in the maintenance of certain principles and softening the formal relationships
created by law. Where, for example, in law a prisoner was the
property of his captor, in chivalry he was ensured good treatment
during his captivity; where, in law, the payment of a ransom
could be demanded before he was released, in chivalry he might
be released on parole in order to make arrangements for raising
the sum needed for his ransom.

The laws and customs of war did not distinguish between combatants and non-combatants. However deplorable it might be to
an observer (and Froissart often deplored it), when a town was
taken by assault, the inhabitants as well as the garrison were at the
victor's mercy. Usually the commander and men of gentle birth
were made prisoners, noble women (if there were any) were
spared and a few rich townsmen from whom good ransoms
might be expected, escaped death. But the remainder—unless
they had managed to flee—might be, and often were, massacred.

The non-combatant's life, then, was not secure. Neither were
his liberty nor his goods. When taken prisoner, he was carried
away for negotiations over his ransom. His cattle, grain and wine
were appropriated without recompense by the commander of the
invading army, while his gold, silver and other valuables were
seized by the soldiers and became their property.

While therefore warriors, in very many instances, sincerely
desired to engage in deeds of arms and to win fame for prowess,
there were also opportunities for material enrichment. Froissart
indeed sums up the advantages of the victory at Poitiers by uniting the two ends. All those who accompanied the prince, he says,
'were made rich with honour and goods'.[34] Warfare was expected
to be profitable and the most remunerative course was the taking
of prisoners who could pay large ransoms for release. Broadly
speaking, the knight who made the capture was entitled to
negotiate and keep a large part of the ransom.[35] Noble prisoners

were sometimes held for long periods pending the transfer (in specie) of the sums agreed upon.

The release of great prisoners might, however, be the subject of political as well as financial bargaining. The king therefore—or at least the English king—reserved the right to hold such captives and to conduct the negotiations himself. Their captors were, of course, suitably recompensed: John Copeland who had managed to capture David, King of Scotland, in 1346, had been very handsomely rewarded, as every man in the prince's army must have known, and Thomas de Holland had received a large sum for capturing the Count of Eu and handing him over to the king. The possibility that the coming expedition might make some valuable captures was formally noted in the indenture made between the king and the prince. There was even a clause safeguarding the king's rights should the 'head' of the war be captured.[36]

It must be added that prisoners held for ransom were usually well treated. If they were knights, they were regarded as honourable guests who happened to be subjects of another king. They might be released on parole and arrangements were made in the terms of truces for them to move across the frontiers in order to pay instalments of their ransoms or to return, as in good faith they did return, to their captors if such instalments were not paid. Honourable treatment also was usually given to hostages and to envoys.

To sum up, while war was terribly cruel for non-combatants and while the archers shot with grave intent to kill and had to defend themselves with all their might against the massive weight of mail-clad cavalry, conventions had arisen which governed the conduct and, in some measure, softened the rigours of war for members of the knightly class.

For them, war had some of the elements of a game or a dangerous sport reserved for nobles. Training was expensive and exacting. Tournaments were great social occasions. Knights of the Golden Fleece and of the Star as well as Knights of the Garter were invited to, and participated in, the contests. And the rules and spirit and splendour of the jousting field tended to be carried to the battlefield. It was magnificent but it was not war. Edward III, though an accomplished knight and a lover of ceremony and splendour, discouraged the holding of tournaments. King John on the other hand encouraged them.

Individual achievement, whether on the jousting field or the battlefield, was prized not only as a military but also as a social distinction, for individual achievement was proof of prowess, the most esteemed of soldierly qualities; and prowess consisted in a union of acquired skill in arms with great daring.[37] So greatly was prowess valued that generalship was overshadowed. Command went to the king, a member of his family or a great noble with but slight regard to fitness for the office; honour went to him who fought most valiantly. There was no 'general staff', no maps, no adequate knowledge of resources. Older knights had no doubt acquired some knowledge of tactics, but many campaigns were marked by an absence of strategy.[38] They consisted in devastation—combining insult with injury—along a line of march which might lead towards the enemy capital or to no clearly defined objective. It has become usual to consider these enterprises as raids rather than campaigns, but the contemporaries of the Black Prince did not distinguish the one from the other. The king himself with a large army in Normandy or Henry, Duke of Lancaster with a medium sized army in Gascony used the same measures as a humbler commander fighting on the Scottish border. The enterprises differed in scale rather than in kind.

CHAPTER II

THE PREPARATIONS

THE spring and early summer of 1355 formed a period of busy preparations for the coming war. In accordance with the undertakings given to Charles le Mauvais and to the Gascon lords, plans were made for the dispatch of troops to Normandy and to Guienne. The king also declared that he would lead an army against his enemies. There were, therefore, to be three expeditions, related in purpose but distinct in their theatres of operations. At no time had England put forth such efforts as she did in this summer to provide men, horses, arms and shipping for the furtherance of the war against France.

To the archbishops, the chancellors of the universities and the chief officers of four orders of friars, the king explained briefly the reasons for the renewal of the war and asked that prayers should be said for himself and his men.[1] That request alone would have made all England aware of the new policy.

Other measures affected other aspects of the national life. It was necessary of course to arrest suitable ships and assemble them in the first place in the Thames estuary and at Southampton or at Plymouth. It became necessary—as was common in periods of war in the fourteenth century—to control the movements of men, of provisions and even of prices. No one was to go overseas without the king's express consent;[2] no corn was to be exported except to Calais.[3] As the needs of the great expeditions gave rise to the hoarding of wine and an increase in its price, orders were given for the inspection of wine cellars throughout London, the listing of quantities of wine in store and for compulsory sale at the ordained price to the magnates and other lieges so that the national effort might not be delayed.[4] The great demand for armour had led to enhanced prices. Armourers' stores, therefore, were to be examined, their goods appraised and put on sale at reasonable prices to 'the magnates and other lieges about to set out for the defence of the realm'.[5]

As rumours reached England of French preparations for the destruction of English shipping and the invasion of English territory, orders were given in the southern counties that no ship should put to sea unless it were well armed, that all ships in harbour were to be kept close inshore, and that the men of these counties should provide themselves with arms meet for the defence of their regions.[6] Beacons were to be set up on the hills 'as is customary' so that men might be warned of the arrival of enemies and go promptly to 'the places where most danger is feared'.[7]

It was during the months of May and June that the men were recruited for the expeditions one of which forms the subject of this work.

The force the prince was to lead falls into two distinct parts— his personal following and the retinues of the magnates appointed to accompany him. In order to obtain men for his part, the prince turned first to his earldom of Chester, a region long distinguished for the number of soldiers it had furnished for the royal armies. Distinct from England in government, possessed of avowries [8] in which criminals fleeing from justice might find shelter, it had found large contingents for the conquest of North Wales, for the wars of Edward I in Scotland and for the armies which fought in France in 1346-7.[9] Cheshire men, moreover, were serving under a Cheshire commander, Sir Hugh Calveley, in the minor war which continued in the early fifties in Brittany in spite of the truce.[10]

For purposes of administration, Flintshire was linked with Cheshire, while North Wales was also administered by the prince's officers. The three areas thus associated were enjoying the benefits of peace. The mineral wealth of Flintshire was being developed and Chester had become a market for a large part of North Wales.[11] Though Welsh national feeling had not died down, the age-long hostility of Celt and Saxon was softened. In these circumstances Welsh soldiers had been used in English armies fighting in Scotland and in France.[12] Flintshire, therefore, and North Wales as well as Cheshire were areas from which troops might be obtained.

For recruiting purposes, the three areas were of course quite distinct. From Cheshire, only archers were raised. From Wales, the men raised were usually half archers and the other half armed with lances. Cheshire archers received higher rates of pay than Welsh archers. Moreover, Englishmen resident in Wales never served in Welsh units.[13]

Before the middle of the fourteenth century, soldiers drawn

from these three areas went to war in uniforms (*cotecourtepiȝ*) of green and white and wore hats of the same colours.[14] By this time, the practice of providing clothing for troops was becoming fairly common, but it is claimed that the Welsh were the first troops to appear on a continental battlefield in uniform.[15] How the uniforms were made is not clear. The justice or the chamberlain (of Chester) bought the cloth. It was the chamberlain's duty in 1347 to 'deliver to each (man) a short coat and a hat of both colours, the green on the right',[16] but the only reference to tailoring I have found occurs in a charge of 50*s.* for 'cutting and sewing the said *cotecourtepiȝ*' (1328).[17] From the entries for both the Cheshire and the North Wales men in 1355, it might be inferred that the soldiers received the cloth and were responsible for its making up.[18]

In 1346 and 1347, the archers chosen from these areas for the French war were always paid in advance for the number of days estimated to be needed for their journey from the county boundary till they reached the port of embarkation or till they joined the prince. When the number is stated, it is usually fourteen, fifteen or sixteen, the route being via Sandwich or Dover.[19] Such payments were no doubt indispensable for subsistence on the journey. They would also lessen the difficulties of the conducting officer. There were occasions when Welsh troops refused to set out till payment had been made.[20]

With the prospective renewal of war in 1355, the prince turned to the old sources of supply for fighting men. It is not to be inferred that his titles and his connections with the region had yet gained for him great popularity in these parts. He had never visited his principality. Not till 1353 did he visit his earldom of Chester and then the occasion was a threatened rising which he quelled by a display of force, followed by very heavy fines.[21] He had not led an army in battle and, although it is likely that after his victory and his return to England in 1357, strong personal attachment would have been found, in 1355 recruitment can have had little relation to sentiment.

In April or May 1355, the prince conferred with some of his Cheshire knights and esquires concerning fees of war and then issued his orders. From the various divisions of the county of Cheshire, three hundred of 'the best and most skilful archers', were to be raised by the normal processes ('choose, test and array') and, in addition, 'the hundred best and most skilful archers that can be found in the county'.[22] Moreover, the prince's needs were to come before all others.[23] From Flintshire, one hundred archers were to be raised [24] and from North Wales one hundred and forty men. (Whether these were archers is not clear.) [25]

The leaders of the Cheshire men were to be as follows: Macclesfield Hundred, Sir John Hyde and Robert Legh; Eddisbury Hundred, Robert Brown; Wirral and Broxton Hundreds (jointly) Hamo de Mascy and Hugh Golbourne; Nantwich Hundred, Sir John Griffyn.[26] Gronou ap Griffith was to lead the men of North Wales.[27] For the men of Flintshire no leader is mentioned.

The knights received 2s. a day, the esquires and Gronou ap Griffith 1s. a day, Cheshire archers 6d. a day, archers of Flintshire and men of the North Wales contingent 3d. a day.[28] This last group was divided into seven vintaines, each twentieth man (vintener) being paid 6d. a day. There was also one Welsh chaplain who received 6d. a day.[29]

The usual green and white uniforms and hats were provided— one suit for each man.[30]

The three contingents were to proceed to Plymouth and the Cheshire men were to reach that port by mid-July.[31] They would have to provide for themselves as they travelled and wages were paid, as usual, in advance: to the archers of Cheshire and Flintshire for twenty-one days; [32] to the men of North Wales (who had further to travel) for ten days; [33] to the knights from the date of their leaving home until their arrival in Plymouth—a vague period, probably settled by agreement with the chamberlain of Chester.[34] Sir Howell ap Griffith was to travel 'by reasonable days' journeys'.[35] (His wages were paid by the chamberlain of North Wales.) The knights also received payment in advance of half a year's fees.[36]

Letters of protection were made out in favour of members of the prince's company to last till mid-June 1356 [37] and some further letters to run till July 28th, 1356.[38]

From Chester there was a well established route to Shrewsbury and thence down the Severn Valley via Bridgnorth, Worcester, Tewkesbury, Gloucester to Bristol.[39] It is very likely that our soldiers took this road. At Exeter, they would join the road which came from London via Salisbury, Shaftesbury and Yeovil down to Plymouth.[40]

The distance from Chester to Plymouth is about 275 miles. If

the Flintshire men started from Flint, they travelled an additional
12 miles. If some of the Cheshire men were assembled at Middlewich or Nantwich and proceeded straight to Bridgnorth, their
journey was about 12 miles less. It would seem that an average
distance of about 13 miles a day was needed to bring the journey
within the number of days for which payment had been made.
The going was easy, the hours of daylight long, the task well
within the men's powers—provided satisfactory meals could be
had. It may be that some of the archers had to shoot, skin and
cook their own rabbits.

As for the troops from North Wales, if indeed they received
only ten days' wages for so long a journey, they may have endured severe hardship. It may be that the chamberlain of North
Wales had forwarded to the prince so much of his current revenues that he had not in hand enough money to pay for the same
period as the Chamberlain of Chester paid. Indeed, it would not
have been possible to make such large disbursements at Chester
had there not been money in hand from the large fines imposed
on the county in 1353.[41]

The operation was not carried through with perfect smooth-
ness. In spite of the proclamation that the prince's needs must
come before all others', it was reported that some of the Cheshire
archers who had been 'chosen, tested and arrayed' to go to war
in his company, had joined the companies of other persons.[42]
With or without permission, Robert de Fouleshurst was serving
the king under another leader [43] and there were men who had
joined the company of Henry, Duke of Lancaster.[44] Before the
army sailed from Plymouth, a small number were deemed to be
too ill [45] to accompany their fellows to France and there were
deserters—a score of the men of Flintshire, fourteen of the men
of North Wales and four of the Cheshire men.[46] Among the four
was a Richard of Wistaston who vanished with 6*l.* which he had
received as wages 'for himself and his companions'.[47]

The Cheshire archers constituted the first group in the prince's
following. A second group consisted of men recruited by what
was becoming the normal method of the period. They were not
raised by commissions of array and were not necessarily drawn
from clearly defined areas, nor were they elements in the feudal
levy, for the days of active service in that cumbersome mechanism
had passed. The feudal levy was indeed being—and by the 1350s
had been—superseded by a system in which military service was

voluntary and all who served—even the magnates—were paid. The innovations made it possible to organize forces for campaigns in more distant theatres, to improve discipline and to incorporate men who, for one reason or another, were attracted to the military life. Service overseas was based on contracts (embodied in indentures) made between the king and particular individuals. These contracts specified the number of men (by categories) to be brought, the period of service, sometimes the place where the men were to serve and always the rate of pay and the 'regard' or bonus payment. They also stated (or it was understood) that compensation would be paid for horses lost in the war and they might cover the allocation of the 'advantages of war'. The troops thus raised remained under the leadership of the contracting party and their wages were paid by the leader (who had himself received payment in advance from the king for the full body for say a quarter or half a year).

From the middle of the 1340s, as it became necessary to dispatch expeditions to Gascony, Scotland, Picardy and Brittany, the system was extended and the number of men a contracting noble or knight undertook to raise or hold in readiness, might be large. Ralph, Earl of Stafford, for example, agreed in 1354 'to stay with the king for life with a hundred men at arms in times of war and of peace'.[48]

Similar indentures bound men to the service of the prince. In 1347, Sir John Hyde, Sir John Willoughby and Sir Thomas Furnival engaged to stay with the prince for one year and Sir John Fitz Walter for half a year.[49] The terms of the agreements include a statement of their own fees, a statement of the number of men who are to accompany each knight, arrangements for the food of the knights and their men, for wages and, in some instances, for the number and maintenance of their horses. In 1353, Sir John Sully was retained for life 'to be of the prince's special retinue both in peace and war with one esquire'. The terms of the indenture illustrate the general background of the knight's life. His annual fee is 40l. and it is to be paid out of the issues of a Devonshire manor belonging to the duchy of Cornwall. During peace, he and his esquire 'shall eat in hall and his chamberlain shall eat in hall or be at wages of 2d. a day. He shall have five horses at livery of hay and oats and shoeing and four grooms. . . . In time of war, he shall have court rations or be at livery or wages . . . and shall have nine horses . . . He himself shall be mounted by the prince. . . .' When summoned to meet the prince, he shall be allowed his travelling expenses.[50]

The second group in the prince's personal following consisted then of men-at-arms and archers raised by captains who had entered into contracts with the prince to provide such and such quotas. The names of many of them appear in the pages of Henxteworth's journal; they received the standard rates of pay (knights 2s. a day, men-at-arms 1s. a day, mounted archers 6d. and foot archers 3d. a day); their total strength is not stated but since they, the Cheshire archers and the prince's personal staff, amounted in all to 433 men-at-arms, 400 mounted archers and 300 foot archers, a rough estimate of their numbers is possible.

A third group consisted of members of the prince's household and administrative staff, not recruited for the expedition but accompanying him as part of their normal duty.[51] Some of their names will be given on a later page.

We pass from the prince's personal following to the retinues of the magnates appointed to accompany him, namely the Earls of Warwick, Suffolk, Oxford and Salisbury, Sir John de Lisle and Sir Reginald Cobham.[52] De Lisle's company amounted to 100: himself, 20 knights, 39 esquires and 40 mounted archers.[53] The sizes of the other companies are not known but they must have been larger, probably much larger. The magnates were contracting parties in the sense in which we have used these words above. They had received half a year's wages from the king in advance.[54] They travelled down to reach the port in July. De Lisle and his men arrived on July 9th.[55]

Efforts to determine the total strength of the force rest on three foundations. In the first place, the chroniclers give figures: Avesbury gives 1,000 men-at-arms, 2,000 archers and a large body of Welshmen.[56] Knighton mentions 800 men-at-arms and 1,400 archers.[57] Walsingham says there were 1,000 archers and 1,000 men-at-arms.[58] Secondly, an indenture between the king and the prince, dated July 10th, 1355 (when the preparatory work might be regarded as complete), defined the force as the prince's retinue of 433 men-at-arms and 700 archers (400 mounted and 300 on foot) together with the troops of the magnates.[59] Thirdly, ingenious but not wholly conclusive attempts have been made to deduce the number of men in the retinues of the magnates from various payments made for 'regards' and for shipping. The calculations are too intricate to state here but they may be summarized thus: the total number of men in the prince's force is believed to be about 2,600. Divided militarily, the groups are believed to be: just over 1,000 men-at-arms, 1,000 horse archers, 300 to 400 foot archers, about 170 Welshmen.[60]

The force thus constituted is far from anonymous.* The chroniclers mention the names of many of the nobles and gentry; records afford the names of several hundred others. Grants of letters of protection, grants of rewards for good service,[61] the nomination of attorneys (legally empowered to act on behalf of a soldier during his absence from England)—all are enrolled. Even the deserters and the invalids who returned to their homes from Plymouth are mentioned by name,[62] while Henxteworth's journal reveals the presence of scores of other men.

In composition, the body is probably fairly typical of the expeditionary forces of the period. The king and the Duke of Lancaster being engaged elsewhere, leadership falls to the prince. With him on the one hand are four of the leading nobles and on the other, the archers from the banks of the Dee, the Mersey and the Weaver. To these are added a sprinkling of men from almost every county in the land. The Scottish marches have their duty of looking northward but, from Westmorland comes a knight, Roger de Clifford, who is joining the Earl of Warwick's company [63] and there are several humbler men from Yorkshire.[64] There are also a few foreigners classed as Almains.[65] To turn from geographical and social distribution, there are, as usual, a considerable number of criminals of one kind or another. The proportion of men indicted of homicide is probably rather high.[66] Others have been indicted of theft, rape, abduction, prison-breaking; and there are some against whom the machinery of the law is about to be set in motion and for whom it is necessary to obtain respite.[67] In one respect, the force is not typical: it was not usual for a leader to have foot as well as mounted archers in his retinue.[68] The emphasis is indeed on archery and this fact, coupled with the absence of miners and skilled craftsmen (used in siege operations) and of pioneers (used in opening the way for great wheeled convoys), may point to the nature of the campaign it was expected would be undertaken in Gascony.

Communication between members of the different sections may have presented occasional difficulties. Between Welsh and English

* See Appendix C.

there was the barrier of language, but between the speech of the northern and the southern counties of England there were still wide differences of vocabulary and pronunciation while the prince and the earls spoke the Anglo Norman of the English court. Probably they understood English. (Froissart records one occasion some years later when the prince spoke in English.) On arrival at Bordeaux, the English leaders had to work with the Gascon lords who spoke the French of south-western France. Some of their men spoke Bearnais. Wengfeld, Burghersh, Chandos, Loring and others of the prince's entourage must have spoken both French and English.[69]

Of the four magnates, all had served in the Crécy campaign. Robert de Ufford, Earl of Suffolk was now fifty-seven years of age, Thomas Beauchamp, Earl of Warwick was forty-two, John de Vere, Earl of Oxford was forty-two, William Montacute, Earl of Salisbury was only twenty-eight. In the previous March (before the breach with France had been formally announced) orders had been given for ships to be assembled to convey Warwick and others to Gascony.[70] Apparently, however, he travelled with the main body. Oxford had already served in Guienne under Derby (later Lancaster).[71] Suffolk had had a long career in war and diplomacy. In 1340, he had been captured by the French, imprisoned in Paris and had gained his release by the payment of a large ransom to which the king himself had contributed 500l.[72]

While rank and retinues gave the earls prominence, there was a group of men whose capacity, training and experience made them valuable in the council and the business affairs of the expedition. Sir James Audley, Sir Richard Stafford and Sir John Chandos had also been at Crécy. Audley, a valiant soldier with lands in North Staffordshire and Devon, was retained in the king's service for many years.[73] Stafford (brother of Ralph, Earl of Stafford) had served with Derby in Gascony and subsequently been employed in various offices by the prince. He had been one of the commissioners appointed to investigate the prince's lands at the time he was granted the principality, and later he had accompanied Sir William Shareshull on eyre in North Wales.[74] Chandos was keeper and surveyor of the prince's extensive forests in Cheshire.[75]

There were many others in the company whom the prince had known for years as officers or friends. Foremost among them were Sir John Wengfeld, the chief of his administrative staff (and called in 1358 'Governor of the Prince's affairs');[76] Sir Baldwin Botetourt, master of the prince's great horses; Sir Bartholomew de Burghersh, justice of Chester; Sir Nigel Loring, the prince's chamberlain; Sir Stephen de Cusyngton, Sir Roger de Cotesford, Alan Cheyne, William Trussell.

Among the household staff were Nicholas Bond, squire of the prince's chamber; Dietrich Dale, usher of the prince's chamber; Henry de Aldrington (tailor); William de Bakton (butler); Richard Dokesey (baker); Robert Egremont (pavilioner); Geoffrey Hamelyn (keeper of the prince's armour); John Henxteworth (who kept the journal of payments); William Lenche and Henry de Berkhampstead and John de Palington (servants). There were also two friars preacher and three clerks described as the parsons of Collesdon, Scoter and Wythingdon.[77]

Magnates, officials, servants, most of them were well-known to one another already. They ensured a good deal of capacity for the staff work of the coming campaign. Not uncommonly the names of Audley and Chandos occur together and, if some deference was due to the opinions of the earls, it is clear that the views of these two men carried weight with the prince from the outset. Chandos Herald calls them his 'chief advisers'.[78]

To the earls the task of accompanying the prince to Gascony was a duty incumbent of men of their rank, a recognition of their fitness for war, an honour (for which of course they were in receipt of fees); to Chandos, Loring, Stafford, it was part of the lot of men who followed careers in the prince's service; to Audley, it was professional activity for which he received an annual fee; to criminals, it afforded an opportunity of righting themselves with the law and returning to normal civil life. Yet many hearts must have been moved by something warmer than duty or business or freedom from arrest for, in spite of the ardours of long marches, the rigours of a sea voyage and the discomforts of camp life in a foreign land, the expedition promised adventure, opportunities for personal distinction and even for personal enrichment.

While the magnates and the men were making their way down to Plymouth, steps were being taken in London to safeguard their interests during their absence. Scores of letters of protection were issued [79] and, in various places where legal action was pending against an archer or a leader, orders were given for the operation of the law to be suspended till his return.[80]

The prince's interests also were carefully reviewed. He, Wengfeld and other members of his council would be absent from

c

England for many months but some of the problems of administering his principality, his duchy and his earldom—more especially his earldom—were anticipated. To a dozen queries concerning forests, woodlands, castles, manors, raised in advance by his officers in Cheshire, clear answers were sent.[81] Further instructions were issued concerning game in the forest of Macclesfield and concerning matters which were to be held over till the prince's return.[82]

The impending journey and its personal and financial implications were also considered. Many members of the household were to accompany the prince. A large sum, therefore, was provided to enable them to buy outfits for the expedition and a sum was paid to the two friars preacher to help them to make suitable preparations.[83]

A new seal was made for the prince's use in Gascony.[84]

A merchant was appointed for a short period to buy gold for the prince's use: it would be a convenient medium in which to carry money and it would be accepted in payment for purchases overseas.[85]

Wages of war and the bonus payments known as regards [86] had already been paid, the totals being as follows:

The Prince of Wales	.	.	.	8129*l.* 18*s.* 0*d.*
The Earl of Warwick	.	.	.	2614*l.* 4*s.* 0*d.*
„ „ „ Suffolk .	.	.	.	1428*l.* 6*s.* 8*d.*
„ „ „ Oxford .	.	.	.	1174*l.* 13*s.* 10*d.*
„ „ „ Salisbury	.	.	.	1124*l.* 2*s.* 2*d.*
Sir Reginald Cobham	.	.	.	652*l.* 0*s.* 8*d.*

The prince pressed for, and gained, repayment of a loan made to his aunt, the Countess of Hainault.[87] He also received 500*l.* owing to him from Sir Thomas Wogan of Ireland.[88] These might have been useful sums but they were slight in comparison with the load of debt already contracted and the expenses which loomed ahead.

On June 21st, the king took two steps in the prince's favour: he granted him all the moneys forthcoming from the recent sessions of Sir William Shareshull and the other justices in Cornwall and Devon [89] and also, in view of the prince's inevitable, abnormal expenses, he granted him 1,000 marks annually from the customs of the port of London.[90] At this period (late June and early July), the prince was paying off many debts but he had recently made lavish gifts.[91] His finances were indeed in an unstable state. Creditors needed some assurance of the way his debts would be dealt with should he not survive the coming expedition. Before he left London, royal letters patent announced that if he died in France, his executors would hold all his castles, manors, lands and rents in England, Wales and elsewhere for three years after his death in order to discharge his debts from the revenues.[92]

The last important business in London was the completion of the indenture between the king and the prince defining the prince's powers in, and the king's contribution to, the coming expedition. This took place on July 10th.[93] On or about July 12th, the prince left London. He reached Plymouth about the 26th.

If the arrangements had worked out as planned, the army should have set sail immediately. There were not, however, enough ships available for the purpose, nor apparently were they expected to be available for some time.[94] The delay (which extended to six weeks) had unfortunate results. It must have affected the morale of the waiting troops. It certainly affected the plans for the autumn *chevauchée*, embarrassed the prince's finances and caused grave difficulties in feeding the men.

The inescapable, financial troubles are revealed in a letter to the Chamberlain of North Wales in which he states that he 'must incur far greater expenses during his sojourn at Plymouth . . . than he anticipated' and orders him to try to borrow 100*l*. and to send that sum by August 16th.[95] It was calculated that by the end of September, large sums would be levyable in Cheshire, South Wales and North Wales.[96] The three chamberlains were urged to do their utmost to ensure that the full sums were collected and transmitted to the prince's receiver general.[97] An officer was sent also to Dorset to deal with the collection of fines which the sheriff of that county had been urged to levy.[98]

For the victualling of medieval, English armies there is ample evidence of the movement of supplies in bulk (for example to North Wales, to Scotland and to Calais), but details of feeding arrangements during marches through, or at camps in, England are scanty. The archers from Cheshire, Flintshire and North Wales no doubt provided for themselves as they proceeded southward and westward to the port of embarkation. How they were fed at Plymouth is not clear. The town had a population of perhaps two thousand people.[99] The sea and the river Tamar afforded supplies of fish but the hinterland was poor.[100]

For the prince's own following, orders had been given in April for the sheriff of Cornwall to accumulate stores in Plymouth: wines from Dartmouth, Fowey and other ports; 300 quarters of oats and 100 quarters of wheat, and brushwood 'in a place as near to Plymouth as possible and where least damage will be caused'.[101] A report on the stores available was to be sent promptly and the prince's officers would come down later. Bartholomew de Burghersh (the son) or his deputy appears to have been sent down in advance—probably to make preparations—and orders were given for supplies to be delivered at 'the place near Plymouth where he is to be lodged'.[102]

Had the expedition sailed promptly, it may be that the accumulated supplies would have sufficed. The delay upset calculations and may account for the 'far heavier expenses than he had anticipated' already mentioned. For the maintenance of his own household, wheat totalling $37\frac{1}{2}$ quarters was obtained, probably in Devon and Cornwall.[103] Other supplies of (unclassified) victuals were obtained in Devon, Somerset and Dorset, the total value being over 1,067*l*.[104] Though instructions were given for the prompt settlement of the debts thus incurred, many months passed and much discontent was caused by delays before payment was completed.[105]

During these weeks of delay, the prince lived at Plympton Priory, four or five miles from the port, and dealt with business arising from the duchy of Cornwall and from his finances.[106] If the relation between his revenues and his expenditure was causing some misgiving to his creditors, he was leaving in England a very comprehensive statement of his borrowings, his purchases and gifts made by him or on his behalf.[107] Meanwhile, the men waited nearer the port. Horses, ammunition, armour, hurdles, gangways were ready. Only two things were needed: sufficient ships and a favourable wind. It was not till September 9th, that the force set sail.

In addition to the assembly of men and materials and their transport to the base, the preparatory work included some broad arrangements for the conduct of the coming campaign together with some measures of a more political nature.

In the enforced leisure of the long delay at Plymouth and during the voyage, the leaders must have discussed the operations they expected shortly to undertake. It is unlikely that Edward III had laid down details for their guidance and it is unlikely that they drew up plans for themselves or for the prince, except possibly the allocation of troops and commanders to the three traditional parts of the army. Routes, distances and surface features beyond the English marches were unknown to them. On such expeditions, local guides were usually employed and, since armies 'lived on the land', their movements were governed in a large measure by the supplies they were able to find.

For some aspects of the campaign, however, plans had been prepared in advance and approved by the king. As the king's lieutenant, the prince has very extensive powers over the administration of Gascony, its officials and its revenues. Concerning finance, the soldiers have already received pay and 'reward' for six months' service. Should the king desire the prince to stay longer, payments for another six months are promised. On major military questions, the prince has power to act according to his judgment. He may make truces or armistices. If prisoners are taken, he shall have their ransoms. If, however, the 'head' of the war falls into his hands, that prisoner shall be reserved for King Edward but the prince shall have a suitable recompense. The prince shall have several of the 'advantages' of war. He may grant away lands gained in war. Finally, should he be 'besieged or beset', the king will rescue him and several nobles have promised to give all possible help. Under such circumstances, he may make a truce or armistice or take such other steps as seem necessary.[108]

No express limit to the prince's powers in the command of the troops is stated. There is no reference to a Council. Only one function is mentioned for the other leaders: 'If the prince incurs any expenses in those parts by the advice of the lords who are appointed to go with him, such costs shall be made good to him.'[109] They were, however, years older than him and it must have been understood that they would advise him not only concerning expenditure but also on other matters. At Bordeaux and elsewhere, the prince called together a Council. No doubt these 'lords appointed to go with him' were among its members.

As regards the more political aspects of the great enterprise also, some preparatory work had been done. A group of documents [110] drawn up in July 1355, define the prince's powers and implicitly reveal the aims of royal policy.

First comes the recovery of lost territories. The prince has power 'to seize into the king's hands all lands, towns, castles, franchises, customs, profits of mints and other things belonging at any time to the duchy of Guienne'.

Closely allied to this is the recovery of lost allegiances. In the march land there were men whose loyalty wavered with the wavering fortunes of the opposing sides. Not only smaller lords but great houses like that of Foix pursued policies of calculated self-interest. In January 1353, for example, when Jean d'Armagnac was about to begin his campaign, some lords who had gone over to the English side, hastened to ask pardon for their conduct and begged him to allow them to join the French.[111] With such dubious or wavering loyalty the prince is empowered to deal. He may admit to the king's peace those who 'wish to come or to return' to the English side; he may grant pardons for felonies and transgressions committed, remit banishments and outlawries, hand over the lands of rebels to those who serve faithfully and to those who wish to join the English side.

A third aim is the engagement of new friends and additional forces. The prince is empowered to negotiate and make agreements with men of any rank and of any kingdom or state with a view to firm friendship and allegiance. He may also receive homage and fealty both in Aquitaine and in France.[112]

To these three aims a fourth may be added. It is the maintenance of friendship with tried supporters. Through the difficult years, the houses of Buch and Lebret had remained faithful to the English cause. Their constancy was now rewarded. On July 6th, King Edward granted to the Captal de Buch his rights in the towns of Benauges and Ilaz, a saltworks in Bordeaux, the castle of Castillon near St. Emilion and various other properties. The grant was made in express recognition of past, and expectation of future service.[113] A few days later, the work of Bernard Ezi, Lord of Lebret was recognized. By virtue of his services in the wars in Gascony, he had received grants from Henry, Earl (later duke) of Lancaster. These grants the king now confirmed.[114]

Though the prince might have a very hazy notion of the military operations he was about to undertake, he had received a clear statement of the political aims he should seek to achieve. He was the king's lieutenant with all the resources of the government of Gascony at his disposal, and he was to take with him from England 'a sum of money sufficient for the conciliation of the people of the country (viz. Gascony) and such other purposes as he shall think proper for the king's profit'.[115] While he waited at

Plympton Priory, the sum of 10,000 marks was paid over to his treasurer for conveyance from the Exchequer to the Constable of Bordeaux 'to pay for victuals and to the people of those parts for the furtherance of the war' as the prince should direct.[116] Not generalship only but statesmanship or at any rate statecraft, would be needed.

Though knights, men-at-arms and archers arrived at the port of embarkation fully equipped for war, it is evident that during a campaign archers would need further supplies of arms. We turn, therefore, briefly to the making, storage and transport of bows, arrows and bowstrings.

While inventories of stocks held in English castles in the mid-fourteenth century reveal the presence of crossbows, it is the longbow that is the typical weapon of war. Its range is inferior to that of the arbalast, but its superior rapidity of fire makes it far more formidable on the battlefield, and the victories of English arms at this period are due in large measure to the skilful use of archers combined with cavalry. Great mobility is gained by mounting the archers, but the bow is too long to be used by a rider. The archer descends before battle.

The crafts of bow-making and arrow-making are distinct but almost invariably associated. Bowyers and fletchers produce their wares for sale; sometimes they contract to supply them at agreed prices; sometimes they are impressed (like other craftsmen) to work 'at the king's wages'.

Bows are white or painted and sold by the dozen.

Arrows are usually arrows without qualification, but they may be 'without heads', 'with heads', 'with heads hard and well steeled'. They are supplied in sheaves containing two dozen each. Arrow heads are forged but the work is seldom mentioned. At Chester Castle in 1359, there is a store of 4,000 of them waiting to be put on arrows. They are valued at 52s. 5d.[117]

Bowstrings are supplied by the dozen and the gross.

There are four main occasions for ordering quantities of these arms: the equipping of archers arrayed in a county, the furnishing of castles, the transport of quantities direct to the scene of war on the Scottish border or to a southern port for shipment to France, the maintenance of a large stock in the Tower of London, the great national arsenal. Two instances will make clear the scale and the nature of orders for the Tower. From the castle of Bamburgh on January 30th, 1356, King Edward issued instructions to four-teen sheriffs (responsible for nineteen counties) to supply arms amounting in the aggregate to 9,900 sheaves of arrows and 5,600 white bows. Half of these goods were to be delivered in London before Easter and the other half before the quinzaine of Trinity.[118] The second instance is the appointment in 1359 of William de Rothwell, the keeper of the king's privy wardrobe in the Tower of London, to 'take in London and elsewhere as many armourers, fletchers, smiths and other artificers and workmen as are required for the making of armour, bows, bowstrings, arrows, arrow-heads . . . and put to them to work at the king's wages . . . to buy and fell timber fit for making arrows . . . also to buy 1,000 bows, painted and white, 10,000 sheaves of good arrows and 1,000 sheaves of the best arrows with heads hard and well steeled . . . 100 gross of bowstrings . . . and feathers of the wings of geese and other necessaries. . . .'[119]

It must not be inferred that such orders are, or can be, carried out promptly and in full. The execution of the instructions in our first instance can be followed in large measure in the Sheriff's returns and it is clear that few counties supplied the quantities demanded by the appointed date. The sheriffs have bought up the supplies available within their area. They report their pur-chases and the prices, the place at which the goods were as-sembled, the mode and cost of transport to London. The sheriff of Somerset and Dorset, for example, has fulfilled the request to supply 300 white bows and 400 sheaves of arrows. The bows (costing 18d. each) amount to 22l. 10s.; the arrows have cost 26l. 13s. 4d.; the goods were assembled in carts and wagons at Dorchester and sent to the Tower in charge of a mounted clerk, and the total cost of collection and delivery is 74s. Hereford on the other hand, from which 1,000 sheaves were asked, has supplied only 363 sheaves (at 16d. each), while Bedford and Buckingham, commanded to provide 600 sheaves, have sent only 260 (at 18d. per sheaf).[120]

It is from stores of arms thus made or accumulated in the Tower that William de Rothwell supplied quantities as the king directed. What quantity he supplied, if any, for the expeditionary force before it sailed to Bordeaux, I have not been able to trace. (The archers would have supplies with them and bows and arrows could, of course, be obtained in Gascony.) Early in 1356, big supplies were sought in England for the prince's troops and sent out to Bordeaux with the reinforcements, as we shall see.

As the fourteenth century advances the role of the horse grows more important. Monarchs, princes, great nobles and the supreme pontiff are surrounding themselves and their emissaries with greater splendour. Dignity is sought not only in the appointments of the court but in the size of mounted bodyguards. Bishops on their journeys to Avignon, and abbots and priors on their way to mother houses, travel with more mounted servants than was their wont. Pilgrimages to Canterbury and Compostella have a more recreative character: the journeys are less arduous when made on horseback than on foot. Tournaments retain their appeal and increase in splendour. The Garter, the Golden Fleece, the Star are companionships not only of skilled fighters but of skilful riders. The management of the horse enters into every feat of arms. The horse's oats, hay, litter, harness are the subject of innumerable instructions.

Changes in the art of war and the organization of armies also enhance the horse's importance. It becomes usual to mount some or a large part of the archers. Warfare tends to become large-scale devastation effected by quickly moving troops. Armies, therefore, need more horses per hundred men than they needed in the preceding century. Moreover, the increasing weight of the armour worn by the knight together with the adaptation of armour to the horse, lead to the need for sturdy mounts, called destriers, some of which are very valuable. Sumpter horses and cart horses continue to be indispensable.

The proportion of horses used as mounts, as sumpters and for haulage no doubt varied widely. Froissart, describing warfare on the Scottish border in 1327, says that the Scots dispensed with vehicles and cooking utensils while the English set out with carts and tents but left them at Durham.[121] For the campaign of 1359, however, the English took over to France a very great quantity of material (cooking equipment, tents, forges, handmills) which was carried in four-horsed vehicles brought from England.[122] Between these extremes, the more typical campaign called for vehicles wherever roads were suitable for wheeled transport. Some such carts or lorries might be specially constructed for service overseas.[123] Armour, a supply of arrows, some horse shoes and nails and a small quantity of food and wine would have to be transported almost everywhere.

For the breeding of horses the king had his stud farms and supervising officers.[124] The prince had studs at Macclesfield, at Byfleet, at Prince's Risborough and at Woking.[125] He bought scores of horses (and gave away scores). But the provision of horses for an army was not of course the business of the king or the prince. The horse had been an element in the service due from those who held land by feudal tenure; it became—or might become—an element in indentured service. A leader contracted to supply a certain number of men *and* horses for a given period. The king on his side undertook to give compensation for horses lost in war.

This obviously necessary guarantee on the part of the superior contracting party, led to the principle that the king must be safeguarded against fraud by a formal appraisal of the horses taken on service. The work was carried out—usually at the port of embarkation—by a clerk trained for the purpose and a capable knight. The horses were clearly marked and the list (showing owner, colour of horse and value) was sent to the king.[126] The same principle applied in indentures made between the prince and various knights. When horses were lost in the wars, claims were sent in and, after due verification (and often after long delay), they were paid.[127]

When preparations were being made for a campaign in France, two further steps were necessary: the king undertook to provide transport for the horses or to defray the cost of shipping them; he had also to ensure that suitable means were available for getting the horses on board.

A last measure may be mentioned. Whenever the king deemed it necessary, the export of horses was forbidden or limited to animals of small value; and the effectiveness of the regulation could be tested by directing the authority controlling a port to furnish an annual statement showing the number of horses which had passed through the port during the preceding year.[128]

A prohibition of this kind had been ordered in January 1355 when the authorities at the Cinque Ports, Boston, Kingston upon Hull and ten other ports were required to prevent the shipment of horses for sale and to permit only the movement of small horses for their owners' use.[129]

It is unfortunately not possible to trace in any detail the sources of supply, the numbers or the values of the horses taken on the prince's expedition of 1355. His personal following needed a minimum of 833 for the 433 men-at-arms and the 400 mounted archers whom he had contracted to provide.[130] To these must be added horses for the men-at-arms (and possibly for some of the archers) in the magnates' companies, horses for a proportion of the prince's household and administrative staff and horses for the knights retained for a period or for life and also for their grooms.[131]

Lambkyn Saddler from whom the prince had recently bought saddles, bridles and other harness, supplied some saddles for the expedition to Gascony.[132]

For the appraisal and marking of the horses, John Deyncourt and three other men were appointed.[133] But it was agreed (between the king and the prince) that if men-at-arms preferred to purchase their horses in Gascony, they might do so and such horses would be appraised by the Constable of Bordeaux. The constable was also to appraise and mark horses bought from time to time by men-at-arms to make good losses sustained in war. Compensation was to be paid to the prince for all duly verified losses.[134]

The permission to buy horses in Gascony instead of in England may have been intended to lessen both the difficulty of obtaining mounts in England and the need for shipping at a time when two other expeditions were being prepared. (The Duke of Lancaster's expedition sailed from the Thames estuary in July without horses.) Since the permission was confined to men-at-arms, it may be inferred that horses for the mounted archers were assembled at Plymouth together with those of the leaders. Of the lists of the horses valued and marked, no copy, so far as is known, remains; nor have I been able to trace an account for the forage taken on board for the journey. Two farriers went out from England with the expedition.

The measures taken for shipping the horses at Plymouth we shall treat on a later page.

For the movement of an English army overseas in the middle of the fourteenth century, the following steps were taken: A port of embarkation was chosen; suitable ships were requisitioned; mariners were engaged or impressed; the requisitioned ships together with some of the 'king's ships' were sailed to the chosen port; efforts were made to co-ordinate the arrival of the troops, horses and supplies with the arrival of the ships.

Research has not yet thrown enough light on the condition of harbours and the state of harbour installations to show how far the choice of a port was governed by ease of shipment. In some ports, quays had been built; in some, there were windlasses; at some, pilots were used. The Thames estuary, Sandwich, Dover, Portsmouth, Southampton, Plymouth were used at different times as starting-points for expeditions proceeding to France. From Chester, troops sailed to Ireland. The Earl of Derby's expedition to Gascony had sailed from Southampton in 1345 and the king's large army from Portsmouth in 1346.

In times of peace, the king's serjeants-at-arms were instructed to 'arrest' ships to convey ministers appointed to offices in Aquitaine and Ireland or to transport victuals to the king's castles in France. During wars, they received more extensive powers and, at times, 'admirals' were appointed to take charge of the group of ports 'from the Thames northwards' and 'from the Thames westwards'. These admirals (or their deputies) were empowered not only to arrest ships and impress mariners; they had also disciplinary powers over all men serving in the fleet and they administered a form of maritime law.

In the 1340s and 1350s, therefore, owners and masters were accustomed, during the truces, to the requisitioning of a limited amount of shipping and, in times of crisis, to demands for all vessels above a stipulated tonnage. Ships engaged in the transport of wool to Flanders, of victuals to Calais, of grain and salt fish to Gascony together with ships plying between English ports, were suddenly diverted from commerce or trade to serve military needs. Since ships often had to wait considerable periods for wind, it is evident that neither the date of their arrest, nor that of their arrival at the chosen port, nor that of the departure of the expedition itself could be accurately forecast.

Merchant ships probably served the purpose of transports satisfactorily. War stores and equipment differed little from ordinary cargoes; the voyage across the Channel or the Irish Sea was short; discomfort could be endured. When, however, it was necessary to convey large numbers of horses, special measures had to be taken.

In some instances, merchant ships were 'fitted out for the king's service', that is to say adapted for defence and offence. As warfare at sea resembled warfare on land in that the arrow and the flung stone were used till the vessels grappled and hand to hand fighting began, a raised deck was advantageous to archers and a station high on the mast could be used for projecting arrows or stones. Some merchant vessels, therefore, were withdrawn from commerce; their bodies were raised at stem and stern and on the parts so raised, beams were laid across which formed the floors of the castles, the sides being strengthened by cleats fastened on under the floor beams.[135]

A third class of vessel was built expressly for war though it might at times be used for the transport of goods. Such vessels were built with castles fore and aft and with crows'-nests. Generally they were large. They formed the nucleus of the royal navy and were known as 'the king's ships'.

Authentic pictures of typical English vessels of the period are few. Contemporary coins and the seals of many Channel ports depict ships but these works cannot be regarded as sound evidence. The artists were not ship specialists; they worked in a very limited space, had to adapt their designs to the circular frames and were more concerned with decoration and symbolism than with accurate representation. The beautiful illustrations of Froissart's chronicles date mainly from the fifteenth century and are for the most part the work of continental artists. The English vessels used as army transports in the middle of the fourteenth century differed widely in displacement. A few may have approached 200 tons. The great majority were less than 100 and many were as low as 50. They had one mast and one large square sail, a hawse-hole for the anchor cable, a wide variety of ropes. By this date, a rudder was in use instead of a steering oar.[136]

Much of the work of a modern admiralty was conducted by the Clerk of the King's Ships from an office in the Tower of London. He supervised the conversion of merchantmen, the construction of king's ships and the purchase of all kinds of gear for vessels used in the king's service except the gear needed when horses were to be conveyed.

For the shipment of horses special gangways (*pontes*) were constructed. They were wide enough to take vehicles and may have been used for that purpose, the vehicles perhaps being loaded with provender or baggage and being intended for the baggage train in France. Since they were ordered afresh for each large shipment of horses, they appear not to have formed part of the harbour equipment.

Finally, hundreds of hurdles—measuring 7 or $7\frac{1}{2}$ feet by 4 or $4\frac{1}{2}$ feet—were made for the horse-boats. When large numbers of horses were brought to a port where they might have to wait days or even weeks before being taken on board, enclosures would be necessary; and that was true also when they were taken ashore and allowed time to recover after the voyage. The main purpose of the hurdles, however, was, no doubt, to separate the horses while they were on the ship. That purpose has been achieved in more recent times by suspending planks from the roof or ceiling. The way in which the hurdles were held in position I have not been able to determine.

The provision of gangways and hurdles was the work of the sheriffs of coastal counties who received instructions direct from the king.[137]

The vessels thus obtained and adapted to transport an expeditionary force had, of course, to be manned and, while voluntary engagement on the sailors' part must have been common, masters of the chosen ships were authorized to impress enough men to make up their crews, the men being taken from specified counties. The crews were (by modern standards) large and all members received the same wages.

As early as April 24th, the prince revealed that his part of the army would assemble at Plymouth.[138] In the absence of statistics, it is not to be inferred that Plymouth was at that time the most important port in the south-west. It was, however, the most westerly port that was reasonably accessible from England as a whole and, in view of the medieval sea routes, its advantage over Southampton in respect of distance from Bordeaux, was greater than it is today. By the mid-fourteenth century it was commonly, but by no means invariably, used for vessels proceeding on royal business to Bordeaux. From Plymouth, the king's daughter, Joanne, had sailed in 1347 and his daughter, Isabel, in 1351. Bernard, Lord of le Bret, sailed thence in 1352, and a fleet of the king's ships was assembled at Plymouth in 1354.[139] On the other hand, ships could be more readily 'arrested' in the busier port of Southampton.

It was from Plymouth that the prince sailed but there is ample evidence that no small part of the shipping for the expedition had been assembled at Southampton. It is in fact likely that some ships destined to convey troops to Gascony were already waiting at Southampton at the end of April, for orders had been given on March 10th to requisition ships of thirty tons and upwards in the southern ports for the conveyance of Warwick and other mag-

nates;[140] and Warwick had not sailed. On April 27th, arrangements for collecting ships for the prince's expedition were made
known: they might be arrested in almost any port in England
and it was to Southampton that they were to be sent.[141] On
May 6th, the Sheriff of Southampton was directed to send to the
port of Southampton hurdles and gangways for shipping the
horses of the Earls of Warwick and Suffolk;[142] and a pay roll
reveals that on May 8th, forty-four ships earmarked for the
prince's needs were lying in that port.[143] Further, on May 31st,
John Deyncourt (the sub-admiral towards the north) took up his
duties in connection with this expedition at Southampton.[144]

On the other hand, though I have not been able to trace the
issue of orders for the assembly of ships at Plymouth, there is no
doubt that ships were expected there, for the Sheriffs of Cornwall
and Devon were directed on May 6th to send hurdles and gangways to Plymouth for shipping the prince's horses.[145] Further, in
mid July, when the King of Navarre had arrived from Bayonne
with a few ships, instructions were given for these ships to be
transferred to the fleet required for the prince 'at Southampton
or Plymouth as the bearer of these letters shall direct'.[146]

Ships therefore were assembled at both ports. The prince's
expedition was intended to absorb Warwick's expedition. The
shipping arrested for Warwick was made available for, and hence-
forward regarded as part of, the prince's fleet. It was certainly
intended that the horses of Warwick and Suffolk should be taken
on board at Southampton. It is possible that Warwick, Suffolk
and their retinues embarked in that port. When the *Saint Esprit*
was chosen for his 'hall', the prince wrote from Plympton (where
he was waiting within sight of Plymouth) to the Mayor of
Southampton directing him to make some alterations in the
vessel.[147] And it was the Mayor of Southampton, John Clerk,
who commanded the ship in which the prince eventually sailed to
Bordeaux.[148]

All the steps which administrators could take to obtain suitable
vessels, to impress mariners and to provide the means of shipping
horses were taken in good time and there is a note of urgency in
the orders. Ships were to reach the port of embarkation by
June 11th [149] and an official was sent down early in May to pay
the wages of mariners on board ships which had already been
assembled.[150]

William of Walklate was sent to Sluys to fetch the *Big Cog* to

England so that by Whitsuntide it might be ready for service wherever it should be required.[151] The *Margaret of the Tower*, the *James* and the *Giliane* of London were also to be manned and made ready for service.[152] The good men of Exeter were directed to build a barge by midsummer and to man it.[153]

Detailed instructions were given for the fittings of the horse boats. The Sheriffs of Cornwall, Devon and Southampton were each directed to provide 2,500 hurdles and 15 gangways. Of the latter, some were to be 20 feet in length and some 15 feet. Those supplied in Devon and Cornwall were to be made with all speed and delivered in the port of Plymouth to Henry le Hewe by June 14th. Those made at Southampton were to be delivered in that port by the same date.[154]

But the urgent orders must be related to the factors governing their execution, namely the weather and the process of assembly: one vessel after another coming into this or that port is 'arrested' by, or on behalf of, the admiral and unloaded; the master reports the size of the crew needed to sail her to Gascony; the admiral himself authorizes the impressment of men in this or that county but sends the information to London; a commission is made out for the impressment; the captain having got his men and provided some victuals, proceeds to Southampton or Plymouth.

It is well known that the prince's departure was delayed and the chroniclers' evidence has been the basis of many inferences that the sole reason for the delay was a prolonged spell of 'contrary winds', that in fact one may reckon forty days backwards from September 8th and conclude that the fleet, already assembled at Plymouth and fully prepared to sail, lay in harbour from the end of July awaiting a change of weather.

The truth is less simple. Adverse winds might imperil or delay the start of any expeditionary force—the king had 'tarried for wind' in 1346—and the weather in July 1355 had been unsuitable for a fleet bent on a voyage to Gascony.[155] The prince himself refers to it,[156] and it had played havoc with the expedition of Henry, Duke of Lancaster who had sailed down the Thames on July 10th but, on seeking to steer south and west down the Channel, had been unable to make headway.[157] But the prince reveals another reason: at the end of July the amount of shipping needed to transport his army had not reached Plymouth.[158] This also may perhaps be partly ascribed to the weather since ships requisitioned in east- or south-coast ports which had not sailed to Plymouth before the July winds began to blow, would have had great difficulty in sailing down Channel against the gale.

The situation must, however, be viewed in its entirety. Efforts were being made to equip and dispatch two expeditionary forces at the same time, to embark these forces at three widely separated ports and to prepare a third expedition for the autumn. The machinery of government was hampered by the slowness of communication and the method of seizing ships as they came into port one by one at unpredictable dates. Adverse weather, of course, played a part but the conditions of the time rendered co-ordination of land and sea movements imperfect. In July 1355, the demand for ships was greater than the country's resources could supply at short notice. The use of two ports for one expedition probably complicated the arrangements and the permission to buy horses in Bordeaux [159] instead of taking them from England, must have caused difficulties in estimating the need for horse boats.

The principal cause of the delay was lack of ships and at the end of July, the prince did not expect an early solution to the problem. He sent agents to try to get more money for his immediate needs [160] and, whatever his disappointment, was probably not surprised by the situation.

For the urgency and precision of the orders issued in the spring had gone. Orders were being executed as fast as circumstances permitted, but not as fast as the plan-makers had intended. The time-table had in fact broken down. The prince had stated that he would be in Plymouth by July 1st. He arrived about July 26th. The ships were to be in port by June 11th. Yet on July 16th, orders were sent out for more ships to be added to the fleet and even later (July 29th) the prince sent instructions to Southampton about some alterations to be carried out in one of them. [161] Not till July 22nd were men appointed to value the horses that were to be taken to Gascony. August dragged on and it was early September before all the ships were assembled, the hurdles taken on board and fitted and the last horses led up the gangways. Chandos Herald says the ships were 'loaded with victuals and jewels, hauberks, helmets, lances, shields, bows and arrows.'

The prince, he continues, embarked 'and all the noble knights. There might one see the flower of chivalry and of right good bachelry who were very eager and desirous to acquit themselves well.' [162] Hoggeshaw, the acting admiral, had a guard of thirty

D

archers and thirty men-at-arms.[163] Deyncourt, sub-admiral of the king's fleet towards the north, who also accompanied the ships, had twenty archers and seven men-at-arms.[164] The prince travelled in the *Christofre*.[165] On September 9th, the great fleet set sail for Bordeaux.

Admirals and sub-admirals may have had complete lists of the vessels sailing in the fleets under their command. Surviving lists are less comprehensive. When they relate to payments made to owners or masters *after* a voyage they are valuable. When they name ships which are to be manned, or supply details of payments to mariners serving on ships that are waiting in harbour, it is evident that they are less valuable. With due caution, therefore, we draw into one table the names of vessels that had been requisitioned or manned for the prince's passage to Bordeaux.[166]

List A: William of Wenlok, clerk, received from the Exchequer on May 8th, 1355, the sum of 380*l.* He went to Southampton and paid twenty-eight days' wages to the mariners serving on the under-mentioned ships lying in the port. In his statement of account, he says explicitly that the mariners were there 'for the prince and other people going to Gascony'.

Port	Ship	Tonnage	Mariners
Seaton	*Margaret*	30	14
Lynn	*Saint Mary Cog*	80	22
,,	*Michael*	50	14
Weymouth & Melcombe	*Margaret*	80	22
,,	*Peter*	90	24
,,	*Clement*	70	20
,,	*Saint Mary Cog*	90	24
Warham	*Saint Mary Cog*	80	26
Lymington	*Saint Mary Cog*	70	24
,,	*Nicholas*	60	22
Hamelhoke	*Nicholas*	70	24
,,	*Gracedieu*	160	42
,,	*Katerine*	120	32
,,	*Welifare*	70	22
,,	*Saint Esprit*	100	30
Southampton	*Trinity*	100	
,,	?	70	22
,,	*Margaret*	30	14
Shoreham	*Welifare*		22
,,	*Welifare*		18

Port	Ship	Tonnage	Mariners
Shoreham	*Welifare*	50	16
,,	*Katherine*	50	16
,,	*Benedict*	60	18
,,	*Godier*	40	18
Rye	*Nicholas*	120	22
,,	*Jonette*	40	12
,,	*Dieulavance*	66	18
Hythe	*Margaret*	50	14
	Saint Mary Boat		14
,,	*Alice*	30	14
,,	*Saint Mary Boat*		
	of Rudynge	30	14
,,	*Godier*	38	14
,,	*Godbiete*	38	14
,,	*Christiane*		
	of Poole	30	14
Winchelsea	*Jonette*	120	30
,,	*Saint Mary Cog*		50
Dover	*Glythe*	50	20
,,	*Cronipher*	50	20
,,	*Lancaster*		20
,,	*Navdieu*	50	20
,,	*Faucon*	40	20
Sandwich	*Blison*	110	30
,,	*Cog John*	140	36
,,	*Margaret*	120	30

List B: On May 28th, 1355, the masters of the following vessels were authorized to impress mariners for their ships in order to sail with the prince at the prince's wages to Gascony:

Master	Ship	Mariners
William Barrett	The *Juliane*	36
John Gobet	,, *Margarete*	26
William Henry	,, *Nicholas*	24
William May	,, *James*	26
John Burges	,, *Gregory*	20
Stephen Stonyng	,, *Saintmarybote*	15
Simon Steven	,, *Mighel*	26
John Lewe	,, *John of Yarmouth*	26

List C: Between March and May 1355, the following masters were authorized to impress men to sail their ships and the copies of their commissions are enrolled in the French Rolls. In the first ship in this list, the prince himself sailed.

Master	Ship	Mariners
John Clerk	The *Christofre*	100
William Ashenden	,, *Cristofre*	80
Robert Gofair	,, *Saint Marie*	80
William Passelewe	,, *Jerusalem*	70
Thomas Clerk	,, *Edward*	60
John Blosse	,, *Claws*	60
John Horset	,, *Holk*	60
John Ram	,, *Alice*	45
John Wille	,, *Thomas*	40
Robert Andrew	,, *John*	40
Walter de Manthrop	,, *Trinity*	130
John Sperman	,, *Rodecog*	35
Paul Portsmouth	,, *Edmond*	35
John Rok	,, *Anne*	30
Hamond Lovetoft	,, *Faucon*	30
Robert Hull	,, *Isabelle*	30
Robert Fikeys	,, *Saint Marybote*	25
Thomas Ram	,, *Mariote*	25
Bartholomew Stigeyn	,, *Welifare*	42
John Maikyn	,, *Plenty*	35

List D: This ship was 'assigned to be the prince's hall' and the prince ordered some repairs to be effected in it in July 1355

The *Saint Esprit*.

These then were some of the ships which it was intended to use for the passage of the expeditionary force to Gascony. That others also were chosen and that Wenlok and his fellow clerks paid a series of visits to the port or ports of assembly I have no doubt. A summary of their payments made during May, June and July to mariners serving on vessels requisitioned for the movement of the prince's and the magnates' troops, amounts to more than 3000*l*.[167]

The fleet no doubt took the medieval sea route, sailing almost due south till it came within sight of the French coast. The voyage is reported by the chroniclers to have been smooth, but repairs were needed in some of the horse boats (and some horses were lost) before the destination was reached. The work was carried out by Cheshire archers from the companies of Hamo Mascy and Robert Brun who were duly given additional pay when the ships put into port.[168] By September 20th the fleet lay in the Garonne under the walls of Bordeaux. To John Clerk, master of the *Christofre*, the prince made a gift of 10*l*. The hundred sailors in her crew were also rewarded.[169]

CHAPTER III

THE FIRST RAID

THE English force spent a fortnight in Bordeaux. Very few of its members had seen this great fortified city [1] whose fourteenth-century walls came close to the quayside and encircled the commercial and administrative centres of the greatest wine-exporting region in the world. Within the walls stood the cathedral of St. Andrew, the castle, several religious houses, a mint, factories producing vessels for the storage and transport of wine, warehouses and all the buildings needed by the merchants, shop-keepers, civil servants, soldiers and other members of a trading centre which was greater than any English provincial town and may have been not much inferior in population and commercial importance to London itself.

Outside the walls flowed the Garonne, far wider than the Thames and used for transport between the many riverside towns both on the Garonne and the Dordogne.

The neighbouring countryside resembled that of many an English county. Sheep and goats grazed in the fields, pigs nosed for acorns in the woods of Entre Deux Mers, oxen drew carts along the roads, windmills stood on the hilltops and thick woods lay within a few miles of Bordeaux. The region, however, produced little corn and it devoted wide areas to the vine. [2]

The troops arrived at the height of the *vendange*, the season (between the last day of August and the beginning of October) in which the grapes were gathered. For this occasion containers and vehicles of all kinds were pressed into use. Every person who could be obtained by obligatory or paid or voluntary service was employed and the whole community devoted itself to the harvesting, pressing and storing of its chief product. There was no fast or feast day in the diocese during this busy period. [3]

There is no reason to suspect the cordiality of the welcome offered by any section of the community to the prince and his men. The town was wholly loyal to the English king; no royal person of such eminence had visited it for more than half a century; the prince was young and distinguished in bearing. Moreover, Bordeaux's privileges had been scrupulously respected by

43

English kings and its prosperity was heightened by successive *chevauchées*. As for the Gascon lords who had assembled to meet the prince, not only was he the eldest son of their liege lord, he had also come at their express invitation and, implicitly, he had come to achieve ends very dear to their hearts. Whether they be regarded as long-suffering men in need of powerful support against French encroachments or as grasping fellows who desired to plunder their neighbours, the prospect of campaigning with him would be agreeable.

At a solemn meeting held in the cathedral on the day after the arrival, the formal relationship between the various parties was made clear and recognized. In the presence of the clergy, the lords, the officials, and the representatives of the town, the prince promised to respect the rights, liberties and customs of the city and province; his status as defined in his father's long statement[4] was proclaimed; the oaths of the Gascon seigneurs were received.

Among these seigneurs the most prominent was Jean de Grailly, usually known as the Captal de Buch, lord of various domains in the 'landes', a Knight of the Garter, one of the most accomplished soldiers of the period and already well known to the prince. With him were his neighbour in the 'landes', Bernard, Sire d'Albret, representative of a house which for several generations was loyal to the English side; Amauri de Biron, Sire de Montferrand; Auger de Montaut, Sire de Mussidon; Guillaume de Pommiers; Guillaume Sans, Sire de Lesparre; Guillaume Amanier, Sire de Roson.[5] These men were members of the *petite noblesse* of south-western France, inferior in wealth and influence to Jean d'Armagnac and Gaston Phoebus, Count of Foix. They had brought fighting men—Gascon and Bearnais—to augment the prince's army;[6] they were of course called in to the council, for they had local knowledge and a clear conception of the course the campaign ought to take.

Another group of men who joined the expedition before the end of September (and apparently at Bordeaux) are described as Almains. They included William Qwad, Ingelbrith Zobbe, Bernard van Zedeles and Daniel van Pesse. And there were three men whose official work was of great importance to the expedition, namely John de Chiverston, Seneschal of Gascony, John de Stretelee, Constable of Bordeaux and Thomas Roos, Mayor of Bordeaux.

It must be supposed that in the king's mind, the general purpose of the prince's campaign was linked in one strategic whole
with the purposes of the other campaigns it was intended to
launch in the same summer. The king was to invade France from
the north-east, Lancaster was to aid the revolt of Charles of Navarre
in Normandy while the prince made an attack in the south-west.
The direction the southern campaign should take, had not,
however, been defined. English and Gascon leaders, therefore,
were assembled to consider plans for joint operations. The outcome as stated by the prince and by Baker, was simple. Jean I,
Count of Armagnac, lieutenant of the King of France in Languedoc
and commander of the French forces in the region, had done much
injury to the English and to the Gascon lords who remained
faithful to the English cause. It was decided, therefore, to ravage
his land of Armagnac, and the decision was clothed by the prince
in a phrase of almost constitutional rectitude. 'It was agreed,' he
wrote, 'by advice and counsel of all the lords being with us and of
the lords and barons of Gascony.'[7]

The situation was, however, more complicated than the prince's
brief statement implies, for no considerable force could operate
in the region without taking into account the power and territories of the Count of Foix.[8] This young and capable noble had
been at the battle of Crécy, had mingled in the turmoil of French
politics in the succeeding years, had held the office now held by
Jean d'Armagnac, was Armagnac's hereditary rival and—most
important—had been imprisoned in the Châtelet at Paris for
eighteen months. By release or escape, he had left his prison just
before the prince landed at Bordeaux. Deprived of his lieutenancy,
subordinate to his enemy, suspected by the French, he had good
reasons for coldness to the French side. His aid would have been
invaluable to the prince. Froissart, who made of him the most
striking portrait in the vast gallery of his chronicles, is silent about
the part he played in 1355. Baker however reveals that on three
occasions, as the path of the prince's troops crossed parts of the
count's domains, they refrained from plunder and destruction and
on November 17th, the count had a conference with the prince.[9]
The careful respect for his property and the pre-arranged meeting
are evidence of an understanding. The Count did not go to the
help of Jean d'Armagnac and the Marshal of France, nor did he
side with the prince; but he placed no obstacle in the prince's
path and some Bearnais troops joined the expedition. It is in the

light of this tacit understanding that the decision to ravage Armagnac must be read.

It has become usual to describe the operation on which the
prince was about to embark as a raid. That word, though derived
from Old English, is not the word our forefathers used. It is more
Scottish than English and it came into general use as Scott's
novels were widely read. The original meaning of raid was road.
Our ancestors, however, thought of the operation as a ride: in
Latin the verb was *equitare*, in French *chevaucher*. Earlier French
writers had distinguished between *l' host* (*expeditio*), an important
war for the defence of the country, and *la chevauchée*, an operation
against, say, a rebellious lord.[10] That is to say a *chevauchée* was an
operation of warlike character on a relatively small scale. By the
fourteenth century, *chevaucher à l'aventure* is used to describe the
actions of the famous *routier* Amerigot Marchès and *chevaucher de
guerre* covered activity regarded as specifically military. *Chevaucher*
had in fact come to have a flavour of the mounted soldier with
his twin activities of fighting and plunder.

But by this time, military art comprised a third phase. Armies
fight and 'live on the land'; armies may be allowed or encouraged
to plunder; they must also be used to destroy the means of living.
Destruction, therefore, of habitations and of the means by which
life is maintained becomes an important part of a *chevauchée*.
While modern strategy consists in cutting off supplies at the
source, destroying them in bulk, or disrupting their transport,
medieval leaders were obliged to destroy them 'on the spot'.
Once the work of destruction is started, it may go further than
strict military needs require. If a town has been besieged and
resisted its attackers for some time, its ultimate capture may be
followed by a combination of butchery, plunder and destruction
which is irrational but intelligible. On occasion, undefended
villages may suffer the same fate. And, at a time when timber
forms so large a part of almost all buildings, the most useful means
of destruction is fire. It makes no demands on transport, requires
no muscular effort and is all-consuming.

Medieval warfare is not solely, nor even largely, battles and
sieges. For weeks and even months at a time, it is military pressure
exerted by the destruction of life, property and the means by which
life is maintained. But the commander must keep in mind his
principal aim. It may be to seek out the enemy's main force and

bring it to a decisive encounter; it may be to create a diversion compelling the enemy to divide his forces and change his plans; it may be to punish or terrify the inhabitants of a region in order to demonstrate the penalties of hostility. If the commander's main aim is to attack, he will take such victuals as he needs but have little time for pillage and destruction. If however his aim is diversion or retribution, his policy may be that of the typical *chevauchée* and the governing factors are the nature of the region, the season of the year and the morale of his troops. Two local considerations may restrain indiscriminate pillage and destruction: the property of the church is commonly, but by no means always, respected; the property of an ally or a friend must be spared. At times, therefore, control of the troops is tightened up.

But the practices of pillage and destruction are detrimental to the morale of an army, for they imply that the military commander is indifferent to the lot of the civilian population. Further, ordained destruction sanctions the most purposeless violence with works of art and little household treasures. It is but a step to the abandonment of all restraint in dealing with the local population. A subordinate leader may occasionally 'mount his horse, ride through the streets' and 'save many lives of ladies, damosels and cloisterers from defoiling', or the king, on grounds of prudence rather than principle, may allow his adviser to 'ride through the streets' and 'command none to be so hardy to put fire in any house, to slay any person nor to violate any woman'. But the raiding force is not usually restrained by humane considerations and, as Froissart says, 'in a host such as the King of England was leading, there must needs be some bad fellows and evil doers and men of little feeling'. In short, in the worst raids, 'evil deeds' and murders may go hand in hand with robbery and arson.[11]

Broadly, the operation proceeds in this way. A large number of horses are made ready; carts will be used if the roads are suitable for wheeled traffic. The army carries its own supplies or obtains them legally till it reaches the frontier. From that point onwards, nothing except the property of the church or of a friend need be respected. The commander will seize food in bulk; marauders will take what victuals they desire; men are free to pillage or even accept money for refraining from pillage.

On reaching a village or town, the troops usually have little difficulty in overcoming civilian resistance. Valuables are collected and loaded into carts or heaped on the horses' backs; cattle are driven away or killed; the work of destruction begins. Granaries, ricks of hay, corn or straw, barns, cattle-sheds, houses and their contents are fired. Wooden bridges are broken, windmills and watermills are burnt or rendered unserviceable, wine vats emptied. In wine-producing regions, knowledgeable men can damage or kill growing vines.

News of the army's approach spreads very quickly and, as clouds of smoke by day and a red glow by night mark the invader's route (or routes, for a large force might move in columns), the inhabitants, seized by panic, flee and thus facilitate the work of the troops: a deserted town stocked with a winter's supply of food and fuel, is a suitable place for a halt and some good meals. But the army never lingers long and there are days when the men have little to eat and the horses little to drink. Always there is the danger of ambushes, of homesteads having been fired by their occupants in order to destroy food and shelter, of houses in walled towns being set on fire at night by concealed enemies or drunken soldiers, of bridges being broken to delay the invader's advance.

To these minor risks and difficulties of the raiding force must, of course, be added an encounter with national forces coming to the defence of the ravaged region, luring the invaders into difficulties, seeking to cut them off from their base, compelling a pitched battle. Finally, in a sparsely peopled area (for example, the Scottish border), it may be impossible either to live on the land or to find guides: the army loses its way, loses touch with its line of supplies and is in dire straits.

Such in outline was a typical raid in the thirty years before the prince entered Gascony. Large scale material destruction and the constant use of fire had become a regular practice. Nor was such work confined to English armies. French troops operating on the borders of Flanders, took the same measures and, at times, burnt and destroyed supplies in their own country lest English invaders should profit by them,[12] while the Scots conducted warfare with heartless ferocity in Northumberland, Durham and Cumberland.[13] In July 1346, the King of France informed King David of Scotland that as England was practically denuded of troops he had an opportunity of wreaking the utmost damage if he would invade England.[14]

By this time the practice had become so much a part of policy that it was included in indentures. The Earl of Northampton,

on appointment in April 1355 to command in Brittany, was empowered '*chevaucher de guerre* against enemies by land and sea, to
take and knock down towns, castles, fortresses as he judges to be
in the king's interests. . . .'[15] It had also become a subject for
argument in that slowly accumulating body of principles, inter-
nationally recognized, which was held to govern the conduct of
war.[16]

Whether the prince's operations in southern France be regarded
as full-scale warfare or as a *chevauchée*, it was inevitable that they
should follow the pattern so widely prevalent. He and all his
principal lieutenants had accompanied Edward III in 1346, when
he ravaged the coast of Normandy and carried fire and sword to
the gates of Paris. They knew the work of Henry, Duke of Lancaster, who had campaigned in Poitou and Guienne, and of others
who served in the smaller affrays during (and in spite of) the
truces. These campaigns had afforded scope for knightly combat
as well as for the ignoble practice of destruction. That the coming
campaign would afford the invaders more opportunities for the
latter than for the former no one could have foretold. They must
have been prepared for both.

A fortnight after its arrival in Bordeaux, the English part of the
expedition was ready to leave for Armagnac. The *James* of
Exmouth had been sent straight back to England on the prince's
business.[17] (The other ships appear to have stayed in the port
for some time and may have been used to take wine to English
ports.) Cargoes had been discharged and the horses unshipped by
means of hoists.[18] Quantities of provender had been bought and
the horses 'rested'[19] (probably given time in the fields for exercise
as nature prompted after the debilitating confinement of the
voyage). Quantities of goods, including bows and arrows, had
been sent upstream to Saint Macaire where they were probably
taken into the convoy as it passed,[20] and large disbursements had
been made to English and Welsh leaders in the prince's retinue.[21]
We shall not enter here into the financial machinery employed
nor shall we distinguish between the several kinds of payments
made. It is sufficient to note that money was available for purchases
and the payment of wages, and that both sterling and French
currency were in circulation in Gascony. Certain men appointed
to remain in Bordeaux had also been paid.[22]

For the prince's household, there were purchases of meat, fish, firewood and salt. Of the prince's more personal affairs, the records afford a few glimpses: money was provided for his private use and for gaming. A medicine chest was made and a dozen boxes to contain confectionery, while quantities of striped material were obtained to be tailored for his clothing He also received a gift of two falcons from the lord of Lesparre.[23]

The force set out on Monday, October 5th. (Both Baker and Froissart state that the departure was hurried.[24] October was late for the beginning of a campaign.) It followed the road along the valley of the Garonne through Langon as far as Castets en Dorthe, then struck southward through the 'landes' to the neighbourhood of Arouille, thus:

On	Monday to Villeneuve d'Ornon	.	.	4	miles
,,	Tuesday to Castets en Dorthe	.	.	25	,,
,,	Wednesday (rest)	.	.	.	.	0	,,
,,	Thursday to Bazas	.	.	.	10	,,
,,	Friday (rest)	.	.	.	.	0	,,
,,	Saturday to Castelnau	.	.	$11\frac{1}{2}$	,,
,,	Sunday to Arouille	.	.	.	25	,,

Baker comments on the two longer marches for they both caused the 'loss of many horses'.[25] The animals may have been overloaded or overdriven. More probably they were suffering from 'transport fever', a condition still found in horses that have been moved long distances by ship or rail. The malady commonly occurs about three weeks after they have reached their destination and, unless quickly treated, proves fatal.

During this first week, the troops and horses were subsisting on food brought from Bordeaux or bought on the journey. Hay was bought at Ornon, hay and oats at Castets en Dorthe, corn and wine at Bazas, meat at Castelnau. Some wine was also bought for the Welsh troops and a large sum was paid in compensation for damage done by these men at Castets en Dorthe.[26]

The force was now approaching 'enemy territory'. In the open country near Arouille, the column was divided into three corps.[27] The vanguard was placed under the command of the Earl of Warwick and Sir Reginald Cobham with John Beauchamp, Roger (afterwards lord) Clifford and Sir Thomas Hampton who was the standard-bearer.

The main body was commanded by the prince with whom were the Earl of Oxford, Bartholomew de Burghersh, John de Lisle, Lord Willoughby de Eresby, Roger de la Warre, Sir Maurice

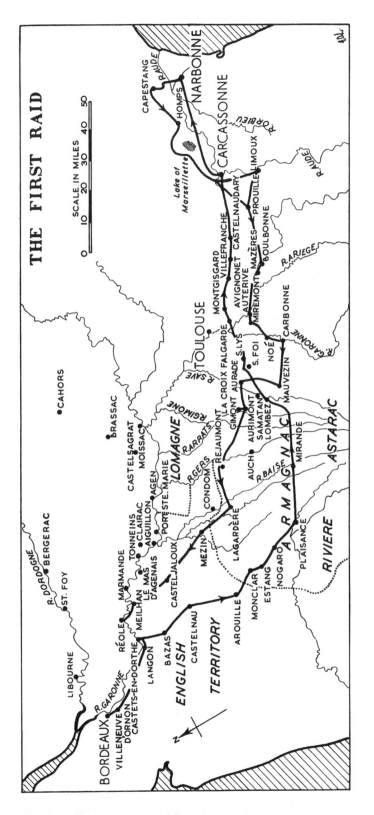

Berkeley, John Bourchier, Thomas Roos, and three Gascon lords, the Captal de Buch, John Sire de Caumont and Aimeri de Biron, Sire de Montferrand.

The rearguard was under the command of the Earls of Suffolk and Salisbury, and with them was Guillaume de Pommiers, leader of the Bearnais.

From this point onwards the march assumes a different character. New knights have been dubbed (as was common before battles); standards have been unfurled; the force moves in three corps which may act separately, one or two being detached for work or for night quarters at a distance from the main line of route; the purchase of provisions ceases; pillage and destruction begin;[28] armed resistance may be met.

Since, however, such resistance was slight, and an account of the campaign tends to be a rather repetitive narrative of minor incidents, we shall trace the route followed, indicate the speed, and pause to consider the situation at Toulouse, Carcassone, Narbonne and Carbonne. Finally, we shall review the campaign as a whole.

The territory lying immediately ahead of the army was (in Baker's words) the 'famous, beautiful and rich' land of Armagnac.[29] Sloping down from the foothills of the Pyrenees towards the Garonne, its surface deeply furrowed by many tributaries of that river, it was a fair land. It was, moreover, the domain of the lord whose policy had been so hostile to the English cause.

During the two days the army spent near Arouille the first acts of war occurred. The town was regained for the English side and the troops were allowed to go out to take victuals and forage and to set fire to properties on enemy territory. On Tuesday (October 13th) the fighting began. Three towns were taken and burnt, the fort of Estang was captured, the castle of Monclar surrendered and troops entered the town. It was a satisfactory start and the more experienced leaders probably recalled two commonplaces of the camp: the storming of fortresses is costly in human lives; one of their group, Sir John de Lisle, had been fatally wounded. Secondly, soldiers who spent a night in a captured, walled town incur grave risks: in the darkness, Monclar went up in flames. The prince escaped but, during the remainder of the campaign, where there was no monastery or castle available for his quarters, his tent was erected in the open.[30]

After two days' pause, the forces advanced on Friday (16th) to the fortified place, Nogaro, and on Saturday, reached Plaisance. From this town the civil population had already fled, but the Count of Montluzon and other lords had remained in the castle. They were captured by the Captal de Buch.[31]

Here the main army stayed all Sunday while one corps turned westwards, took by assault the castle of Galiax and burnt it. Plaisance which had sheltered the army for two nights, was burnt on Monday and the force moved eastwards along the road leading towards Auch, the capital city.[32] The easterly direction was maintained at the cost of crossing ridge after ridge and river after river, mainly, it may be supposed at fords and, as (according to *Froissart*) the summer had been dry,[33] the water-courses probably presented no serious obstacles. The average day's journey was however only about eight miles.

By Monday evening the army reached Bassoue. This was church property (it belonged to the Archbishop of Auch) and completely respected: only the officers in charge of victualling were allowed to enter. On Wednesday (21st) the army passed near Montesquiou, came down to the bank of the Blaise at Mirande, a well garrisoned town belonging to the Count of Comminges, and the prince had his quarters in the Benedictine abbey of Berdoues, a little distance upstream. The abbey was already deserted but its goods and fabric were respected. As for the town of Mirande, though the army remained near it all Thursday, it was apparently not taken. The soldiers are said to have rested and it is likely that no attempt was made to gain possession, for a siege would have taken time and an assault would have been costly in lives.[34] Moreover, the road from Montesquiou to Mirande led away from Auch. Auch also was not to be besieged.

On Friday (23rd) the prince and his troops left Armagnac. Circumstances which he could not foresee caused him to traverse another part of this county a few weeks later but, in view of the declared purpose of the campaign, it is convenient to consider his achievement. In a letter written at Christmas to the Bishop of Winchester, the prince stated that he had ridden 'through the land of Armagnac harrying and wasting the country, whereby the lieges of our most honoured lord (the king) whom the count had before oppressed, were much comforted'.[35] Baker's terse narrative supplies no details beyond those already quoted. Froissart makes no reference to this region at this time. Wengfeld says, 'My lord (the prince) hath ridden through the county of Armagnac and hath taken there many walled towns and hath burnt and destroyed them, save certain towns which he hath strengthened. And then he went into the county of Riviere and took a goodly town which is called Plaisance and which is the chief town of the land and he burnt and destroyed it and all the country round about.'[36] In short, there had been no substantial resistance anywhere. Such French forces as were in the south-west were either local garrisons without cohesion, incapable of holding up the English invasion, or the royal troops under the command of the Constable and the Count Jean d'Armagnac. The latter had been at Agen on the day the prince left Bordeaux but had withdrawn to the east.[37]

If the troops kept mainly to the route described by Baker, they had covered a distance of about eighty miles; they had spent ten or eleven days in the county and they were sufficiently numerous to have done a great deal of destruction and consumed or carried off a considerable quantity of food.

But neither in the prince's letter to the Bishop of Winchester nor in Wengfeld's letter is there any pause after their references to Armagnac. From the continuity of the narratives, it would be inferred that while the avowed, primary aim of the campaign had been achieved, the prince was pursuing other ends, not declared but probably well understood by the bishop and certainly clear enough to himself and the English and Gascon leaders. It may be judged that the enterprise on which they had embarked was deemed to be prospering, that it was carried forward by its own momentum, that the leaders felt strong enough to risk an encounter with a French army and adventurous enough to desire some fighting. They decided to advance eastwards still crossing the ridges and the rivers in spite of the difficulties of the march. They may have had Toulouse in mind.

Passing into Astarac, the force reached Seissan on Friday (23rd) and here occurred an instance of indiscipline important enough to be recorded (by Baker): notwithstanding the prince's strict orders, the town was fired and could not be saved.[38] As in Armagnac, the news of his advance spread far in advance of his columns. Inhabitants fled before his troops arrived, but left stores of food. On Saturday (24th) the three corps camped separately, the vanguard at Tournans, the main body at Simorre (in the valley of the Gimone), the rearguard at Villefranche (a mile upstream), each having victuals without the trouble of foraging.[39]

On Sunday (25th), continuing eastwards, they saw Sauveterre on their left, passed by but did not take the fortified town of Lombez, forded the Save and spent the night in the large deserted town of Samatan. On the following day, the town was burnt (and a convent in it) and the army entered the domains of the Count of Comminges which they ravaged with fire and sword, crossing the rich, well-cultivated plateau of Touch, passing through Sainte Foy and reaching Saint Lys for the night (26th).[40]

They were now within a dozen miles of Toulouse. In that large, fortified town were concentrated the forces of the Count of Armagnac and his fellow-lords whose duty and interest lay in opposing this invading army which had spread havoc in their territories.

What form the opposition should take lay with the count to decide. The French could come out and compel the prince to fight a battle in the open or, by staying within their walls, they would compel him to lay siege to their town. Both forces, of course, employed 'coureurs' and, as intelligence came in, it became evident that Count Jean had made preparations: the bridges over the Garonne had been broken down; the many houses outside the city walls had been destroyed so that besieging troops would have no shelter. Jean intended that the prince should not pass Toulouse. He was awaiting an attack from the west.

Tuesday (October 27th), described by Baker as a rest day, was a day of decision. Having come so far and with such ease, what was to be the ultimate objective? To continue the march eastwards was to go straight to Toulouse. If the Count of Armagnac emerged, a battle, it may have been felt, would turn in their favour. Even so, unless the town capitulated forthwith, there would have to be a siege; and sieges, if they lasted more than a few days, were wearying operations calling for artillery and costly assaults. If, however, Count Jean did not emerge, the siege would be even longer. Small fortresses—provided they did not command river crossings—might be by-passed by keeping out of bow-shot or by risking casualties. But Toulouse was not a place of that kind. It was the capital city of the region, the focus of communications, the natural rendezvous for French troops, the only point at which the Garonne could be crossed (if anybody even considered a crossing desirable); and its garrison was commanded by the man whose 'oppression' of English subjects had formed the ostensible (and perhaps the real) reason for the direction the campaign had taken. To by-pass Toulouse—were it possible—

E

would be contrary to military prudence. In any case it would not
be possible, for a great river barred further advance eastward.
If the *chevauchée* was too enjoyable to be dropped, then the force
might turn north, south or west. It could not go east.

The English decision was audacious to the point of the fool-
hardy. Had it failed, posterity would have treated it with contempt.
Its success has led historians to leave it unnoticed in a campaign
lacking military interest. The decision had a threefold boldness.
The great fortified town should be by-passed with all the risks
involved in leaving a powerful hostile garrison in the rear at the
only bridge left standing. The great river should be crossed without the aid of a bridge; in fact two rivers should be crossed in
one day with a ten-mile march as a prelude. The crossings should
be made at points where Jean d'Armagnac—if he had the will—
could station his archers and men-at-arms on the opposite bank
and kill his enemies as they struggled through the waters or sought
to climb ashore.

Great speed, pluck and discipline were needed—and good
fortune. 'There was never a man in our host that knew the ford
there, but by the grace of God, they found it,' wrote Wengfeld.[41]
They found a ford (probably between Rogues and Pinsaguel, a
little above the confluence), marched the troops ten miles to it, got
them across the great river—men, horses, baggage-carts—moved
forward a couple of miles, plunged into the Ariège, a narrower but
swifter river, crossed that also and made their camp at La Croix
Falgarde, all in one day (28th). The prince stated that the two
rivers were 'very stiff and strong to pass', and admitted that he had
had some casualties.[42] Baker described the Garonne as 'swift,
rocky and terrifying', the Ariège was 'still more dangerous than
the Garonne'.[43] Wengfeld made the situation clear: 'Our enemies',
he said, 'had broken down all the bridges on the one side of Toulouse and the other, save only the bridge in Toulouse, for the
river goeth through the midst of the city.' There were great
forces, he continued, in that city, yet the English troops had
effected the passage.[44]

Audacity had succeeded. To Jean d'Armagnac such a movement of troops was probably unthinkable for, as Baker says,
'never till this day had horsed troops crossed these waters. That
is why the people in the district, panic-stricken, unwarlike in
temperament—for they believed they were secure behind their
rivers—not knowing what course to take and unable to flee, made

no resistance.'[45] And Jean himself had opposed no resistance! In a single day the strategic situation had been completely changed. The prince could now—if he wished—penetrate deep into Languedoc. It had been a memorable achievement and should still be regarded as noteworthy.

The night following this daring and exhausting movement was spent at La Croix Falgarde.[46] An attack on Toulouse from the south may have been considered and rejected. Some slight demonstration (probably a reconnaissance in force) within view of the city walls was apparently made, and there was pillage and burning in the locality.[47] But the leaders' aim was to proceed eastward and, though the evidence does not warrant the inference that they had in mind a firm objective, they followed the eastward route across southern France for another week. The 'land of Toulouse' was described as 'very rich and plenteous'.[48] The three corps were often employed on separate tasks and numbers of small towns and small strongholds were easily gained.[49] Baker supplies the main itinerary. On Thursday (29th) they moved through Castanet and in the evening camped on the bank of the Hers at Montgiscard. The town had been taken by force at the cost of some casualties. It was, of course, plundered and burned. Froissart tells the story in his usual style and then adds an unexpected note of pity for the fate of the men, women and children of this town.[50] Two spies, captured in the town, reported that the Constable of France was at Montauban hoping that the prince's army would be held up in a siege of Toulouse.[51]

The next day (30th) the prince advanced along the old Roman road, the Via Domitia, through Baziège and Villefranche to Avignonet. The inhabitants had fled before his arrival and the various corps were quartered in the town and suburbs for the night. Some of the richer people had taken shelter in the castle but it was taken by storm and they became prisoners. There followed the usual pillage and destruction and here, as also at Montgiscard, the soldiers burnt some windmills.[52]

On Saturday (31st) the army burnt Mas Saintes Puelles with its Augustinian abbey and reached Castelnaudary, a large town, feebly fortified but stoutly defended. It was taken by storm amid much butchery. Its men were held to ransom or, if they declined, they were manhandled.[53] Sunday (November 1st, the feast of All Saints) was a rest day for the army but some of the men went out and gained possession of a town whose inhabitants purchased their security by a payment of 10,000 gold florins. Castelnaudary, town and castle, was subsequently burnt and with it a church, two convents (of the Friars Minor and the Carmelites) and the hospital of St. Antony.[54] Monday (2nd) was spent in a march through Saint Martin la Lande, Las Bordes and Villepinte to Alzonne, and on Tuesday (3rd) the force reached the important town and great fortress of Carcassonne.[55]

Here, as in several other towns in southern France, human habitations and military protection were very clearly separated in space. The town (*le Bourg*) of Carcassonne, rich, large and defenceless stood on the left bank of the Aude, the castle (*la Cité*) on the right, the two banks being connected by a stone bridge which had not been broken. The town was well stocked with wine and provisions; refugees had poured in from all the countryside and, as the army drew near, very many of them had gone with such valuables as could be carried, to the Cité in which already the burgesses had stored much of their portable wealth.

In the light of their experience, the leaders would conclude that the town could be taken without serious difficulty and both the prince and Baker in their terse narratives, imply that the army entered an almost deserted town and took up its quarters without opposition.[56] Froissart, however, states that chains had been stretched across the streets and that the townsmen—bidaus armed with lances and bucklers—strenuously resisted the attackers; that the English horsemen dismounted and with banners and pennons flying, leapt over the chains and, sword in hand, fought the bidaus while archers poured arrows into the bucklers and in the end, the bidaus withdrew across the bridge to the Cité.[57] This may be a magnified version of a minor episode. The army lodged in the town in safety and had plenty of food and wine.[58]

There remained however the Cité. Situated on a hill rising to 150 feet above the level of the bridge, this immense bastion was one of the most formidable essays in military architecture of the period. Its double row of towers and lofty walls enclosed a small fortress-town which dominated the eastern exit from the Bourg. If it were adequately provisioned, it might resist a siege for months. A halt of such duration was not in keeping with a *chevauchée*. Moreover, a force which, in spite of broken bridges, had crossed the Garonne and the Ariège could readily find a way across the Aude—if indeed a further eastward advance was desired. It might even use the stone bridge and risk the showers of arrows which would pour down from the Cité. And it might consider the situation which would arise if large French forces should be assembled in its rear. Possession of the Cité was not at all indispensable, but it would be advantageous to the prince: it would increase his military security, his wealth and his prestige.

A further factor needed consideration. Though the inhabitants had deserted the Bourg, they were near at hand; though they could not prevent the destruction of their town, they could, and did, offer to negotiate terms for a payment in return for which the town should be spared. During Wednesday and Thursday (4th and 5th), while the army rested, representatives argued over the terms. On the side of the Carcassonnais the sum of 250,000 *écus d'or* was proposed in return for the preservation of the Bourg from fire. To this offer was added a plea from the local clergy that the prince would not allow the town to be burnt or to suffer any further damage, but neither the inhabitants nor the clergy could negotiate the surrender of the Cité.[59]

The offer was rejected and the rejection deserves consideration. It was an immense sum, far greater than would be available in the town for immediate payment and probably greater than could have been raised quickly by loan in the circumstances prevailing in Languedoc in the autumn of 1355. Baker does not say the sum was insufficient. He regards it as irrelevant: the prince's purpose was not to raise money but to demonstrate the justice of his cause. He also holds that the apparent steadfastness of the occupants of the Cité in their loyalty to the French king was really fear of his vengeance. Though these statements are obscure, they merit examination in the light of the circumstances. There may well have been reasoning among the French that terrible as was the immediate power of the prince, a *chevauchée* was a passing phenomenon; that sooner or later (as in Normandy in 1346), French authority would be restored and therefore (on the level of expediency) resistance would prove better than surrender. On the other hand, the Cité was impregnable; time was on the side of its commander; there is no ground for doubting his fidelity or that of his garrison to the French crown; the prince was obliged to bear in mind the certainty that French armies were moving to meet him. With great reluctance, the fact that the great military prize would not be gained, had to be accepted.

Under the circumstances a bargain over the commercial town

must have been unacceptable. While the prince was well aware that the hope of financial gain animated a large part of his army, he himself might be regarded as inspired by loftier or, at any rate, different motives. Furthermore, though in the inconsistencies of human affairs it was expedient to connive at various practices in the troops, he himself had not, so far, been a party to a sordid transaction of the kind proposed. In the light of Edward III's claim, the people of Carcassonne had to be regarded as his father's subjects and, since they offered resistance, as rebels and therefore his father's enemies. As Edward's lieutenant, he could not bargain with them. Their proposal was refused with haughty disdain.

No more time was to be wasted. Instructions were given that on Friday morning the town should be burnt, with the usual provision that church property should be respected. The destruction, however, was complete.

Froissart says that the army crossed the bridge over the Aude and that, in passing the foot of the hill on which the Cité stands, it was assailed by great stones flung by the artillery of the fortress. He may be referring to a section of the troops.[60] It is unlikely that an attempt was made to take the whole army out by that route. Baker says the army withdrew (*recessit*) and its journey that day was 'heavy-going, stony and marshy'.[61] It was no longer on the Roman road that it was marching, but along the left bank of the Aude and soon along the southern edge of the lake of Marseillette. Trebes was burnt; the surrounding country was devastated and quarters for the night were found or made at Rustiques (November 6th). After skirting the lake of Marseillette, the force passed through Serame (which it did not destroy: the town belonged to a friend of the prince) and reached Canet (November 7th). On Sunday (8th) it crossed the Orbieu in two sections, one passing over an unfinished bridge at Villedaigne, the other using a ford at Raissac d'Aude and, after a journey over the hills between Moussan and Bizanet, it reached Narbonne.

This town, famous since Roman days, had enjoyed great commercial importance but the approach from the sea was becoming more and more difficult for large vessels as the channel gradually silted up. Though its maritime importance was diminished, it remained a flourishing trading centre in the midst of a prosperous region. Stone bridges spanned that arm of the Aude which still flowed, in declining volume, through the town.

It resembled Carcassonne in that its Bourg and its Cité stood on opposite sides of the river. The Cité was well fortified, garrisoned, and equipped with artillery capable of projecting missiles into the Bourg. It was believed that quantities of gold, silver and jewels were stored within its walls and that it also sheltered rich men whose capture might lead to the payment of big ransoms. Treasures and ransoms, however, could not be gained without a siege.

When the army approached Narbonne, the women and children moved into the Cité. The invading troops fought their way into the Bourg, took their quarters in the houses and enjoyed the large stores of food and wine, but a shower of missiles flung by the balistae in the Cité, poured into the Bourg by night and day. Among the casualties was Jean de Pommiers. Clearly the town could not be occupied for long without serious losses. Several heavy assaults were made on the Cité on Monday and Tuesday (9th, 10th) but all were stoutly repelled. Withdrawal, therefore, became imperative. The city was fired and the soldiers made their way through the blazing houses into the open country, followed by the Narbonnais who managed to smash and pillage some of the prince's wagons. Held in among the retreating English soldiers were prominent Narbonnais whom the prince had taken as hostages. They had to accompany the troops as far as Cuxac d'Aude where those who could pay suitable ransoms were released. The remainder were executed.[62]

The withdrawal from Narbonne (November 10th) was a check to a force which had enjoyed for so long an easy passage through French territory. Since, as we have stated, it is not possible to infer what ultimate objective the Anglo-Gascon leaders had in mind, or indeed whether they had any definite objective, it is not possible to reconstruct fully the situation confronting them. The Gascon lords who had asked King Edward to send his son to Gascony and who had pressed him to attack Armagnac, had had their wishes fulfilled. The power of the French king had been flaunted by a daring incursion deep into his territory, inflicting great injury on his subjects. Fear of the prince's approach had spread across southern France causing the inhabitants of Montpellier and even Avignon to prepare their defences. With friends gratified and enemies insulted and injured, some aims, it might be held, had been achieved. As for the knights and archers, many of them had journeyed nearly three hundred miles from their homes to the English seaport. They had now travelled a similar distance from the French port and were maintaining themselves from the abundant supplies of a fertile region and enriching themselves with plunder. No serious opposition had been met. Yet opposition there must be, for the French king could not allow the work of devastation to continue with impunity. Moreover it was almost mid-November. As the winter advanced, even hardy troops would need warmth and shelter at night.

From different sources but almost at the same time, news arrived that King Edward had landed in France, that the pope wished to communicate with the prince and that French forces were massed in the prince's rear. Only a little later it was reported that French troops were moving from Montpellier.[63]

Two bishops riding from Avignon had sent a messenger to ask for a safe conduct in order that they might deliver the pope's request that the prince would negotiate with the king of France. The request was in keeping with papal policy throughout the period. Letters were in fact sent to all four earls and to others in the prince's circle and to Jaques de Bourbon, Jean de Clermont and other French nobles begging members of both sides to use their influence to bring about a truce. Moreover, the prince had been empowered to make a truce. On the other hand, the moment chosen was inopportune. The bishops were informed that they should confer with King Edward and, in a letter written six weeks later, the prince described the episode in terms which emphasized the correctness of his procedure.[64]

Correctness also appears in the major decision of policy for the force under his command. A French army, prisoners revealed, had at last taken the field and was following the Anglo-Gascon army in the direction of Narbonne. 'We took counsel whether we might best withdraw,' wrote the prince, 'and we turned again to meet them.'[65]

From Narbonne, the most eastward point reached in the raid, the prince's troops had marched northwards. They had paused before Cuxac d'Aude (which was fortified), completely destroyed Ouveillan (November 11th) and a detachment had begun a siege of Capestang. Negotiations were started for the payment of money in return for which the town should be spared, but at this point news was received of French forces near at hand in the west and of a force moving from Beaucaire in the east. The Council's decision was made: operations at Capestang were discontinued; the army turned westwards.

The change was one of direction rather than of method. For the moment it was necessary to face the French army and from now onwards, the ultimate objective is quite clear: it is to reach the march land near Bordeaux with as much of the accumulated booty as can be convoyed without endangering the column. But the practices of the great raiding force remained unaltered. The devastation continued; prudence alternated with boldness in the choice of route; there were days of hunger and discomfort and days of feasting plenty; at its own pace, it made its way back to its base.

On leaving Capestang, the leaders expected that the French and English forces would meet in battle within three days, and at Homps (November 12th) they learned that officers of the Count of Armagnac had actually spent the previous night there. Why Armagnac did not stand and force a decision must remain a matter for conjecture. Whether the prince could have overtaken him as he withdrew towards Carcassonne must equally remain undetermined. (The English army had had a very difficult march on Wednesday (November 11th), along stony roads where they could get neither food nor water for cooking. Only wine and oil were available and the horses had actually been allowed to drink wine.) After leaving Homps, the army split into groups. The town of Pepieux and the castle of Redorte were taken and the main body spent the night (November 12th) at Azille where a great store of muscat wine was pillaged.

The journeys made on November 13th and 14th are most difficult to trace. According to Baker, that of the 13th was long and extremely wearying. It passed over rocky roads where no water could be got and ended in a camp made wretched by lack of water and lack of shelter. On 14th, he says, they crossed their former track. By Sunday (15th) the route is quite clear again. The most recent French scholar holds that from Azille the prince, determined to avoid contact with Armagnac's army, made a detour northward via Siran, Lalivinière, Ventajou, Peyriac, Villalier, Conques, and camped his three corps in different places near Pennautier for the night of Saturday (14th). That is to say, he passed north of Carcassonne.[66]

On the following day (Sunday, 15th) a part of the troops moved westward along a good road through rich, open country, passing Montreal and increasing its speed because the prince was to be entertained in the great religious house of the Friars Preacher at Sainte Marie de Prouille. Here the prince and many of his suite were admitted to the brotherhood and a very substantial gift in cash was presented on behalf of the prince by Richard of Leominster, one of the Friars Preacher who had accompanied the expedition from England.[67]

Meanwhile another part of the army swept round southwards sacking and burning Limoux, Lasserre, Fanjeaux (with its score of wind mills) and Villasavary.

The combined force proceeded on Monday (16th) to Belpech where town and castle were quite separate. The former was taken by force, the latter surrendered. But Belpech was spared damage by fire, for it belonged to the Count of Foix.

Travelling westward on Tuesday morning (17th), they reached the valley of the Hers where news of the prince's approach had preceded him. The friars had made ready their hospitality at Prouille and awaited him. Today the Count of Foix awaited him and gave him a cordial reception at the abbey of Boulbonne. Count and prince spent several hours together riding downstream mainly through the count's domains and, as Baker puts it, 'out of respect for the count and his neighbours, there was a truce to fires on that day'.[68]

The Ariège was crossed again and the main body camped at Miremont which they subsequently burned. A short march on the 18th brought them to the Garonne at Montaut where, at normal times, ferry-boats were available for a crossing. The boats had of course been removed but, to the astonishment of the inhabitants, the feat of three week's earlier was repeated. Heavy rain was falling and the men learned subsequently that had they arrived one day later, the flood waters would have rendered a crossing impossible. Baker attributed the success of this second hazardous venture to divine providence. Without a pause, they moved up the left bank. One detachment actually recrossed the Garonne, took Marquefaue and returned, while the remainder advanced to Carbonne, took it by assault and lodged in the town for the night. They must have been wet and tired.

The rain ceased however and on Thursday (November 19th), in calm and delightful weather, the men rested. It was the first real halt since leaving Narbonne and, in view of the laborious journeys and work of the preceding days, they needed a pause for recuperation.

Now that the Anglo-Gascon army was encamped west of the Garonne, a new phase of the military situation opened. Jean d'Armagnac had not forced an encounter, nor sent his men up-stream to oppose a crossing of either of the formidable rivers, nor taken any effectual steps to hinder the progress of the raiding force which had continued its destructive practices within a few miles of the great strongholds of Carcassonne and Toulouse. He could not now bar the route to Bordeaux but he might seek to embarrass the retiring army by attacks on detachments, by break-ing bridges, by harassing the rearguard. This he did. The evi-dence however is not sufficient to permit a reconstruction of his tactics—which were doubtless opportunist—nor an assessment of their results, save that they very materially increased the diffi-culties of the prince's task.

The difficulties were due to the season of the year and the load of booty his men had acquired. By this time, the hours of day-light were short, wintry weather had begun, roads were soft, rivers were swollen and he could not expect to find a bridge stand-ing anywhere. Yet he must contrive to get his men into the warmth and shelter of winter quarters as soon as possible, and must resist the temptation to chase attackers back toward Toulouse. The first need was to choose a good route.

Day to day decisions, particularly the choice of route and halting place were made in the light of 'intelligence'. Medieval com-manders, of course, used reconnaissance forces, 'coureurs', scouts, spies, and extracted information from prisoners. (A Scottish prisoner, Froissart relates, 'was so sore examined that for fear of his life' he divulged his leader's plan. On the other hand it was a French prisoner who, to gain a reward revealed to King Edward the vital ford of Blanchetaque which enabled his army to cross the Somme.)[69] These resources were available to the prince. He also used local guides. Two grooms had shown him the way from Castets en Dorthe at the beginning of the journey.[70] There was, however, a 'guide for Gascony', named Arnold Bernard, who at the end of the campaign received 9l. for his services.[71]

The route actually followed from Carbonne to Bordeaux may well have been the best. Baker writes boastfully of some skir-mishes and small engagements but, behind his words, may be read the hardships of the march and a determination on the prince's part to avoid a large-scale action. Moreover he reveals, though tersely, the difficulty of crossing the rivers. At the Garonne itself, the movement had been as smooth as a drill (*equites singuli, successive . . . transierunt*).[72] At the tributaries, scattered men sought a hazardous crossing where they thought it might be possible (*transierunt districte . . .; cum districcione magna . . .*).[73] In one place, he states clearly that it was hoped that a river the army had crossed would serve as a barrier against the enemy.[74] Further, there were three bad nights—two in places without water and the third in a place where they arrived very late and passed the darkness in expectation of a battle on the morrow. Between Thursday, November 19th, and Sunday, November 28th, there was only one rest day and the average distance covered works out at about twelve miles a day. This does not differ greatly from the pauses and distances in the earlier part of the campaign but, when allowance is made for the conditions under which they were now travelling, it will be inferred that for both men and horses these days formed a period of great discomfort.

There was contact between sections of the armies on Friday, Saturday and Sunday (November 20th, 21st, 22nd). French forces had moved out of Toulouse—probably with the intention of making an attack on the English flank or of pressing the English back to the river. News of the French movement reached the English camp during the night of Thursday–Friday. The prince says that Jean d'Armagnac, the Constable of France, the Marshal Clermont and the whole French force camped within two leagues of the English rearguard. Baker says it was known that the French were divided into five strong columns. On Friday morning, a party of eighty lances under Burghersh, Audley, Chandos and Botetourt, was sent out to gain information and, in a skirmish, captured more than thirty French knights (including the Count of Comminges), killed many waggoners and destroyed their provisions. A considerable body of French troops then retired, not towards Toulouse but westward. Later in the day, a few were found taking refuge in the church of Mauvezin where their right of refuge was respected. (They were deprived of their arms and their horses, but not held to ransom.) The greater part however fled across the Save, broke the bridges and encamped in safety on the river bank at Lombez and Sauveterre where, in the light of their fires, they could be seen by the English troops encamped on the eastern bank, 'but there was between them and us a great, deep river'.[75]

The following day (21st) these French troops moved northward.

The English also—still east of the Save—moved under pouring rain down the narrow and difficult roads in the valleys of the Aussonne and the Save as far as Aurade and on Sunday (22nd) crossed their former track (the high road from Auch to Toulouse), forded the Save and towards dusk, approached Gimont. Here, however, the French troops were able to impose a check. Well placed on a hill outside the town, they offered sufficient resistance to hold the English force at bay till midnight. During the delay some English troops were sent five miles upstream and gained possession of Aurimont. Here the main body spent an uncomfortable night while the vanguard passed what few hours remained at Celymont. The French had diverted the army from its shortest route to its objective and had not given up Gimont. The opposing forces were near enough for another engagement.

Another engagement was certainly expected on the English side. Before sunrise, on the following morning (23rd), while the transport men were kept in Aurimont, the whole fighting force was arrayed for battle in the fields. There they remained for hours till a reconnoitring body brought news that the greater part of the French force had withdrawn from Gimont during the night. The fortress itself, though lightly garrisoned, was strong enough to endure a long siege.

The prince's council was assembled to consider policy. 'And, forasmuch as we perceived that they would not have fighting, it was agreed that we ought to draw to our marches.' [76] But there was no relief yet for the troops. They crossed the Gimone and the Arrats and on Tuesday (24th), after a long day's march, they had to bivouac in open country. Here, once more, they were short of water. Horses, allowed to slake their thirst in wine, died and the work of transport became even more laborious. The enemy were still following up and it was with great difficulty that the scattered groups managed to cross the Gers. That flood, it was hoped, might serve as an obstacle to the enemy. They then forced their way into Réjaumont (25th) and had their first rest since leaving the bank of the Garonne (Thursday, 26th). Here a prisoner captured from the French, reported that between Jean d'Armagnac and the Constable of France there was deep disagreement, the latter reproaching the former for his inactivity and for the unworthy performance of his troops. [77]

Friday (27th) was spent in another long march and a difficult crossing of the Baise. From their various camps south of Condom, they were gathered on Saturday morning (28th) to cross the swollen Osse and enter the thickly wooded country which lay on the western boundary of Armagnac.

At last the army had reached the march land and the enemy had ceased to follow. Arduous and dangerous though the closing phases of the march had been, they had not wholly prevented the work of destruction, for firing a town required little time and effort. Aurade had been burnt. Réjaumont had had to be taken by force and therefore (*ideo*, says Baker) it was burnt.[78]

But the campaign was now at an end. Standards were furled. Prompt steps were taken to liberate the Gascon sections of the army. Before they left, the prince promised them another expedition for the following summer and even greater 'profit'. They expressed their satisfaction and their willingness to follow his lead. Then all the Bearnais troops and many of the Gascons were allowed to return to their homes.

Saturday night (28th) and all Sunday (29th) the English and Welsh troops spent at Mezin. It was now neither necessary nor permissible to forage. Supplies of bread, hay and oats were obtained by payment. Nor, of course, was it permissible to fire houses. For one that was burnt, compensation was paid.[79] Monday (30th) was spent in a long march through the moorland to Casteljaloux and on Tuesday (December 1st) the force pushed on northward through the forests, one section (led by paid guides) going to the abbey of Montpouillan and the other straight to La Réole.

At La Réole, the prince's council, in formal session, decided the location of winter quarters and a few days later the prince reached Bordeaux.

As for the booty, though Froissart emphasizes the quantity and regards the Gascons as very grasping, he gives no details of its disposal. Probably very many of the articles were regarded as individual possessions. His summary is 'You should know that in this journey, the prince and his men had very great profit',[80] and it was this kind of profit to which the prince referred in his farewell remarks to the Gascon troops.

Assessments of the character and importance of the *chevauchée* have varied widely. Though the sources are almost entirely English (or, as in Froissart's chronicle, broadly favourable to the English cause), there has been no dispute over the three main features of the operation, namely that an Anglo-Gascon force proceeded from Bordeaux to Narbonne; that it did very much damage and that no French force resisted it. It is concerning the purpose of the expedition, the means employed and the reasons for the inaction of the French leaders that differences of view have been advanced.

These differences spring largely from two circumstances. In the first place, to some minds the whole episode is paradoxical. A large army moved across hundreds of miles of 'enemy' territory without fighting a battle. Such an operation, they feel, cannot justly be regarded as military. (Military historians have largely ignored it. Oman dismisses it in two sentences.) Moreover, this army, fully equipped for war, used its energies in pillage and destruction. Such activities offend the moral sense of modern times and therefore lead to unqualified condemnation. Further, the man whose status and domains made him the natural, and whose royal appointment made him the official, protector of the region, witnessed this army at its evil work and did not oppose it. His inaction seems inexplicable.

The second (and less important) circumstance lies in the nature of French studies of the campaign.[81] By most careful work, French scholars, studying the prince's movements in their own localities, have gone very far in the identification of Baker's place-names and thus produced a more accurate itinerary than would have been possible for English scholars. Their researches, though gaining in detail, have suffered somewhat in breadth. Concentrating on the activities of English troops in limited areas, they have lacked the perspective of the broad, national, and indeed international, background.

Now, it is only against the full background of the Anglo-French conflict that a just view may be gained. We gather up here, therefore, some earlier passages on the aims of the force.

The campaign in the south was part of a three-pronged attack on France conceived in the minds of Edward III and his counsellors. Though the functions of the three prongs are not recorded (and, by modern minds, perhaps not readily inferred), it must be held that they were considered to form a strategic whole. In any case, France was as vulnerable in the south as in the north and a blow struck from Bordeaux might (as the event showed) prove as effectual as one struck from Calais or Saint Vaast de la Hogue. Coinciding in time with the other attacks, it should serve to divert

French forces from the north. It was a military means for the achievement of the great political end, namely the pure sovereignty of the English monarch in those regions he claimed to rule independently of the French crown.

Given this general aim and Bordeaux as the base, the prince's counsellors had decided that the blow should be struck first in the county of Armagnac. By bringing retribution on a persistent opponent of the English cause, it would serve as a demonstration of England's might. But the conception of the work to be undertaken may be seen in the financial arrangements. Half a year's wages and fees had been paid in advance and another half year's wages and fees had been guaranteed. The great engine of war had not been set in motion for a mere ten days' work in the ravaging of a single county. Military and financial provision had been made for a much greater campaign. The lesson taught in Armagnac could be driven home much deeper in French territory. Moreover, the leaders enjoyed the work. Far from avoiding a fight, they were seeking one. They moved straight toward Toulouse, waited a whole day within ten miles of that city and, being no doubt well informed by scouts that Jean d'Armagnac proposed to remain within its walls, decided to advance along the great main road of southern France. Their purpose was still political but their military objective was vague. It might be Carcassonne, Narbonne, Beziers, Montpellier or even Avignon. (Fear of their approach did, in fact, spread along that artery of communication.) The council would decide in the light of circumstances. After the intelligence received near Capestang, the council's decision was clear: the army would return to Bordeaux, taking with it as much as possible of the great quantity of valuables it had gathered on its march.

Yet the original purpose of the campaign had been clouded by the circumstances of the march. French writers have indeed regarded both this campaign and that of 1356 as having no aim but pillage and devastation of enemy territory, and Mr. Belloc has been cited in support of this view since he stated that the prince regarded towns as "objects for plunder." These judgments arise from mistaking the means for the end. Edward III had not financed this expedition, nor had the leaders embarked on it, solely for pillage and devastation. If Jean d'Armagnac had emerged in force from Toulouse on October 26th or 27th, the prince might never have crossed the Garonne. Jean's resolute inactivity facilitated the worst deeds of the invader, deprived both sides of military glory and gave the enterprise an appearance which has deceived subsequent generations.

We are now in a position to review the campaign as a whole. Viewed as a military operation, it was successful. A march of four hundred miles across enemy territory, accompanied by systematic devastation was carried through with scarcely a check. If French forces had sustained no decisive defeat, it was because they had not ventured to oppose the invaders. If it brought little military glory to the English, it spelt deep humiliation to the French. That the campaign 'had not conquered a region' is true but irrelevant. Conquest was not its purpose. That 'the prince's enterprise was absurd' is a view we need not discuss, for it is founded on a misconception.[82] That his campaign lacked a strategic plan is in some degree true, but it is almost a truism of all warfare in the fourteenth century.

Viewed in the light of political considerations, again the campaign was successful, for the Gascon subjects of King Edward were strengthened and exalted in their loyalty, and ready for another such operation in the following year.

A still further aspect of the campaign was regarded with satisfaction because of its consequences for France. The region in which the Anglo-Gascon army had operated was rich and assessed highly for taxation. The complete destruction of Carcassonne, the virtual destruction of Narbonne and a score of other towns would cause a very serious loss of revenue for the French crown. To the prince's advisers, this aspect, verified from the tax-accounts found in the towns they had occupied, was very gratifying.

Finally, by pillage collected and by money exacted as ransoms or the price of immunity from attack, very many members of the expedition had been enriched. National advantage and personal advantage had been combined. Service with the prince had its rewards.

Concerning the prince's methods of campaigning, two broad condemnations have been made by French critics: he avoided battles and sieges, and he resorted to pillage and destruction.[83] With the absence of battles in this autumn *chevauchée*, we have already dealt. The responsibility lay with Jean d'Armagnac. But the era furnishes other examples of unwillingness to stake all on a decisive encounter. In the strange episode at Buironfosse, the kings of England and France had agreed on the date and site of

F

a battle, but it did not take place. Even in the autumn of 1355, when King Edward invaded northern France, King John did not force an engagement on the invader. And in 1359, when Edward again invaded France, the dauphin Charles avoided battle. The policy of Jean d'Armagnac, therefore, was not necessarily inconsistent with the military practices of his age. We will return to his circumstances later.

The avoidance of sieges was a feature of the typical raid. In his classic campaign of 1346, Edward III did not assault castles or closed towns. He 'passed by the strong castle of Rolleboise' and he 'passed by the city of Beauvais'.[84] Sieges were costly in time; assaults were costly in soldiers and artillery. A fortress situated in a mountain pass or at the bridge over a broad river was an unavoidable obstacle, but a leader who boldly got his men across a river without a bridge, or was prepared to incur the risks inherent in leaving an enemy garrison in his rear, was defying the conventional limitations of movement. He cannot justly be reproached for such initiative.

Concerning the charge of pillage and destruction, a threefold answer may be made. First, it is of course true. Secondly, as M. Perroy has recently pointed out,[85] if a *chevauchée* of several thousand men enters enemy territory and is not met in a pitched battle, all it can do is to pillage: it cannot conquer, still less occupy the territory. Thirdly, these practices were not innovations devised by the prince and his men for use against the people of Languedoc. They were, as we have shown, regular features of fourteenth-century warfare and regarded as legitimate and even honourable. The prince and his chief followers had learned the art of campaigning from Edward III. They were 'very eager and desirous to acquit themselves well'. They were in fact the 'flower of chivalry' and many were members of the Order of the Garter. That the 'flower of chivalry' should spend a Sunday with a devout brotherhood at Prouille, while their men only a few miles away were burning down the homes of the burgesses of Limoux, was not incongruous to the mind of 1355. They were neither better nor worse than the men of their age and, when the duty of conducting operations fell to them, they experienced the satisfaction and even the pride that comes from the efficient execution of almost routine tasks. 'We took our road', the prince wrote, 'through the land of Toulouse where were many goodly towns and strongholds burnt and destroyed, for the land was very rich and plenteous; and there was not a day but towns, castles and strongholds were taken. . . .'[86]

To Wengfeld, no soldier but a very experienced steward, who viewed property as the source of revenue, the soldiers' work was gratifying. 'Since this war began', he wrote, 'there was never such loss nor destruction as hath been in this raid'. The taxes provided by the areas now devastated had, he declared, supported a very large part of the French army. He had had access to the revenue records in the captured towns and was, therefore, looking beyond the immediate damage to the future war potential. Further, Wengfeld went on, 'my lord hath not lost in all this march, knight or squire save only my Lord of Lisle who was slain. . .'[87]

Moreover, the baggage train of heavily laden beasts and overloaded vehicles had conveyed the valuables gathered during the long journey, safely to the English base. As Froissart declared, the expedition had brought 'much profit'.

Seen through English eyes, the mission entrusted to the prince had prospered. Great damage had been inflicted on the enemy; the men had returned to their base; the cost in life had been negligible and there was a good store of plunder. Regular methods systematically employed had produced the usual results. Daring policy had been crowned with success. And, if the prince occasionally wrote contemptuously of his opponents' courage, they had displayed little enough. Judged by the standards of the time, the prince had carried through a model raid.

Seen through French eyes, however, the prince's work must have been heart-rending. Though direct evidence from genuine French sources is scanty, it confirms and complements that obtained from English sources and from Froissart. From the one side we have descriptions of the destruction of flourishing towns and small fortresses; from the other instructions for rebuilding or repair. And the promptitude and urgency of the measures taken, form evidence of the calamitous extent of the damage.

The great fire at Carcassonne was started on November 6th. On November 22nd, King John sent a letter of sympathy to the citizens and on the same day an order to the Count of Armagnac directing him to take immediate steps to rebuild the town and put it in a state of defence against future attack. In order to raise funds for the work, the Count authorized the levying of tolls on goods brought into the town, and the task was completed by April 1359.[88]

Before the summer of 1356, similar measures were in hand for the rebuilding of Castelnaudary, Alzonne, Limoux and Narbonne. Among the measures taken to raise money, to ease burdens and to facilitate the work, were the allocation of fines to the expenses of building, the exemption of the inhabitants for a period from the payment of various dues, deferment for the repayment of debts, the impressment of carpenters and masons, and the right to take timber in the royal forests for the building of churches and hospitals. There is specific reference to the rebuilding of mills and to the drafting of documents intended to replace those destroyed in the fires.[89] The need for all this constructive activity points to the great material damage these towns had suffered.

The most enduring effects, however, were not material. Buildings might be replaced but memories remained, and though there is probably no dreadful deed recorded of Languedoc in 1355 but could be paralleled by deeds in Normandy in 1346, the southern raid left a more painful and more lasting scar than the great raid of King Edward. Between the two campaigns there were differences in the season (summer in 1346, autumn in 1355), in the armies employed, and in the racial stock and previous history of the populations affected. The prince's army was an Anglo-Gascon body, the king's almost entirely English. The prince's command was subject in some degree to conciliar control, or, at least, assent; the king's was unfettered. Moreover, the prince's army included men who had a personal grievance against Armagnac. It may well be that the mixed troops of 1355 were held in slacker reins as they sped the work of destruction than were the troops of King Edward. Gross spoilers as were the latter, they witnessed the king's sternness when they overstepped prescribed bounds. When, for example, in contravention of orders, the abbey of Saint Lucien (Messien) near Beauvais was destroyed in 1346, the king promptly hanged a score of them.[90] Baker, however, records the prince's inability to prevent the burning of Seissan.[91] He also mentions the destruction of church property in several places and, in particular, at Carcassonne where explicit orders for its preservation had been given. Even the incendiary strokes appear livelier in the narratives of 1355 than in those of 1346 for, whereas Baker mentions firing nine times in the earlier raid and uses the same word (*comburo*) eight times, in describing the later raid he makes seventeen allusions to the practice but contrives to use a dozen different phrases (burnt, went up in flames, consigned to the flames, burnt to ashes, etc.) to describe it.

We can make no comparison of the methods employed by the soldiers in the two raids, but Froissart leaves vivid pictures of the sack of towns in Languedoc—the wanton ('they took what they liked and burnt the rest'), the discriminating ('disregarded clothing and went only for silver plate and cash'), the indiscriminate ('nothing of value remained. They carried off everything, especially the Gascons, who are very grasping.').[92]

Scenes of this kind must have been burnt into the memories of thousands of people and, when they were accompanied by personal violence and even slaughter, Froissart himself, usually so tolerant of soldierly excesses and so indifferent to the lot of common people, is moved to feeling. At Montgiscard, after mentioning the ill-treatment of men, women and children, he adds, 'It was an occasion for pity.'[93] The men and women of Toulouse (who did not suffer an attack) are described as 'dispirited, and with good reason, for they knew not yet what war was',[94] and the people living east of that city (who felt the full weight of the raid) were 'good, simple folk who did not know war, for they had never had war made upon them'.[95] Baker comments in similar terms on the people living beyond the Garonne: they were temperamentally unwarlike. To the consuls of Carcassonne, King John sent a letter of sympathy, in which he said he had full information about their overwhelming disaster and innumerable losses.[96] And Wengfeld, summing up the situation at the end of the raid, said 'our enemies are sore astonished'.[97] Mentally and morally unprepared to bear with fortitude the horror, misery and grief inseparable from war, they had seen their great bridges broken down, their suburbs razed, their stores plundered, theri cities burnt, their valuables stolen and, in many instances, their fellows killed. The swift-moving, devastating power moved on unresisted, irresistible, spreading havoc wherever it went. Winter found them mourning, bewildered and fearful for the morrow. The ruthless invaders had remained on French soil and were active even in mid-winter; their odious allies were but a few leagues away in Bearn and Gascony. The terrible episode might be repeated unless a powerful protector arose.

The man responsible for the protection of the region was Jean d'Armagnac, now about forty years of age.[98] As a young man he had gained military experience in the defence of the Holy See and he had taken part in the early stages of the Hundred Years War in Flanders and Normandy. With him may be associated, in some measure, Jaques de Bourbon, Constable of France and Jean de Clermont, Marshal of France and military commander of the region between the Loire and the Dordogne. Frenchmen have not been slow to note (and often to condemn) the policy these leaders followed in the autumn of 1355. M. Jeanjean cites three French writers of the seventeenth century and one of the eighteenth, all of whom were bewildered that men in command of forces numerically superior to those of the prince, failed to attack him.[99] More modern scholars are equally at a loss for an explanation.

At least four reasons have been advanced to account for the inactivity of Jean d'Armagnac,[100] namely:
(1) That he was secretly in league with the English.
(2) That he was a coward.
(3) That he and Jaques de Bourbon were at variance about the course to be followed.
(4) That in view of the general situation, great prudence was necessary.

It is most improbable that he had a secret understanding with the English. Though his loyalty to the French cause was not absolute, he had furthered French interests during his lieutenancy, was rightly trusted (according to Froissart) by the people of Toulouse, and could hardly have retained any pro-English sentiment after hearing the stories of the refugees who fled before the prince's devastating army to the shelter of Toulouse.

Concerning his courage, we have no evidence to support or refute the view. It is, however, necessary to distinguish between knightly bravery *per se* and responsible leadership.

The third and fourth reasons may be considered together. That there was disharmony among the French leaders is likely. A prisoner captured in the closing days of the campaign, reported that there was deep disagreement between Armagnac and the Constable who is said to have reproached him that he had done nothing for France and that his soldiers had repeatedly and shamefully taken to flight. If that be true, the responsibility for policy falls wholly on Jean d'Armagnac.

Kindly critics find some difficulty in defending Jean's policy. His position, however, deserves examination. Notwithstanding the assertions of the earlier writers that he had greater forces under his command than had the prince, we have no accurate figures of the strength of either side. Moreover, the equivocal attitude of his rival, the Count of Foix (who actually welcomed the prince on November 17th within thirty miles of Toulouse), must have given Jean grounds for caution. His own policy of destroying houses outside the city walls may have made him unpopular. Froissart states that the citizens of Toulouse desired to fight but that he restrained them, holding that they were quite unfit to match themselves against the experienced troops in the prince's army.[101] It is likely that he had not envisaged the possibility that the prince might, or even could, cross the Garonne. And, if he felt unsure of his power to defeat the prince's force, he may well have decided that it was wiser to save his resources than to plunge rashly into action which must end in calamity. Chivalry lauded boldness in the individual but paid less attention to the further qualities needed in the general. Jean was not alone, as we have shown, in avoiding pitched battles and, if his role in the autumn of 1355 was inglorious, it was less disastrous for France than the leadership which had brought her so low at Crécy and was to bring her still lower at Poitiers.

CHAPTER IV

BETWEEN THE RAIDS

NEWS of the great raid had, as we have seen, spread quickly across southern France and northwards also to the French king. What was the amount and the quality of the information that reached England? and at what date was it received? Immediately after his arrival at Bordeaux in September, the prince had sent a dispatch to England—probably in the *James* of Exmouth.[1] He sent no further formal communication till Christmas. It is likely, however, that a little was known, for the pope was very well informed and papal envoys were constantly active; many wine-carrying vessels left Bordeaux for England in the early autumn and the two sub-admirals, Hoggeshaw and Deyncourt, returned with some of the vessels which had conveyed the army to Gascony. Deyncourt was, however, back at Southampton by November 22nd and Hoggeshaw (who travelled in the *Thomas* of Dartmouth) had reached England on October 27th.[2] The common talk of the seaports and the oral reports of reputable officers could not have afforded reliable information about the progress of the campaign in November and the return of the army to its base.

Late in December two important communications [3] were sent from Bordeaux to the Bishop of Winchester, one of the 'guardians of the realm' during the king's absence. The first was a report by the prince on the autumn campaign. It is formal in tone and (except that it omits dates) is of the type a commander-in-chief might make in almost any century. The route followed, the council's decisions, the reasons for refusing to treat with the papal envoys, the damage done in Armagnac and elsewhere—these form the substance of the dispatch; and there is a brief account of the skirmishes between Carbonne and Gimont. Five men are mentioned by name in the dispatch—Audley, Botetourt, Burghersh, Chandos and Felton—but without praise or blame. The dispatch contains no request for help or instructions concerning further operations, nor does it make any recommendations.

The second communication is a letter from Sir John Wengfeld

to the Bishop of Winchester. It is friendly in tone, covers much
of the same ground as the prince's dispatch but adds a few points
of interest: the prince, earls, barons, bannerets, knights and squires
are in good health; only the Lord de Lisle had been lost in the
campaign; the pope's serjeant-at-arms had been in his (Wengfeld's) custody and he had used the serjeant's services to interview men who had acted as guides to the Constable of France.
Wengfeld was greatly impressed by the destruction the army had
wrought, particularly because of the resulting loss of revenue to
the French king. Once—only once—he uses the verb 'spoil'
(*gastames*). It is of the towns in the viscounty of Narbonne.

The two letters would be of great value to the king and his
advisers but, in estimating their significance, it must be remembered that neither the king nor (so far as is known) his advisers
had ever travelled across southern France, nor was any source of
contemporary geographical information available for even the
best informed men save the testimony of travellers. This, of
course, is implicit in Wengfeld's letter. He tells the bishop that
Carcassonne is 'greater, stronger and fairer' than York, and is at
pains to describe the position of Narbonne by reference to the
Mediterranean, to Montpellier (a university city), to Aigues
Mortes (an important seaport at that period), and to Avignon.
He even says—probably very inaccurately—that it is 'little smaller
than London'. The two letters by themselves, therefore, convey
news that the expedition has travelled a great distance, done very
much damage, had very little fighting, suffered few losses and is
back at its base. The information, though inexact, was no doubt
the best it was possible to send about military operations in that
area at that period. It was in the light of such information that
future policy would have to be settled.

There remained the oral reports of reputable officers and here
the prince took the usual, prudent course: he chose a suitable
agent to bear his dispatch and asked the bishop to get further
information from him. Sir Richard Stafford took both letters to
England.[4] They probably reached the bishop in the second half
of January 1356.

A second letter from Wengfeld conveyed more up to-date
information.[5] Dated January 22nd (1356), and addressed to
Stafford, it reads as a friendly, private communication. On the
other hand, the information it contains is so comprehensive as to
suggest that since Stafford had become a liaison officer between

the prince and the English administration, Wengfeld felt it desirable, or perhaps had received instructions, for him to be kept informed of the course of events whenever a ship was sailing to England. This letter describes in detail military operations by English forces 'since your departure', gives the location and strength of units, mentions the work of commanders and the undertakings that were still in progress. It also reveals the movements of the Count of Armagnac and it ends with a request to Stafford to 'send news to my lord the soonest that in any way you can'. At this period, information was being duly forwarded from Gascony and news from England was earnestly desired.

Had Stafford been instructed to ask for reinforcements? It is impossible to say. But at the end of his letter to the bishop, Wengfeld remarks almost casually 'and by the help of God, if my lord had wherewithal to maintain this war and to do the king's profit and his own honour, he would easily enlarge the marches and would win many places'. At any rate, a few months later, Stafford returned to Gascony with reinforcements.

Wengfeld's letter to Stafford throws light on a more personal aspect of the expedition. In the records of the administration of the prince's estates, Wengfeld's name occurs many scores of times and Stafford's not a few. That the one was a competent official and the other a faithful agent would naturally be inferred. But what kind of men were they? The tone and contents of the letter reveal glimpses of the humanity of both men. 'Right dear lord and right trusty friend', it begins and, after quickly summing up the latest successes in the war, it turns promptly to 'your men', that is to say Sir Richard's tiny personal following who were now necessarily grouped with other commanders. 'And please you to know that my lord John Chandos, my lord James Audley and your men that are with them . . . (and other troops and leaders) took the town which is called Castelsagrat by assault'. . . . The others have now gone elsewhere but 'my lord John and my lord James and those of their company have remained in Castelsagrat and have enough of victuals between this and St. John's day save fresh fish and greens. . . . Wherefore you need not concern yourself about your good folk. . . . The enemy has assembled forces near Castelsagrat . . . and you may well think that there will be a goodly company there for each man to make trial of his comrade.'

From this letter and other evidence, slight in itself but cumulative, it becomes evident that Audley, Chandos, Botetourt and, at times, Burghersh were the prince's handy men for field work, that Stafford was assigned to 'special tasks' (as he had been before the campaign), that Wengfeld remained as 'head of the office' and that these men, who had of course known one another before going out to France, formed a group bound by friendly relations to one another and by common loyalty to their chief: they were part of the 'permanent staff'. Other knights there were of equal ability and greater wealth, but their capacities were not yet so well known. The prince relied on his tried servants. And Froissart's highly coloured story of the prince's solicitude for Audley after the battle of Poitiers,[6] is perhaps best understood not in terms of chivalry as the fulfilment of the obligation of a knight to a fellow knight in distress, but of attachment to a member of the 'headquarters staff' to whom the prince was bound by ties of frequent contact, admiration and affection. The coldly impersonal entries in Henxteworth's journal show that very soon after Chandos and Audley were said to be short of fresh fish, a large quantity of lampreys was bought, packed up and forwarded to them at considerable expense.[7] Gifts of money were common. No comparable gift of food is recorded for months.

At a meeting held at La Réole as the English army was returning from its campaign, the Council had decided on the places in which the component groups should spend part of the winter. It is probable that the groups went straight from La Réole to their quarters: Suffolk and his men to Saint Émilion, Salisbury and his men to Sainte Foy, the prince's men to Libourne, while Warwick and his followers stayed at La Réole. The prince and his household staff went to Bordeaux.[8]

For a short period, military work was at a standstill. The men settled in their new quarters and enjoyed a rest after the rigours of the long march. The opportunity was taken to straighten out the accounts.

Though we are not entering into a formal study of army finance, the payments made at this period are sufficiently interesting and important to deserve mention. We start, therefore, with a short reference to the evidence afforded by Henxteworth's journal. Henxteworth acted as a cashier recording payments of the most diverse kinds as he made them. He accompanied the prince during the autumn campaign and made some payments then, but his work had been far greater before the army set out from Bordeaux and it grew again on its return. For each day on which he made payments, he recorded the total sum in hand, stating the amounts he held in French and in English currency. Often he noted the rate of exchange and sometimes the source from which his funds were drawn.

It was not, however, his duty to provide a statement comparable with a Minister's Account. His disbursements are not grouped; they are not explained; they are simply recorded. On the same page among great sums paid to the leaders for their wages, occur trifling amounts for petty purchases in the kitchen and minor services. Moreover, there is no indication in the journal of the periods for which wages are paid, nor whether sums paid on the same day to different men cover the same period of service. Further, where wages are paid for archers or for grooms, he seldom gives any figures on which calculations might be based. To sum up, while the journal throws light on several aspects of the army's life and activities, it has a limited value as a source for the study of army finance.

Before the prince left London in July 1355, he had received wages and reward for himself and the men of his own retinue for half a year, payment being reckoned (as was usual) from thè day on which they reached the sea.[9] Before the prince sailed, sums totalling more than £7,240 had been paid out in the fees and wages of knights and men-at-arms together with the purchase of victuals.[10] Before the expedition left Bordeaux, there had been large disbursements to the leaders. On its return to winter quarters, large disbursements were resumed.

Some of the foreign knights (e.g. William Qwad and Ingelbert Zobbe) had received their fees in September.[11] Now, foreign and English knights alike received sums in payment of wages. Though the periods covered are not stated in the journal, they appear to have been recorded in the knight's pay-book or some other book: the usual entry is *pro denariis sibi debitis libro memorandorum* and, in a few instances, the words *sicut patet* are inserted before *libro memorandorum*.

The payment of grooms is always coupled with the shoeing of horses and appears to have been part of the duty of the Clerk of the Sea who may have acted as Henxteworth's assistant. Though no indication of the number of horses or grooms is given, periods are sometimes indicated. In September, some entries in this class are 'till the eighth day of October'. In December, the typical entry runs: 'To the Clerk of the Sea for wages of grooms and shoeing of horses of ——'. Sometimes 'during the campaign' (*tempore guerre*) is added and, in one instance, 'for 47 days in the campaign'. Often a knight's personal payment and that for his grooms and horses are entered on the same day.

As examples, the following [12] may be quoted from the entries for December 16th:

	Grooms and Shoeing.			Wages.		
	£	s.	d.	£	s.	d.
Nigel Loring	5	17	6	9	13	1
Richard Plaice	5	18	5	10	1	10
Thomas Bradgate	1	0	5	2	16	3
John del Haye	1	0	6	1	13	9
Richard Baskerville	5	4	9	9	13	3
David ap Blethin Vaughan	1	0	6	39	0	6
Gronou ap Griffith	1	0	6	43	17	6

and these[13] from the entries for December 17th:

Richard de Stafford	11	15	0	36	0	2
Ralph Bassett	15	0	6	32	4	7
James Audley	5	10	7½	12	18	1

Some moneys paid out for the Cheshire archers are recorded on January 2nd.[14] They are paid in advance and in French currency (leopards):

	£	s.	d.
Hamo Mascy, leader of 63 Cheshire archers for their wages paid direct (i.e. to Mascy)	11	18	6
John Daniers for 18 archers staying in Bordeaux	4	1	0
Ralph Mobberly for 32 archers	7	4	0
Hamo Mascy „ 11 „	0	11	0
Robert Brun „ 28 „	6	6	0
John Hide „ 37 „	8	6	6

Most of these were evidently for nine days.

It must be emphasized that deductions based on the comparative sizes of the payments quoted may be unsound. Moreover, Audley received further sums on December 24th and 27th, while Stafford (who was on the point of leaving for England) received 21*l.* on December 29th, the two Welsh leaders cited each received advance payment of 10*l.* on December 24th, and Loring and Bassett also had further sums on January 8th.[15]

Payment of wages may be traced for several months. There were, however, no regular 'pay-days' but, when the army was not on the march, sums due and even payments in advance were available at fairly short intervals. Sometimes the money was paid direct to the knight or leader; at other times it was paid 'through the hands' of the knight's squire or chaplain or associate or an official. Payments continued through the period when the groups were widely separated and, during Stafford's absence in England, payments were made on his behalf to a deputy.[16] If looting was practised in the first half of 1356, it cannot justly be attributed to lack of wages.

As for the currency in which wages were paid, Henxteworth always quoted in terms of sterling but often used (and probably was obliged to use) a quantity of French specie, especially at the end of 1355 and the beginning of 1356. In September 1355 (when the journal begins) and June 1356 (when it closes), one leopard was worth 4s. 6d. sterling, but he duly notes a temporary change of value on May 24th when it rose to 5s. 6d.[17] A couple of payments to men for guarding leopards remind one of the conditions of the time.[18]

The prince and his staff spent several weeks in Bordeaux and many of the leaders were there in December. Two chroniclers give glimpses of what may have been considered fitting for knights enjoying their ease after a campaign. The Anonimalle chronicler says, 'The prince returned to Bordeaux before Christmas, commanding his lords and chiefs to sojourn in various towns in the district and to have ease and refreshment for themselves and their men all the following winter. And thus they remained till the feast of St. Mary Magdalen',[19] while Chandos Herald states, 'The prince . . . abode there (at Bordeaux) until the whole winter was passed. He and his noble knights were there in great joy and solace. There was gaiety, noblesse, courtesy, goodness and largesse.'[20]

As regards the duration of this period of solace ('all the winter', 'the whole winter'), the picture is seriously wrong. For the rest, it is probably true enough. The courts of kings, princes and the greater nobles were crowded with knights, squires, grooms, members high and low of the domestic staff, messengers, chaplains, minstrels. Few could read and, in any case, there was little reading matter. Entertainment of one kind or another, indoors or out of doors, was indispensable and good manners were polished in factitious gaiety. It was in keeping with the prince's character that there should be sumptuous festivity.

But, of all this aspect of the expedition at rest Henxteworth's sober pages of course provide little evidence. A few purchases which served as a material base for life in the court may be quoted. From Saint Macaire on the last stage of the homeward journey, bread and wine are brought down to Bordeaux by water.[21] Then firewood and coal are bought, herrings and other fish, carcasses of pork, almonds, wax, candles. For the horses, hay and corn are bought. Fuel is brought down the river from Saint Macaire and wine from La Réole. Aldrington, the prince's tailor, has cloth and furs with which to make garments for the prince and for one of the friars. On December 16th, there is a payment for 'preparations for Christmas' and on December 24th, rice, honey, almonds, fruit are entered, and two "nakers" (kettle drums) for Hankin the minstrel. There is also a large purchase of sugar (*zucre in pane*). On December 27th, the prince's offering at High Mass on Christmas Day is recorded. New Year's gifts arrive from the Capitalesse de Buch and from the Lord of Montferrand [22]

But the general impression conveyed by the various chroniclers —that the Gascons had gone to their homes, that the prince and his leaders enjoyed a long period of inactivity in Bordeaux, that from their winter quarters they ultimately emerged for some raiding, and that during the following summer the Gascons returned in time to take part in the second raid—is at variance with the facts. On December 20th, the prince gave orders for the earls and bannerets to proceed to their quarters in order to conduct military operations.[23] Before the end of the year the holidaying came to a close; the leaders departed; preparations were made for the prince and his staff to move to Libourne. Men, wine and other goods were sent there in advance.[24]

About January 17th the prince himself went there.[25] Henxteworth and Wengfeld were with him and it was from Libourne that Wengfeld forwarded to Sir Richard Stafford a survey of current military operations.

The division of the army into groups for a period of rest (and perhaps partial reorganization) was both convenient and strategically sound. The places chosen for group-headquarters lay at some distance from the great seaport. La Réole, situated some forty miles upstream from Bordeaux, commanded the highway to Languedoc. Libourne, on the Dordogne, was twenty miles to the east of Bordeaux along the old Roman road, but the men and goods of the expedition were usually conveyed between the two towns by water, though the distance was very much longer. Sainte Foy, also on the Dordogne, lay twenty-four miles east of Libourne. These three towns were bastides. Saint Émilion, standing on a fortified hilltop some distance north of the Dordogne, lay only four and a half miles from Libourne and afforded additional accommodation for the prince's men.

Whether there were casualties or sickness after the exacting autumn march cannot, of course, be determined. For some reason there was a slight decline in the number of Cheshire archers. One man, William Jodrell, was given formal leave to go to England in a deed which is still extant[26] (and may be the oldest surviving English military pass). Six others, all named, also went back, each receiving a gift from the prince.[27] The number of archers serving under Mascy was not constant but the variation may have been due to military reasons. Average winter conditions in Gascony differ little from those of England. The differences in food and drink between the two countries may, however, have been sufficient to affect health. And the obligation of a single and not very populous county to provide for one campaign after another such large numbers of archers, may have necessitated the arraying of some men of indifferent physique.

In any case, the various groups of soldiers were all actively campaigning far from their headquarters in the opening weeks of 1356 and they were accompanied by Gascons.

Nor is their activity surprising for, devastating and decisive as the autumn *chevauchée* might at first sight appear to have been, and difficult as it was to conduct warfare in the winter season, several considerations made a lengthy rest inexpedient.

In the first place, King Edward himself was heavily engaged in warfare in the Scottish borderland. The great three-pronged attack planned for the summer and autumn of 1355, had not been carried through as intended. Henry, Duke of Lancaster, had sailed from the Thames estuary with an army bound for Normandy where he was to join forces with Charles of Navarre. His fleet had met with great difficulties, had ultimately put into Southampton and there the duke had learned that the ally with whom he was to co-operate had made terms with the King of France. That prong, therefore, had inflicted no wound on the French body politic. The prince's army had been the second prong and the king's the third. After much delay, Edward had landed at Calais and, on November 2nd, advanced southward to meet King John who had long awaited him. The two armies had been only a few miles apart and a battle had seemed imminent but, from an obscure set of circumstances, two results emerged clearly: there was no battle and Edward withdrew to Calais. There he received news that the Scots had taken Berwick. He therefore returned hastily to England and immediately took an army northward, recaptured Berwick early in January and proceeded to devastate the Lothians. It was unthinkable that his son's army should idle in the relative mildness and plenty of Gascony while Edward and his men bore the brunt of campaigning in the cold expanses of Northumberland and southern Scotland.

Moreover, the time was opportune for action. The aims of the expedition, as we have shown, were the recovery of lost territories, the recovery of lost allegiances and the engagement of new friends. The prince was empowered to admit to the king's peace those who wished 'to come or to return' to the English side. His task was to reverse the trend which had become marked since Lancaster left Gascony and Jean d'Armagnac became King John's lieutenant. The autumn campaign had provided an impressive demonstration of English power or, at any rate, of French weakness. In a region where allegiance was largely governed by self-interest, a continuance of the demonstration would be advantageous to the English cause.

Further, Jean d'Armagnac had not been defeated. He was taking steps not only to rebuild the ruined towns of Languedoc but also to defend its western outposts.[28] Prudence required that balancing English forces should be near at hand and, once sent, all the circumstances would conduce to their taking the initiative in attack.

That in fact was the prince's instruction: the leaders were to live in the marchland in order to make raids and harass the enemy.[29] It was promptly put into effect. The disposition[30] of the Anglo-Gascon forces in the middle of January 1356 reveals widespread, small-scale campaigns directed largely against the region which Jean d'Armagnac had to defend. The army has been broken into groups: the earls are leading their men on separate or combined enterprises; and the prince's following is divided into several independent or associated commands under such leaders as Burghersh, Chandos and Audley.

G

The prince is at Libourne which (with St. Émilion and Fronsac) forms the headquarters of his troops and those of Elie de Pommiers and Bernard d'Albret.

Far away to the north at Cognac in Saintogne, Bartholomew de Burghersh is in command of 120 men-at-arms and 120 archers. In the same region, the Captal de Buch, the Lord Montferrand and the Lord of Curton have larger forces and there are garrisons at Rochfort, Tonnay and Taillebourg. A combined force drawn from the above together with men serving under the Earls of Oxford, Salisbury and Suffolk and two Gascon lords, is out on a raid towards Notre Dame de Rochemade.

But the greatest activity is in the middle Garonne valley. On both its outward and its return journeys, the *chevauchée* of 1355 had swept south of the Garonne. In January 1356, small groups are at work along the northern bank. Warwick has journeyed upstream from La Réole, has taken Tonneins and Clairac and is now engaged in destroying the supplies of Marmande.

Still further east along the valley, Chandos, Audley, Botetourt and Cobham with English and Gascon troops have taken by assault Castelsagrat and Brassac and have twice conducted demonstration before Agen, burning mills, destroying bridges and even capturing a castle situated outside the walls. Though Jean d'Armagnac was in the town at the time, he has not come out to fight.

The French leaders, Grismouton and Boucicaut with French troops and Lombard mercenaries are at Moissac. A clash with these forces is anticipated.

Such in summary was the situation when Wengfeld wrote from the prince's headquarters on January 22nd. (In view of the distance at which Audley's men were operating, the news from this group may have been a week old.) English forces had not taken all the river towns but there was nowhere along the north side of the valley as far as Moissac (120 miles from Bordeaux) where they might not appear. Five walled towns and seventeen castles are named as having fallen into their hands; and the work was still in progress. The prince's instructions were being carried out and reports were reaching headquarters at Libourne.

Unfortunately, from this point onward very little detailed evidence of the military activities of the winter and spring has survived. Baker summarized the work thus:—'from the places entrusted to them (which they skilfully organized for defence), they went out frequently on expeditions, accomplished great exploits and carried away much booty from the enemy country, but it would take too long to relate the details'.[31] Chandos Herald said that Chandos, Audley and the Captal de Buch camped in the open a long time, went to Cahors, to Porte Ste Marie and towards Agen. Afterwards (he says) they went to Perigueux, camped there a great part of the winter and made many attacks on the castle which (as at Carcassonne and Narbonne) stood outside the town.[32]

Perigueux has had fame thrust upon it because of a declaration of policy on the prince's part. Fearing an attack on the town, the Count of Perigord approached his brother, the cardinal, who in turn got in touch with the pope in February 1356. As a result, a money payment was offered to the prince in return for the immunity of the town. The prince is reported as answering that he would not accept money to spare the town. He would accomplish that for which he had come: to chastise, discipline, master by force of arms all the inhabitants of the duchy of Aquitaine who were in rebellion against his father, and recall to their allegiance and maintain those who were obedient.[33] The tone of the statement attributed to the prince is in harmony with that made under similar circumstances at Carcassonne and also with the general aims we have stated. Shortly afterwards, the town was taken by English troops under the Captal de Buch. [34]

A few details of operations may be deduced from Henxteworth's journal. Castelsagrat was held for some time: work was carried out there at Chandos' command and letters were conveyed there from Bordeaux, payment for both operations being made in March.[35] Perigueux was the scene of important activities: sums were paid in March and April to the Lord of Mussidon for the provisioning of the town, in May to Elys Gerard for a lock for the gate of the town, in May also to John de Stretelee for the repair of the balistae bought for the town, in June (to the same John) for his men garrisoning that town till June 16th; and at the end of June (still to John de Stretelee) for 100 men-at-arms remaining in Perigueux.[36] The financial record thus supplements the chronicler's narrative.

In the spring, the Earl of Warwick reduced Mirabeau in Quercy, the town of le Mas d'Agenais with its castle returned to the prince's allegiance and there were further gains of castles and fortalices.[37]

Whether plunder and destruction accompanied the operations at this period, as they had done in the autumn *chevauchée*, cannot be determined from the slight evidence. Certainly there were no grounds for restraint and the prince's attitude concerning Perigueux implies no softening. Baker speaks of booty and, once more, Henxteworth supplies a sidelight by a payment made in June 'for 215 head of cattle from the booty of Sir John Chandos and his fellows'.[38]

One further incident deserves mention both because of its place and its date. In Poitou, small scale warfare waged by adherents of the English cause had not ceased with Lancaster's withdrawal but continued down to 1356. About the end of July, only six or seven weeks before the battle of Poitiers, there was an engagement between the garrison of Poitiers and an English detachment in which the mayor himself, Albert (Herbert) Guichard, was captured and held to ransom.[39]

To sum up, though the evidence is very incomplete, the general trend of policy and of events in the interval between the great raids is clear. The English force may (or may not) have been waiting for reinforcements or for summer weather or for a diversion to be created by the descent on northern France of another English expedition. Its policy was to harass the enemy, that is to say to maintain military pressure with its varied effects. Of these the chief and the most easily stated, seemed to contemporaries to be the number of strongholds captured: they stressed the loss of the power to fight. That is, of course, of great importance but loss of the will to fight is decisive. The purpose of the expedition was, as we have insisted, to recover allegiances, to gain over those who might be induced 'to come or to return' to the English side; and force was not necessarily the only means that might be employed. The plans and arrangements we sketched reveal a statecraft which may have exceeded the prince's knightly conception. He had money with which 'to conciliate the people of the country'; he had power to pardon all sorts of past disloyalty; he could redistribute rebels' estates among new adherents; he could in fact take almost any course which might advance King Edward's cause; and the ample powers conferred in July 1355 had been confirmed in January 1356.[40] Distasteful though it might be to a chivalrous mind to resort to such means, the king and his advisers were realistic enough to know their value. The moral effects of the autumn *chevauchée*, of the winter and spring raidings, and perhaps of some dangling of material rewards and compensations became evident in a transfer of allegiances. The attitude of the peasants, the townsfolk and the clergy were not likely to be recorded in documents but some of the leading Gascon lords formally changed sides. Among them in April 1356 were the following:—the Sire de Caumont, Jean de Galard (Sire de Limeuil), Gaillard de Durfort (Sire de Grignols) and Bertrand de Durfort.[41] Moisant cites others [42] and the accounts of John de Stretelee show disbursements to various people in indemnification of losses sustained through adherence to the king's side and for expenses incurred in bringing others 'to the king's obedience'.[43]

The transfer was not a simple act of submission to a different king. It was accompanied by agreements about material wealth, for the lord whose estates were scattered in territory held partly by one side and partly by the other, was subject to pressure from both sides. Negotiations, therefore, were complicated. Against certain dispossession of lands to the east was set compensation by new estates or sources of revenue to the west or by the return of estates already confiscated. The transactions inevitably became conditional on further contingencies. But the fact that important lords had become convinced that their interests lay in serving King Edward rather than King John, is evidence that the trend of opinion and events in Guienne had been reversed. The tide was now favourable to the English cause.

At the time Sir Richard Stafford was travelling to England with the prince's dispatch, King Edward was engaged in warfare on the Scottish border. By the beginning of March, the king was back in London and the following information was available for him and his advisers:—the prince's report on the autumn campaign, Stafford's personal statement, Wengfeld's account of operations in January, and a call by the prince for a supply of bows, arrows and bowstrings to be sent to Gascony. Two matters, therefore, required consideration: the advisability of sending reinforcements and the need to send arms, to Gascony.

The times were difficult. French attacks on the southern coast were still regarded as possible; the Scottish border could not be neglected; supplies of arrows were low;[44] an invasion of northern France—should an opportunity occur—would be less costly; and the war in Brittany might be regarded as of indefinite duration. On the other hand, the prince's commission and powers had been renewed in January, his *chevauchée* had had some success and he was in a position to strike again. The full fruits of his work could not be gained unless his needs were supplied. It was decided that those needs should be met primarily from the resources of Cheshire.

The first decision was to raise for service in Gascony 300 archers of whom 200 were to come from Cheshire. They were to be mounted, clothed in the now traditional green and white uniforms, paid wages in advance and sent down to Plymouth where they were required to arrive by Palm Sunday (April 17th) in order to sail in the company of Sir Richard Stafford.[45] Less than a fortnight later, the total number of archers to be enrolled was raised to 600 of whom Cheshire was to furnish 500, clothed as above and paid only eight days' wages, the prince's servants meeting them at Plymouth to pay them more wages.[46] As the county had supplied very many men in the preceding summer for Gascony, this demand of March 1356 was very heavy. It is in fact quite improbable that so large a number could be raised at that date from the palatine earldom.

Even so, there remained the balance of 100 men. For these the king turned to the county of Gloucester. A mandate was issued to the sheriff, to Simon Bassett, to William atte Marche and John de Cornwall, directing them to array 100 mounted archers in the county, to clothe them with one suit, furnish them with bows, arrows and other competent arms and to pay them wages for the period between their departure from the county and their arrival at Plymouth. (These were the usual arrangements.) John de Cornwall was to lead them to the port and William de Bolton to arrange for the transport of some arms from Gloucester to Plymouth.[47]

As regards the larger supply of arms, Robert Pipot had been sent by the prince to obtain 1,000 bows, 2,000 sheaves of arrows and 400 gross of bowstrings and, as the king's demands had denuded the greater part of England of these things, Pipot was sent to Cheshire with instructions to requisition all the available stocks in the county and to ensure that the fletchers continued production till the prince's needs were satisfied.[48] Little John of Berkhamstead was appointed to arrange for the conveyance of all the stocks thus purveyed to Plymouth, the Chamberlain of Chester paying the expense of carriage.[49]

Pipot was then to proceed to Lincolnshire, obtain transport for bows, arrows and bowstrings purveyed in that county and have them also conveyed to Plymouth,[50] while John de Palington was to obtain similar supplies in the city of London and forward them to the same port.[51]

In addition to the archers' mounts, other horses were to be taken to Gascony in the same convoy. A certain Roger Ragaz had bought sumpters for the prince which were awaiting shipment[52] and the receiver of Cornwall had to purvey in Cornwall and Devon thirty of the strongest baggage horses he could find and provide a groom for each horse.[53] Moreover, horses were being sent from England for the earls who were with the prince.

Finally, victuals also were needed in Gascony. Wherever the army was in enemy territory, as much food as was practicable was no doubt obtained without payment, but both the prince and the earls drew supplies also from England. In at least one instance, a boat was chartered to bring provisions obtained by Adam Kentish for the prince's household.[54] The Earl of Suffolk had obtained leave for his officers to buy large quantities of wheat, oats and fish and send them from Gippeswick to Gascony[55] and the king gave orders for sixty salted hogs to be obtained in the western counties and sent to Plymouth.[56]

For the transport of their horses and victuals two ships were assigned to the earls,[57] and orders were issued for the assembly of ships at Plymouth for Sir Richard Stafford's convoy.[58] The preparations were completed by arrangements for the supply of hurdles. This time the task fell to the Sheriff of Devon who was directed to deliver 400 in the port of Plymouth by Easter.[59]

But in 1356 as in 1355, and indeed frequently in the middle ages, there is a gap between the programme and its execution. The country's resources for a war against France are men, arms, horses, ships and in some circumstances, victuals. To the absence of reliable information about the quantity and location of these resources and the planner's inability to move ships without nature's aid, must be added once more the competing needs of other enterprises. During the spring and summer, great quantities of bows and arrows were ordered—for the king;[60] many men were raised both in England and Wales—for the king and the Duke of Lancaster;[61] ships were requisitioned—for the Duke of Lancaster.[62] Reinforcements and supplies needed in Gascony, therefore, were subject to the circumstances of the time.

It was not in April, as had been intended, but about the beginning of June that Stafford and his men left Plymouth. They were in Bordeaux by the 19th of that month.[63] So far as is known, no further reinforcements were sent from England to Gascony for this expedition.

There were, however, a few further orders for supplies:—in July for arrows and quarrels;[64] in August and in September for fish.[65]

During the interval between the two great raids, the pope never relaxed his efforts to bring about peace between France and England. Nuncios were sent to the two kings for the express purpose of fostering amity, and nobles and prelates were directed to aid their efforts. Papal officers were ordered to try to meet the commanders and seek to avert a battle. Letters were sent not only to the two kings, the Prince of Wales and Jean d'Armagnac urging the need for peace, but also to many nobles and to leaders in the prince's entourage urging them to use their influence for the same end. Direct appeals were made to the prince begging him not to invade French territory, to Jean d'Armagnac urging him to stay outside English territory, to the emperor asking him to use his good offices and seek to bring about a conference between King Edward and King John. The pope still declared himself a mediator not a partisan and indeed, whatever his motives or sympathies, his policy had the outward appearance of impartiality. On both sides equally he pressed the advantages of peace; of both sides he demanded redress of injustices committed during the war. Mediation, however, was foredoomed to failure. King Edward could gain nothing thereby unless King John was prepared to concede his crown. And, in the summer of 1356, John felt that he had gained some important successes.

For John had not journeyed south to defend Languedoc against the Black Prince's incursion. He had felt that in a conflict with England, the greatest danger for France lay in the north. Derby's operations in 1345–46 had been damaging, but they were much less important than King Edward's march from Caen via the Seine valley and Crécy to Calais. The prince wrought havoc in the south in 1355, but King Edward intended to invade France and, by waiting in the north, John had been able to confront him. Whatever explanation might be offered of the strange episode in Picardy in November, Edward had retired from France without a battle. For John, the outcome though not a victory, was a success: danger had been met and warded off.

The next danger came from within France and within the royal family. Charles the Bad, the king's talented, enterprising but treacherous son-in-law and lord of great estates in Normandy, was again turning to disloyalty. Himself in the line of royal descent and having claims to the French throne as good as those of Edward III, he had during the winter of 1355–56, secretly plotted with the dauphin himself: King John was to be captured, deposed, imprisoned and then—Charles was to be king. For some years, Charles had enjoyed far greater indulgence than a prudent king could afford to show to so bad a subject. John now acted decisively. On the night of April 5th, 1356, he arrived suddenly at a banquet at Rouen given by the dauphin to Charles and some Norman nobles. He took and imprisoned Charles, had four of the Normans executed and soon had the satisfaction of seeing Godfrey of Harcourt, an Anglophile Norman leader, condemned by the royal court to perpetual banishment and the confiscation of his wealth. In that a most dangerous enemy and some of his confederates had been removed from the stage, this step also was a success for John.

But the step had been taken too late for, worthless as Charles was, he enjoyed the secret sympathy of many French nobles and sympathy for Charles was almost equivalent to disaffection towards John. Moreover, Charles' brother Philip of Navarre promptly declared war on John and—as might have been foreseen—applied to Edward III for aid. Circumstances were assuming their accustomed pattern: France's peripheral discontents were England's opportunities. Henry, Duke of Lancaster, who had recently been appointed as Edward's lieutenant in Brittany was now directed to co-operate with Philip's friends in Normandy. He landed with an English army at la Hogue on June 18th and moved quickly southwards in typical raiding fashion as far as Verneuil but, when King John with a French army approached to meet him, Lancaster retired. Whether the grounds for his sudden withdrawal to the Cotentin were fear, a desire to save his booty or the hope of luring John further northwards into wooded country, the result could be regarded for a time as a third successful stroke on John's part.

He had shown as much decision as his opponents, but he had not the stature needed for the heavy tasks of kingship in mid fourteenth-century France. Now about thirty-seven years of age and king since 1350, he had had a long but unprofitable apprenticeship in the arts of war and government. In 1340 he had been the French leader in the war against the English in Hainault and, in 1341, in the war against John de Montfort in Brittany; and he had been sent as the king's lieutenant to Languedoc in 1344. Personally brave and full of chivalrous notions, he had not the gifts of generalship. Fond of banquets, tournaments, rich clothes and fine gold and silverware, he sustained his extravagance by measures which exceeded his rights. Like Edward III, he was driven to financial expedients but, whereas Edward could borrow from Florentine bankers under the security of a monopoly of wool, John, the ruler of a country whose commerce was less advanced, resorted to confiscation, arbitrary taxation and the debasement of the coinage.

Like Edward III also, he founded a new order of chivalry, the Order of the Star. Its insignia and equipment were impressive in their splendour, its meetings were occasions of great festivity and its practices no doubt enhanced the prowess of its members. But the order did little to increase the military strength of the French people. It may even have decreased its potential strength, for chivalry emphasized individual rather than corporate accomplishment in arms; it placed supreme value in cavalry; its members came to regard warfare as a knightly game rather than a deadly conflict. 'War in his eyes', it has been observed of John, 'was nothing but a tournament on a large scale.'[66] Had it been so in fact, the French knights might have added undying glory to their nation's arms. At Crécy they had faced, and at Poitiers they were to face, English armies inferior in numbers but better integrated, setting greater store by their archery and treating battle as a contest for life.

In point of civilization, standard of living and size of population, France was the first state in Europe and, in a theoretical way, capable of producing the largest army. In point of political development and military organization, however, her progress had been less notable. National consciousness was growing but slowly. The machinery of national administration was neither so well developed nor so efficient as that of England. The king as chief executive had quite limited power and was still expected to carry out the functions of government from the revenues of the royal domain. He had neither an effective military machine nor the financial resources for maintaining one. When war occurred, therefore, he was obliged to demand taxes for, in France, as in England, the greater part of the army now consisted of paid men. But in spite of much ingenuity in devising varied ways of exacting money, the taxes were intensely unpopular. Hence the resort to devaluation of the currency which temporarily enabled the king to meet his debts and pay for troops. The principle of national service had been established and so modified that those who could not, or would not serve, might buy exemption, the money thus gained also being available for the pay of hired troops.

Of such hired troops there was no lack in France at this period. Military life was attractive in itself and the circumstances of the time fostered it. Wars were frequent; there were crusades in Spain, in Prussia, in Rhodes; family quarrels over inheritances and even less worthy reasons led to private war. The king, therefore, could obtain the services of men-at-arms or infantry, and the recruiting ground was as wide as the nation itself. Younger sons of noble families, bastards, poor lords, commoners, archers, arbalesters, artillers were glad to accept pay for the duration of a war. They were not of course recruited direct into the king's service, but gathered somewhat as in England into 'companies' by lords who brought them into the royal army. In this way, the freed villein, the commoner who had acquired land, the lord who had fallen into poverty, the foreigner might carry and use arms and thus enter the worthiest occupation of a free man.

On the organization of the military potential thus made available, the *Ordonnance* of April 30th, 1351, throws a good deal of light. Explicitly or implicitly, it recognizes the conditions of the time: the rising cost of living and the dependence of voluntary service on adequate pay, the problem of discipline among men in whom individualism is stronger than loyalty, the need of organization, the opportunities for dishonesty. Rates of pay for all ranks are raised—in some instances they are doubled; an oath that the soldier will not withdraw his service is to be asked for; every man must belong to a company, that is to say he must be subordinate to a captain; the high command (under the king) is vested in the Constable, the two Marshals of France and the master of the arbalesters; horses are to be marked on the flank, described by their colour and valued; rigorous steps are to be taken to inspect the companies lest captains should draw pay for non-existent members.

These reforms point to evolutionary trends in France not widely different from those which had operated in England. In both countries, the feudal levy had been very largely superseded; great nobles as well as knights accepted royal payment for military service and raised bodies of men who served under them; men of relatively humble birth (like Du Guesclin, Knolles or Calveley) might rise to importance, even to eminence. It may be added that King John had a Council of War consisting of members of the royal family, his chief commanders and selected advisers. He had also a rudimentary intelligence service.

Two great difficulties, however, faced the king. The first, as already stated, was the financing of large-scale operations. The second was the conversion of a heterogeneous mass of men into an efficient, military instrument. It would take time, great skill and great determination, for the task posed problems that were moral as well as organizational. The infantry, hastily raised as a war began, had little training and the arbalests which they and the Genoese mercenaries used, were very clumsy weapons in comparison with the English bows. The French army had neither brought its archery up to English standards nor combined its use effectively with that of mounted troops. Moreover, the 'companies' necessarily differed widely in size, efficiency and dependability. They were professional soldiers, interested in the continuance of war and inclined to rapine. Grouped in 'routes', they were very soon to give the word 'routier' the connotation pillager.

Even if these defects could have been promptly remedied, there remained the intractable problem of cohesion. Courage and fidelity to knightly standards (as seen in the return of scores of French knights liberated on their honour to get their ransoms) abounded and were potentially of military value, but no vital unifying principle animated the body. National sentiment was still weak. The different social groups felt little loyalty to one another and a right of withdrawal which differed little from desertion, was still recognized. The nobility, theatrical in their zeal for chivalry with the opportunities it offered for the display of magnificent accoutrements, regarded the profession of arms as their exclusive sphere. For infantry they had little esteem. They disliked the use of the arrayed townsmen and held aloof from the mercenary troops whether Genoese or *roturiers*. Moreover, they were not adapted in spirit to the devices of the skilled commander: the sudden concentration, the feint, the surprise, the sudden flank attack. They preferred the challenge, the chosen place and date and the formal combat.

Finally, the maintenance of discipline in an army so lacking in cohesion presented very great difficulties. Froissart refers several times to the medieval commander's task of preventing men during a march from getting in front of the marshals and, during a battle, from rushing away to capture individual prisoners. Both tendencies violate the fundamental principles that the fighting men must be disposable exactly as the commander wills. But there might be a worse violation: the fighting men might withdraw their services—even at a critical moment. John's *Ordonnance* of 1351 contains a very mild attempt to prevent such a withdrawal.[67] Efforts were to be made to obtain an oath that members would not leave a company without the captain's permission and— it was a hope rather than a regulation—men so leaving, or a leader so leaving, should notify the commander of their 'battle' or corps. In short, provided the formalities were observed, the deserter might escape penalties. On the field of Poitiers, there were many who judged the situation to be disadvantageous. They withdrew.

To sum up, in so far as he was able to obtain sufficient money, John could raise a very large army but that army was less formidable than its numbers might suggest.

In July 1356, he had the satisfaction of seeing the English force which had threatened to march through Normandy, fall back before him and retire to a remote part of the Cotentin peninsula. Early in August, he rounded off his northern campaign by the siege and capture of Breteuil. By now, action against the force which threatened his kingdom from the south had become urgent. He chose Chartres as the place and September 1st as the date for the assembly of a large army.

CHAPTER V

THE SECOND RAID AND THE
BATTLE OF POITIERS

THE military operations conducted by the English forces in the
opening months and the spring of 1356 had had limited
objectives. The summer brought a large scale campaign beginning
on August 4th at Bergerac and comparable in several ways with
that of the preceding autumn. The undertaking sprang naturally
from the circumstances of the time. The campaign of 1355 had
been gratifying to the Gascons, profitable to Gascons and English,
desolating to the French, and accomplished with very light losses.
These facts alone would have afforded grounds for a similar
enterprise in the following year, preferably with an earlier start.
The prince had in fact promised the Gascons that he would lead
another *chevauchée*; reinforcements had arrived from England; the
Gascons were ready to march. A *chevauchée* into any part of the
French kingdom would diminish the revenue and prestige of
the French king.

It remained to decide the direction in which the raiding force
should march. In this respect the two raids differ widely. The
decision to proceed against the territories of Jean d'Armagnac
had given purpose, animus and direction to the opening phases
of the autumn campaign. No such motives governed the opening
of the second campaign. The route taken is known but the reasons
for the choice of route remain obscure. It is clear enough that a
second march into Languedoc would have encountered the resistance of Jean d'Armagnac and that the use of the entire Anglo-
Gascon force for a raid in any other direction would have given
Jean an opportunity to seize the great English base. In the event,
the prince marched northwards, passed near Bourges and thence
to the Loire valley.

In a letter ostensibly explaining the course of his campaign,
he wrote that he had expected to find the French king's son, the
Count of Poitiers, at Bourges and that 'the sovereign cause for
our going towards these parts was that we expected to have had
news of our father . . . the king, as to his passage'. Both grounds
are rather vague expectations. Neither carries sufficient weight to

justify the view that a clear, military plan determined the choice of route. Bourges was a strongly fortified city the siege of which would not have commended itself to the leaders of a *chevauchée*.

It has been supposed that the prince intended to join forces with the Duke of Lancaster in the Loire valley and the fact that the two leaders were not far apart in the opening week of September lends plausibility to the view. It is indeed the kind of junction more modern minds would expect leaders to try to bring about. It must, however, be borne in mind that at the outset of his march, the prince was very badly informed about Lancaster's whereabouts, that as he journeyed northwards he allowed his troops to loiter, that he wasted time on a siege and that, if he had any such junction in mind, he did not proceed in a businesslike way to attain it. It is more likely that he received news of Lancaster's movements two or more weeks after his departure from Bergerac and then adapted his plans.

No dominant strategic plan determined the march. 'It was our purpose to ride forth against the enemies in the parts of France,' wrote the prince. The Bourges road looked as promising from Bergerac as the Toulouse road had looked from the borders of Armagnac but there was no clear intention of laying siege to either town.

The second *chevauchée* then resembled the first in its lack of a clear objective and there is no ground for believing that it differed in other essential respects, namely that the army 'lived on the land' through which it passed, that the troops carried off valuables, and that they inflicted widespread destruction especially by fire. The evidence, however, for these normal phases of the *chevauchée* is less detailed. Whereas in their treatment of the first raid, all the sources refer freely to looting and destruction, the prince himself mentioning 'harrying and wasting the country', and Baker delighting in instances of havoc, the treatment of the second raid contains far fewer examples of these things. In a long letter sent to the Mayor, Aldermen and Commonalty of London, the prince makes no reference to any damage done by his army on its march. Baker is equally silent. It may be that wilful devastation was now regarded as routine practice, no more calling for mention than meals, or that the victory of Poitiers made the mention of minor damage superfluous. The Eulogium, however, gives a few instances of burning and Froissart and the Grandes Chroniques supply descriptive notes of the northward march which show that the second *chevauchée* differed little from the first in this respect.

Concerning the conduct of operations, the part played by the prince grows somewhat less shadowy. The surviving accounts of the first raid reveal very little of his personal authority and influence. Apart from his anger at the outset and his refusal at Carcassonne to compromise his position as son of the rightful ruler of France, he scarcely emerges from the narratives of the march. There had, it is true, been no opportunity for a display of valour but the chronicles contain no word of his labours, wisdom or foresight. In the second raid, Baker depicts him as a prudent commander who foresees danger, sends his scouts ahead, moves his camp often, inspects all sections of this force and addresses his troops.[1] Such praise may be regarded as a conventional tribute but it is likely that with increased experience, the prince sought to play a real, and not merely nominal, part as Commander-in-Chief. In his letter to the Londoners, the significant phrases 'we took counsel' and 'it was agreed' reveal that on matters of major policy, the Council was consulted. The day to day conduct of the march appears to have been settled by the prince, and, in the operations at Romorantin, he took command.

Before setting out on the second great adventure, the prince went to La Réole, the key fortress on the Garonne and the best centre from which to assess the problem of safeguarding Gascony during his coming absence. Thence he moved to Bergerac, the rendezvous for the contingents that were assembling from various parts of the English domains. Here the allocation of troops was settled.

A substantial force under the command of John de Chiverston (the seneschal), Bernard d'Albret and the Mayor of Bordeaux was detached for the protection of Gascony.

The remaining troops—probably about 7,000 fighting men—were to take part in the *chevauchée*. They consisted of the men who had come over from England in September 1355, the reinforcements that had arrived in June 1356, some lords who had changed to the English side and a body of Gascon lords, knights, men-at-arms, *bidaus* and 'brigans'.

The army began its march on Thursday, August 4th, and travelled northwards along the western edge of the Massif Central. From the valley of the Dordogne it crossed to Perigueux in the valley of the Isle,[2] to Brantome at the crossing of the Dronne

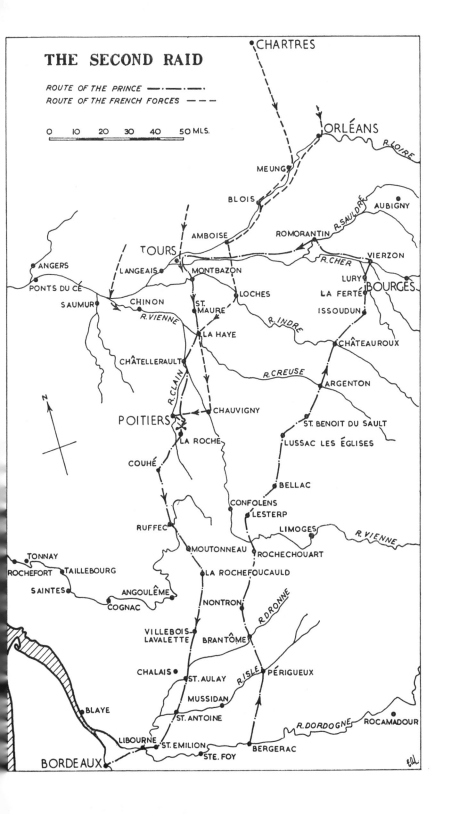

and then passed via Quisser (on the 10th), Nontron (11th) and Rochechouart (12th) to the Benedictine priory of Peruche near Confolens (13th) and to Lesterp (Sunday, 14th). It had covered about one hundred miles in ten days.

During the following week, it marched via Bellac (16th), Lussac les Eglises (19th), Saint Benoit du Sault (20th) to Argenton (Sunday, 21st)—a total of about seventy miles in the seven days.

The troops had advanced through Limousin and Marche, were now on the borders of Berry and approaching the very heart of France. They lived on the land, sending out foragers for miles on either side of their track; they burned towns but spared church property and the property of friends; occasionally detachments engaged in quite minor military operations. No army withstood their progress.

On Tuesday, August 23rd, the march was continued to Chateauroux on the Indre. The town was not taken but the rearguard spent the night at Saint Amand Montrand to the east and the vanguard at Bourgdieu to the west and, because Wednesday was the feast of St. Bartholomew, the army remained in the district another day. Then it marched to Issoudun where it spent Friday and Saturday. On Sunday (28th) it marched along the valleys of the Theols and the Arnon through La Ferté and Lury (on the ancient boundary of the duchy of Guienne), crossed the Cher and spent the night at Vierzon. This week's progress was under sixty miles. Unimpeded, the raiders made their leisurely way. Such conduct cannot be related to a serious effort to meet the English king or the Duke of Lancaster or the Count of Poitiers.

But, at about this point, the character of the *chevauchée* underwent a change. The routine devastation along the line of march was now accompanied by military action against objectives remote from the route of the main force. Secondly, scouts or reconnaissance parties made contact with French parties and there were skirmishes. Bourges, a walled and well defended city was attacked but suffered no more than the burning of its suburbs. Aubigny, a less important place, was carried by assault and destroyed. As the attacking party of 200 horsemen, commanded by Chandos and Audley, was returning from Aubigny, it met a French force commanded by Philip de Chambly, called Gris Mouton. In a skirmish, some prisoners were captured and, from this point onwards, the French king had regular news of the movements of the English army. The prince, on his side, learned from the prisoners that John was preparing to meet him in battle, but the news could cause no surprise. Not until the risk of a clash was nearer need it affect his campaign.

As he advanced along the valley of the Cher, another French force was encountered. Its leaders, the Sire de Craon and Jean le Maingre, called Boucicaut, withdrew to the little town of Romorantin and shut themselves within the castle that stood on the edge of the river Sauldre. It was not the purpose of a *chevauchée* to spend time in besieging castles and indeed, during the preceding fortnight, the army had passed several but, in this instance, it was decided to capture the two commanders. The prince is stated to have declared that he would not leave till they had surrendered or been taken. The operations involved the use of all the power, skill and ingenuity the army could bring by assault, ladders, towers, stone-throwing machines, mining (and, one account adds, 'Greek fire') till finally, after the main part had been gained, the defenders in the keep were compelled by a fire they could not extinguish, to surrender. The prince's aim had been achieved.[3] On the other hand, lives had been lost in the siege operations, no real military advantage had been gained and (so far as is known) no plunder. It may be that the siege and capture of the castle served a psychological purpose: so far the second *chevauchée* had afforded even fewer opportunities for warlike action than the first.

By this time, the fact that the French king was about to move, or already moving, large forces down the Loire valley was at last apprehended. The English reaction was to march along the Cher and the Loire to Tours and wait there four days before moving southwards.[4] This is the turning point of the second raid.

The situation has not been fully understood. Broadly, it has been inferred that the prince sought to join forces with the Duke of Lancaster and that the breaking of the bridges over the Loire prevented the accomplishment of his aim. The truth is somewhat different. Both the prince and Lancaster were engaged in *chevauchées*. If they could inflict damage, procure booty, divert or divide the forces of King John, they would achieve their purpose. The damage had been inflicted and a great quantity of booty collected, but John's forces had not been divided. Neither the prince nor Lancaster had sufficient strength for a battle with the army of the French king. Lancaster had withdrawn. Prudence dictated that the prince also should withdraw.

In considering which route should be taken, the leaders (who of course had no maps and had to rely on such information as they could get) would reason that a wide river lay between the king and themselves, that its bridges would be guarded or broken, that they had a few days' start and that, having the smaller army, they could keep well ahead of their opponent. The best way from Romorantin to Bordeaux lay in going west along the Cher and, at some suitable point, turning south. There was, however, Lancaster's force somewhere north of the wide river. A junction with this force and its experienced leader might make an army which could face that of King John.

Here three points must be made. First, the prince had been in communication with Lancaster. Secondly, Lancaster was under a contractual obligation to aid the prince should he need help. The prince's indenture of July 1355 included a clause running thus: 'The king has promised that if it shall happen that the prince is besieged or beset by so great a force that he cannot help himself unless he be rescued by the king's power, then the king will rescue him . . . and the Duke of Lancaster and (others) have promised and pledged their faith to give without fail all the help and counsel they can in making such rescue.'[5] It is hardly likely that the prince desired at that time to invoke this clause, but its existence constituted a relationship on which the prince would feel that he could rely. Thirdly, the prince's information about Lancaster was that he 'would make haste to draw towards us'.[6] The march to Tours is then a first step towards Bordeaux and Henry of Lancaster is expected to join the prince and not the prince Henry of Lancaster.

The evidence concerning the Loire is misleading. There are weeks when its great sandy bed could easily be crossed by an army which had forded several rivers in Languedoc. At other times, the river is a vast, swirling flood, 465 yards wide between its modern embankments at Tours and wider in the country where it overflows its banks. According to Baker, rains had made it unfordable at this date. The bridges, according to Burghersh and the prince, had all been broken. Baker, however, narrows the statement in two ways: he says that the king 'ordered the breaking' and he says 'all the bridges between Blois and Tours'.[7]

Now the fact that only a few days later the French army crossed the Loire at several points shows that the bridges were intact. They were in fact strongly guarded. As for 'all the bridges between

Blois and 'Tours', there was but one, namely that at Amboise (which, according to le Bel, the English approached [8]). On the other hand, a study of war-time mental states suggests that 'Every bridge along the river is broken; the king ordered it' is the kind of rumour which would spread and be believed in France. Indeed, if it were invented as part of an apologia, it would be believed in England also.

Finally, Lancaster's army was many miles away when the English forces reached Tours.

To sum up, while the decision to start the journey southwards by way of the Loire valley was wise, the halt at Tours served no purpose. Lancaster's army did not reach the northern bank, (Baker's statement that the armies saw one another's camp fires is quite untrue), nor, if it had arrived, could a junction have been effected for the city of course commanded the bridge and the city was held by the Marshal Clermont, the Duke of Anjou and a considerable French force. The English army spent four days on the outskirts of the city (September 7th to 11th), burnt the suburbs and on Sunday (11th) began its southward march.

By now the situation of the English force was serious. King John had already crossed the Loire at Blois, only thirty miles upstream, and parts of his army were crossing by the bridges at Orleans, Meung, Saumur and Tours. The project of a junction with Lancaster had proved illusory. The safety which might be held to lie in a few days' start and in the superior speed of a smaller army, had been thrown away. The situation was indeed creditable and becoming increasingly favourable to the French. The bridgeheads had been held and the congestion and delay resulting from the passage of a large force over a single bridge, had been avoided. With his whole army south of the river and quickly concentrating into one force, John would very soon be in a position to threaten the prince's flank, possibly even to intercept him.

A race began in which each army pushed ahead quickly but John's showed greater determination. From Tours (September 11th) the prince moved southward via Montbazan and Saint Maure to la Haye (13th). He covered thirty miles in two days. From Blois (10th) John came down the Loire to Amboise (12th) —twenty miles in two days; turned south and pressed on to Loches (13th)—twenty miles in one day; and to la Haye (14th)— again twenty miles in one day. He had missed his prey but only by about twelve hours. To the resolute speed he had shown, John now added a stroke of bold generalship. Instead of following the prince's track, he sought to get in front of him. The prince, he would learn from the people of la Haye, had taken his army in the direction of Chatellerault. If not overtaken, that army would proceed either towards Poitiers or up the valley of the Vienne. They would not waste time in laying siege to so well defended a city as Poitiers but they would have to pass within a few miles of its walls. Alternatively, they might follow the Vienne for many miles. Driving his men and horses to great exertions, he would take a different route southwards, reach the Vienne at Chauvigny and, if the English had not been seen in the valley, he would cross the river and make for Poitiers.

Meanwhile, the prince lost even the advantage of his twelve hours' start. Though rumours of the king's determination or the dauphin's strength reached him every day, he seems to have been deplorably served by his intelligence service. That there were errors of judgment is likely, but judgment is made in the light of information and the circumstances affecting civilian morale in Touraine in September 1356 differed from those in the south in November 1355. The Languedocian, powerless before the merciless invader, aware that Jean d'Armagnac would not defend him and that the king was hundreds of miles away, would comply with demands for information. The Tourangeau, half conscious that the invader was retreating and aware that the king was drawing very near, could express his feelings if not in direct hostility, then in lies.

The English army reached Chatellerault on the evening of Wednesday (14th), and stayed there during Thursday and Friday —a period so long that one is driven to the conclusion that the leaders were very ill-informed of their opponents' whereabouts. At this point a chronicler lets fall one of the very rare notes on organization of transport. A fortnight earlier, he had mentioned an instance in which two lords stood back to let the baggage train get in front of them. At Chatellerault he says, on the day before the army's departure, orders were issued for the whole of the transport (*summagia, cariagia et portantes victualia*) to cross the bridge over the Vienne lest on the following day the army's progress should be hindered.[9] Early on Saturday morning (17th), the whole force set out towards Poitiers but, leaving the great trunk road which ran along the western bank of the Clain, it followed the old Roman road along the eastern side and, a few miles north of the city, branched left, keeping wide of Poitiers and making southwards. The intention was, no doubt, to return to the main Paris-Poitiers-Angoulême-Bordeaux road further south.

The outcome of the two commanders' moves reveals that the French king's intelligence service no less than the prince's was astonishingly inefficient. Though both leaders had very considerable forces, though they must have sent out their men wide of their tracks to get food, though they had the greatest interest in discovering each other's whereabouts, though the distance between the armies since Monday evening had not exceeded twenty miles and had been as little as twelve, yet on Friday morning (17th) as John crossed the bridge over the Vienne at Chauvigny, he is reported to have believed that the English had passed southwards before he could strike, while the prince 'wist not truly where the French were' but inferred from the lack of forage that 'they were not far off'. John had covered thirty miles on Wednesday and Thursday. On Friday he reached la Chabotrie and on Saturday morning he entered Poitiers. He had marched round the prince—without knowing it.

But his large, ill-organized army could not maintain the pace of its leader, the more so because numbers of newly joined lords with their trains and their stores of provisions were still joining the royal army, and also because the bridge at Chauvigny slowed down the movement of the mass of followers. On the Saturday, therefore, John's army was extended over miles of the road leading west from Chauvigny and, as the Anglo-Gascon force had to cross this road in order to continue its southward march, an encounter between parts of the rival forces was likely. It is, in fact probable that the English used the forest of Moulière as a hiding place and awaited an opportunity to fall on the rear of the French army or to capture some of the ostentatiously dressed lords who had waited at Chauvigny for the bridge to be cleared before setting out for Poitiers.

An encounter did take place. French riders were drawn northward towards the main English army near Breuil and there was a fight in which Jean de Chatillon and the Counts of Joigny and Auxerre were captured and held to ransom. It was a brief affair and naturally regarded as very favourable to the English side, but it revealed to the English commanders the relative positions of the rival forces. John was as far south as the prince. It would be extremely difficult, if not impossible, to reach Bordeaux without a decisive battle and that battle would have to be fought within a few hours. It was in fact imperative to press on further that very day, to snatch at the possibility of getting well south of Poitiers before the French army could deliver its blow.

Late that evening the two forces lay south-east of Poitiers. The prince had had to await the return of the riders who had pursued the French nobles. He gathered his army at Savigny l'Evescault in the triangle between the roads leading to Bourges and to Limoges. The French king had promptly turned about, taken his army along the road leading towards Limoges and camped a few miles from the city.

Both sides took measures for the safety of their camps during the night. The French constable and marshals organized the body which came to be known as 'the marshals' corps', a mobile, efficient group designed for the night watch, for assault and for scouting. The English, now aware of their danger were vigilant also. An order was issued that no man should get in front of the marshals' banners unless explicitly commanded to do so.[10] This order, given on several occasions, is not a mere precaution against the dispersal of man-power. It is a prohibition of the ever present tendency of knights and men to turn to individual enterprise—whether for glory or for profit—and thus to endanger the efforts and safety of the army as a whole.

For those who hold (and it is inherently probable) that the prince's army contained rival parties,[11] the one prudent and favouring retreat with the accumulated spoils, the other audacious, desiring still more booty and prepared to risk battle, it may be argued that Savigny was so situated that either course would be possible. On the one hand, the woods, great and small, afforded three advantages to the English: concealment for the large baggage train, the means of devising ambushes, the difficulties the French would experience in a full deployment of their great army. On the other hand, southward there was still a way open. Whether prudence or audacity should prevail, the Council would have to decide.

There was another pressing problem, namely the army's supplies. As we have shown, soldiers on *chevauchée* may alternate between days of ample meals and days of scarcity. Their horses may fare similarly and both men and beasts may have to endure periods of thirst. No serious shortages are mentioned during the second *chevauchée* till the army is near Poitiers. After leaving

Chatellerault, there had been few opportunities of seizing food or watering the horses and, by the Saturday evening, supplies were very low. Savigny had a small religious house but it had no stream for the horses. About three miles away lay the Benedictine abbey of Nouaillé. Both houses may have furnished food but their total stores would have been of small value to so large a body of men. The Miosson, a stream flowing through Nouaillé, may have been used for water.

A third preoccupation was the need for information about anything that could be turned to military advantage. For this the *coureurs* scoured the countryside.

Very early on the following morning (Sunday), the Anglo-Gascon force—tired, hungry and thirsty—occupied a gentle slope at the northern side of the wood of Nouaillé. It was here that, should it be necessary, a stand was to be made and defensive measures were begun immediately.

Just as the opposing armies were ready for instant combat, the papacy made a supreme effort to prevent a battle. Cardinal Talleyrand had already seen the prince at Montbazon on September 12th. He now appeared at a most critical moment and did his utmost to arrange terms between the French king and the prince. Chandos Herald describes his emotion, Froissart his negotiating skill, several chroniclers the dramatic quality of his intervention. The Cardinal contrived a truce to last throughout the Sunday and spent the day going between the two armies with proposals.

The French were in a very strong position. The hated invaders and marauders had at last been brought to bay; their force was inferior; their supplies were low; their marching speed had proved insufficient to enable them to escape. If they were determined to fight, their fate seemed certain. Hard terms were not only morally right but a just expression of the situation. The prince is reported to have been willing to offer the restoration of all his prisoners, his booty and the towns he had taken together with a promise not to fight against the French king for seven years. King John's minimum terms are said to have been the surrender of the prince himself together with a hundred of his knights.

Much attention has been given to the divergent accounts of the day's proceedings and very little to the indenture of July 1355 which had made provision even for such an eventuality as that in which the prince now found himself. 'If it shall happen', the terms run, 'that the prince is besieged or so beset with enemies that his person is in peril and no rescue can come in time, then, to save himself and his men, he may help himself by making a truce or armistice, or in any other way that seems best to him.'[12] It is in the light of those words that the terms offered on either side should be considered. It might have been argued that in view of the French king's peremptory demand, the prince's person was already 'in peril' or, in the light of every probability, it would be 'in peril' within twenty-four hours and that he might, therefore, legitimately resort to some 'other way that seems best to him'. No official statement of the prince's reply has survived and we cannot be certain that the remark of Chandos Herald includes the whole truth. The prince appears to have offered a great deal and, when still more was demanded, to have stated—as he had twice before stated to papal representatives—that he had not power to make peace without his father's assent.[13] The negotiations broke down.

Conciliation under the circumstances then prevailing was impossible. The French were on the point of a great victory and in no mood for discussion. The English and Gascons were not prepared to surrender without fighting. At nightfall Talleyrand went back to Poitiers bitterly disappointed and distrusted by both sides. The following morning before sunrise he sought once more to intervene, going first to the French camp, but his offer was decisively rejected. That the English should lack confidence in a French emissary of a French pope intervening in a French quarrel was natural. Moreover, there were men in the cardinal's large retinue who not only favoured the French cause but, when negotiations failed, actually remained to fight on the French side. That the French should dislike the cardinal's mission was natural also. He was restraining them when a victory was rightly theirs. Papal diplomacy had been consistent. Whatever view be taken of its impartiality and sincerity, its intervention at this point was untimely. Its effect was to postpone battle by twenty-four hours.

The cardinal's departure left the stage clear. The hard clash which had been expected on Sunday morning would certainly take place on Monday morning and, since the truce would end at sunrise, the action was likely to begin early.

As already stated,[14] it is not our plan to give an exhaustive account of the battle as a great military engagement. We shall, in fact, deal only briefly with those aspects which have formed the debating ground of military specialists and then pass to aspects which have received less attention.

Though legend pointed to a certain area as that of the battle-field and the finding of battle relics appeared to confirm the legend, doubts remained for very many years about the exact spot on which the battle of Poitiers had been fought. The prince said that it was one league from Poitiers. Most of the chroniclers gave no details of its position. Froissart, however, gave three points of reference. It was, he said, 'near Poitiers in the fields of Beauvoir and Maupertuis'. But Maupertuis could not be identified. The word means 'bad road'. It is a common enough term (there is a Maupertuis on King Edward III's route of 1346 from Saint Lô to Caen), not necessarily a place-name, and it may be classed with the group of names of fields, enclosures, lands such as Mauchamp, Maucourt, Mauregard, or 'passages' such as Malpas, Maupas which have become place-names. A number of antiquaries and surveyors in the middle of the last century realized how aptly the chroniclers' topographical details described the region to the north and west of the wood of Nouaillé and concluded that the little settlement long known as La Cardinerie must be Maupertuis. Their inference was embodied in the French *état major* 1 : 80.000 map and has been widely followed. More recently it has been argued that the inference is wrong. La Cardinerie, it is said, stands *on* the 'bad road' and, in the fourteenth century, Maupertuis was the name of the *road* and perhaps vaguely of the region through which it passed. This road runs north–south a little west of the wood of Nouaillé, crosses the stream called the Miosson at the Gué de l'Homme and joins the road from Nouaillé to Les Roches. It is to the east and west of this road, Maupertuis, that the battlefield lies.[15]

The battlefield may best be described as seen from the air from a point a mile south of the Bois de Nouaillé and looking north-ward. Below is the valley of the Miosson cut fairly deeply into the plateau and at this point taking a mainly westerly course but with many meanders. On the right, running south-east is the road from Poitiers to Limoges. Less to the right is the village of Nouaillé with the fortified enclosure of its abbey. In the middle, just north of this village lies the large wood of Nouaillé through the north-eastern corner of which a road runs northwards. This road crosses the Miosson by a bridge in Nouaillé, rises over a hummock near the present railway station, then crosses the old road, Maupertuis, near La Cardinerie.

Woods great and small still cover much of the extensive region visible from the air, but north and west of the wood of Nouaillé the surface is almost clear. Through this cleared area the old Maupertuis runs southward, dropping down to the valley of the Miosson. Here and there the valley is marshy, and thickets line its southern slopes. The stream may be crossed today by a bridge where formerly stood the Gué de l'Homme. The land partly enclosed in the south-looping meander to the west of this ford is called le champ Alexandre.

At Nouaillé, the bottom of the valley is about 350 feet above sea level. The clear area forming the battlefield is a little over 400 feet. It is not plain but the variations of surface are insufficient to afford cover or to impede the movements of troops. The gently rising hummock on the north side of the wood, however, rises to about 440 feet and south eastward from La Cardinerie there runs a long, narrow but quite slight depression.

At the date of the battle, the land at the northern side of the wood was cultivated: there were vines and, in some places, hedges; the wood may have been more extensive; the meanders of the stream may have been a little different; and a causeway rather than a bridge afforded the means of crossing the Miosson in Nouaillé.

Concerning the composition and strength of the opposing armies, it must be said of Poitiers, as of many other battles, that contemporary estimates differ, and we have no means of determining the exact numbers. Even when the more improbable figures are disregarded, there remains doubt about two features, namely the proportion of Gascons in the Anglo-Gascon force and the number of miscellaneous half-trained men, who for good reasons or bad, had joined themselves to one army or the other.

Modern writers put the total strength of the Anglo-Gascon army at between 6,000 and 8,000 men who may be grouped roughly thus: 3,000 to 4,000 men-at-arms, 2,500 to 3,000 archers, 1,000 light troops of other kinds variously described as *bidaus*, 'brigans', serjeants. Contemporary writers all assert that the French force was much larger than the Anglo-Gascon. It may have included 8,000 men-at-arms, 2,000 arbalesters and a considerable number of lightly armed and imperfectly trained other men, possibly 15,000 to 16,000 in all.[16]

The English force was grouped in the usual three 'battles'. Warwick and Oxford commanded the van. With them was the Captal de Buch and many Gascon troops. The prince commanded the main body. With him were Audley, Chandos, Cobham, Burghersh, Felton and others. The rearward was in the charge of Salisbury and Suffolk. With them were some of the 'Almains' and Denis de Morbek. Probably each 'battle' contained about a thousand men-at-arms, about a thousand English archers and a few hundred Gascon light troops.

King John's army also was grouped in three 'battles' but—possibly as a result of a decision made on the Sunday—it had a novel feature, namely a fourth group designed to be the spearhead of attack. The first 'battle' was commanded by the king's son, the dauphin Charles, Duke of Normandy, the second by the king's brother, the Duke of Orleans and the third by King John himself. The spearhead of attack was commanded by the marshals.

The departure from custom in the use of a specially selected body for the primary onslaught seems to have been an adaptation of French attack to the now established English mode of defence. As the English fought on foot and used archers very effectively, the opening tactic should be designed to cause a very large expenditure of arrows and to ride down the archers by the trampling of the horses. It would be an expensive opening, but it would leave the English lines broken for the massive French attacks which would follow.

Since we are almost obliged to use the same terms and tend to use the same symbols, in describing medieval and modern warfare, it may be useful to stress three features of the medieval army. They concern the army's units or divisions, its discipline and the cartographical representation of battle dispositions. A feudal army had not a well-defined hierarchy of command. It was not 'divided' on functional principles; nor was it 'split' for convenience of operation into units, homogeneous in nature and uniform in size. Nor was it 'built up' of parts integrated into one organic whole; nor was it a military machine the parts or whole of which responded immediately and unfailingly to the will of the commander-in-chief. It was an assembly of groups of men with their leaders whom they recognized by their shields or banners, and a 'battle' was nothing more than a temporary combination of small groups into a larger group.

Secondly, in such an army morale was unpredictable, the more so if the army had only recently been assembled. Numbers, skill, high spirits and confidence might abound but, when cohesion, grouped training and discipline were deficient, the shining instrument might prove to be not tempered steel but a brittle blade.

Thirdly, the use of neat, coloured rectangles placed in parallel on a map to represent a medieval army stationed for battle, may be misleading. Such symbols suggest degrees of organization, of homogeneity and of precision in location that are at variance with the facts.

We return to the morning of Sunday, September 18th. During the darkness, the whole Anglo-Gascon force had been moved from Savigny to the northern end of the wood of Nouaillé. There on a slight eminence facing north-north-west and commanding a view of the plain, clear area, the members of the force were preparing for battle. The wood could conceal the baggage train or afford shelter for themselves. Hedges and vines in the neighbouring fields afforded a certain amount of cover. Wagons had been placed as a barrier at one point of the defences and the horses stationed sufficiently near at hand for quick mounting should the need arise. Archers had taken up the positions they were intended to occupy during the battle and, although a truce was arranged for the day, they improved their defences by digging trenches. Against these gains, however, must be set the fact that the men lacked food and the horses lacked forage.

As the armies lay (according to Chandos Herald) a quite short distance apart and watered their horses at the same stream, the truce afforded opportunities for men on both sides to observe the nature and disposition of their opponents' forces. Nor did they fail to do so. A French reconnaissance party studied the English position and reported that it was 'strong' and 'wisely ordered'; that in front of it lay a serious obstacle, a hedge which had only one opening; that the hedge was lined with archers and not more than four knights could ride abreast through the opening; that the English men-at-arms were dismounted and that the English front line consisted of archers disposed in saw-edge formation.

At the king's request, they added to their report their own conclusion. The customary, overwhelming cavalry charge, so beloved by the knightly order, would not be an appropriate tactic. A single, fierce attack by three hundred of the best armed and most expert French horsemen would make a suitable opening.

It might break through the English archers and, in the rents thus made in their lines, the French troops could follow. But these troops would have to dismount, follow the cavalry quickly on foot and engage in hand to hand fighting.[17]

This advice King John accepted. It was one of the most important and most fateful decisions of his career. Trained, equipped and mounted at great expense, French knights were to engage in a mode of fighting for which they were imperfectly prepared, wrongly equipped and in which they could not use their horses. It is true that English knights had fought thus at Halidon (as the Scottish leader, Douglas, who was fighting in the French army could tell him), and at Crécy (as he knew from his own experience), but there were two conditions in the English practice which did not apply at Maupertuis: the English had been defending, not attacking and the English knights had been combined with archers. If John was reasoning that the dismounting of the knights was the key to victory, he had not fully grasped the conditions of success. In view, however, of the obloquy poured on him by later generations, it should be said that his general arrangements earned the praise of contemporaries, that he did not rush precipitately into action and that his management of his force in this supreme test showed at least as much generalship as his father had shown at Crécy.

Sunday closed with the failure of negotiations and the certainty of battle on the morrow. That night the prince's council met to consider the situation. The dash southward with the accumulated treasure had failed. Hampered by the baggage train, stricken with hunger, watched by a numerically superior army which could, and doubtless would, force battle on them and could even surround and starve them, they were in a perilous situation. On the other hand, the position chosen for defence was good and it had been strengthened. Further, they had shared experiences longer and come to know one another better than their opponents could know each other. It was necessary to choose between prudence and audacity, between retreat (if it should prove practicable) and a fight in which victory appeared most improbable and even survival doubtful.

The night's deliberations led to an important decision which the prince himself summarized in a letter written a month later.[18] 'For default of victuals', he wrote, 'as well as for other reasons, it was agreed that we should take our way, flanking them, in such manner that, if they wished for battle or to draw towards us in a place that was not very much to our disadvantage, we should be the first.' The statement (written after the 'unbelievable' victory had been won) is intentionally obscure but it leaves no doubt that the Anglo-Gascon leaders had thought out a plan for the morrow. Was it to retreat as early as possible? or to stand their ground and retreat only if the attack became too strong to parry? or was it to feign retreat by moving part of the troops southward in the hope of provoking the French to rashness and folly? These questions have received much discussion for, on the following morning, the English were in fact the first to move.

Sunrise on Monday, September 19th, was at about a quarter to six and the absence of comment on the weather in the chronicles permits the inference that the day was fine. Very early, Eustace Daubriggecourt and a small party of knights from the Anglo-Gascon army were sent out in the direction of the French army. Their task may have been to probe for information; more probably it was to divert attention from more important business in their rear. Daubriggecourt had distinguished himself in the mêlée near la Chabotrie on the preceding Saturday. This time he was taken prisoner.

During the skirmish, part of the prince's force was proceeding southwards east or west of, or through, the wood of Nouaillé. This opening step—made in accordance with the council's plan—set in motion the sequence of tactics which marked the day. The vanguard (commanded by Warwick) was escorting wagons containing booty down the slope toward the Miosson and the well-wooded further bank of that stream. Once in that wood, the booty would be concealed; its guard could not be caught in the bottom of the valley and surrounded; both booty and guard would be nearer the road leading to Bordeaux.

Two controversies have arisen from this initial move. One concerns the degree to which it was completed. The other lies in the interpretation of its purpose. Warwick and his convoy crossed the stream—probably in Nouaillé—left the wagons on the further side and returned toward the prepared position from which he had set out, probably crossing the stream at the Gué de l'Homme. Whether the prince and his large 'battle' had followed him we shall not discuss. Concerning the purpose of the movement also we shall be brief. It is now generally accepted that it was intended to be the first phase of a retreat, if retreat should prove practicable. Yet it is possible to see in the movement a feint and to regard the French command as deceived. The use of a small force, ostentatiously exposed, to provoke an attack on an army on a ground of its own choice was a common device. It is possible also to regard the movement as a combination of prudence and audacity, of retreat and provocation for, on the one hand, it placed (or would place) the more cumbersome material near the Bordeaux road and, on the other, it challenged attack for which (as Chandos Herald shows) every man, not archers only, was warned to be on his guard and ready for instant action should an attack be launched.[19]

But our chief concern is with the reaction produced in the enemy. The English movement must have been in progress for some time before it was noticed by the French. Then two things appear to have struck them—one, that the departure of the vanguard left the main body (which some writers conjecture to have been following the van) and particularly the rearguard exposed to attack; the other, that possession of the ford was of critical importance. The king was remote from the scene but his marshals realized that action on their part was necessary. Clermont wished to wait till the situation was clearer; d'Audrehem desired immediate action. Though joint commanders of the 'crack' companies who had retained their mounts and were stationed in front of the dauphin's 'battle', they allowed their different views to govern their actions: one led a cavalry charge against the disappearing English force and the other against the stationary rearguard commanded by Salisbury.

d'Audrehem's column galloped forward and began the descent of the slope towards the stream but, as Warwick and a small body of archers were already returning to the field, the half armed horses were exposed to the archer's fire. Very many of them fell wounded. Their riders were killed or captured and d'Audrehem himself became prisoner.

The other column under Marshal Clermont and the Constable, de Brienne, flung itself against the English rearguard which was still in its station in front of the wood. The function of this column, defined on the previous day, was to force a way through the English archers in order that the French men-at-arms who should follow on foot, might have gaps cleared for their attack. Had the archers been drawn up in straight lines, their fire might have failed against horses which were armoured in front. The archers'

I

stations and grouping, however, permitted cross fire and it was deadly. Clermont, de Brienne and many others were killed.

The prince's (or council's) plan had precipitated two very costly strokes entailing the loss of three of the most experienced French commanders. Responsibility for the direction of the French army now rested with the king but he was still with his own 'battle', far away from the scene of action.

As the broken remnants of the French cavalry withdrew, the first of the great French 'battles', the dauphin's, advanced in armour but on foot, across several hundred yards of country and, tired but still valiant, made their heavy attack. This was the severest part of the action. Masses of men engaged in hand to hand fighting, but the whole Anglo-Gascon force, except a reserve of four hundred horsemen, was holding the position. In the drawn-out struggle, both sides suffered heavy casualties. The defenders were neither broken nor dislodged and after some time, the dau-phin's 'battle' in remnants but not in disorder, gradually made its way back. It had made a gallant attack. Another such stroke, made by fresh men while the tired English were searching for more arrows, bringing up fresh weapons and saving the wounded, would probably have succeeded.

But the next stroke did not follow quickly on the dauphin's withdrawal. Indeed the word 'withdrawal' may imply a greater unity of movement than the facts warrant, for the various accounts of the battle when added together, present a picture of many combats of relatively small groups and of individuals. 'The battle began on all parts', says Froissart, implying not the impact of a sledge-hammer blow but scores of local combats; and he speaks of 'the battles, rencounterings, chases and pursuits that were made that day in the field' and uses such phrases as 'near the king' and 'a little above that'. It is the picture survivors would give of their own limited observations. It is also the kind of action which would result from the impulses of an army so ill co-ordin-ated as King John's. And, in any case, it could not be expected that men advancing against a rain of arrows, would maintain their alignment on a long front. A rush here and there taking advantage of a shortage of arrows among the English archers, a stiff mêlée around a few skilled men-at-arms, a spirited charge by the retinue of a bold French knight, attack heroic but ill organized and, therefore, ragged and wasteful—such is the impression con-veyed by the chronicles. And, on the English side, there is the fatigue and depression inseparable from continued physical, mental and moral exertion prolonged till exhaustion almost overcomes will power.

It was, however, the turn of the next French 'battle,' that commanded by the Duke of Orleans, to advance and deliver its blow. Instead of advancing, the whole body left the field. The reason for this extraordinary conduct must remain a matter for conjecture. Its effect was decisive. Very severe fighting was still to come but (the historian can now see, though English commanders could not), from the moment this large body of troops turned away from the fight, a French victory became almost impossible. The English had a breathing space, French numerical superiority was diminished and other French groups began to consider withdrawing from the field. The departing French troops had taken to horse and left in good order. At King John's command, the dauphin and his brothers, under a very large guard, also left the field. Some Englishmen inferred that the time was ripe for action, leapt to their horses and began a pursuit.

But the time for pursuit had not yet come. The biggest and best disciplined French 'battle' remained intact under the king's command and, at the moment he judged most propitious, he led it (on foot, of course) against the prince's tired army. The attackers had a longer march than the dauphin's men had had to make. The distant sight of this large body of fresh, armoured men with the Oriflamme floating above them, made English hearts doubt the issue. It was a testing time for morale.

To meet this supreme effort of the French king, three steps were taken. During the pause, the unwounded men of the three English 'battles' were made into one ordered force. Next, the Captal de Buch was given a special task: he was to take a small mounted force on a circuit of a mile or two, passing first behind a small hill (near the present railway station), then keeping concealed behind thickets and thus, unseen by the French, get to their rear. That achieved, he was to display the banner of St George as a sign to the prince and then attack the French. Thirdly, the English men-at-arms and the very many horse-archers were given the order to mount.

The king's 'battle' advanced; the prince's mounted men were ready; the signal from the Captal was received; the prince ordered a charge and every man who could sit a horse rode out against the French. It was a bloody encounter. Men fighting hand to hand swayed backwards and forwards and tended, as we have shown, to lose alignment and break into local combats in which—as Baker implies—the English, fully aware of their situation, exhibited the furious energy and recklessness of desperate men. In the midst of the struggle came a shout from the Captal's men, now in the rear of the French, then a charge by these men and the immense moral effect on the French of finding themselves surrounded. The furious fight continued till many fled in panic while the remainder were killed or captured. Among the prisoners taken were the king and his fourteen-year-old son, Philip.

Though many Frenchmen had failed to strike a blow, the long list of French nobles who were killed in the battle and the high estimates of the number of French dead, point to desperate fighting and great slaughter.

We cannot close this summary of the military aspect of the battle without reference to a controversy about the location and disposition of the French army on Sunday and Monday, September 18th and 19th. Place names and topographical details point to the site of the battlefield and to the position of the English force on the Sunday. There is, however, no indication of the exact position of the French (except that they were quite near the English). Nor do the chroniclers, in describing the battle, imply a direction for the French movements (except of course that they attacked the English). Since King John had come down the road leading towards Limoges, it has been inferred that his men spent Saturday night near Beauvoir, that on Sunday they were facing the English position at a distance of half a mile to two miles, and that the French 'battles' were drawn up in the conventional order (in échelon).

French historians have contributed to our knowledge of the English expedition by checking the place names of the route the force followed in Languedoc and by identifying the site of the battle of Poitiers. They have also put forward a view which is not yet fully accepted, that King John's army lay not north-west of the English army, but west of it, that its three 'battles' were not in échelon but in something like a straight line running north-south, that John himself and his 'battle' were stationed on a promontory in the champ Alexandre in a meander of the Miosson, and that the English force, having left its prepared position facing north to north-west, fought the battle near the stream.[20]

No chronicler asserts that the French army had taken up this position; the chroniclers' very silence is significant; it has been forcefully argued that 'the (French historians') thesis is from a military point of view, intrinsically improbable'. On the other hand, certain passages in Baker and Chandos Herald can be interpreted to imply that the French army had taken that position. It may be argued that such a move was wise, at least in intent, and that from the champ Alexandre King John commanded a perfect view of the field. The evidence (which is not wholly consistent) must of course be interpreted in relation to the terrain and also to the character and capacity of the leaders to whom it relates. We leave the last words to the military experts. If the French historians' view be accepted, then the encircling movement of the Captal de Buch must have been a south-westerly loop taking John in the rear from the Gué de Russon, and some other tactics need re-interpretation.

Morale as evinced in the opposing armies, presents interesting problems.

The expeditionary force had among its leaders at least a dozen men who had fought at Crécy while others had served in Gascony in 1345–6 and still others were sons of men who had campaigned with Edward III in 1346. Their experience of warfare against the French was united with the esprit de corps which came of a whole year's active association in operations and with the knowledge that on this occasion, they must fight for their lives. On the morning of the battle, English morale was of the grim order which knows that nothing less than a supreme effort both in fighting and endurance, can save the day. On individual valour the leaders could depend. Of perfect corporate action they were less sure. The battle was not a phase of the *chevauchée* with its easy discipline but a defensive engagement necessitating the tightest control. That control was at times seriously impaired.

After the anticipated cavalry charges, there followed two quite unforeseen events. First came a French attack on foot. Then came the wholly unforeseeable departure from the battlefield of numbers of French troops who had not struck a blow. This astonishing conduct in the enemy proved a very severe test of English judgment and discipline. Even in the temporary relief afforded by the withdrawal of the cavalry, Baker reports that 'our leaders took steps lest the victors should follow the fleeing'. Of the next pause (during the orderly retirement of the dauphin's 'battle') he says that 'as the issue of the day was doubtful so long as the French king and his force lay in the near-by valley, our men would not leave the field in pursuit of the enemy'.[21]

But the itch to pursue was ever present. Lord Berkeley disregarded orders, chased his man and was himself captured. Others also leapt to their horses and began the pursuit. The situation grew utterly confused. A well-placed observer might have seen at one time Frenchmen fighting stoutly in groups against their opponents, a French corps retiring, a very large French corps standing ready to advance and bodies of Frenchmen riding away from the battle. Less favourably placed Englishmen had drawn their own conclusions and were breaking away for a chase as if victory were already won. English commanders had either misjudged the situation or failed to keep a tight hold on their men. The prince was 'abashed'.[22]

Later, when the supreme test came, those who had borne the brunt of attack after attack and were now exhausted, grew dispirited. At this moment the prince prayed for help, then made the critical decision which turned the scales. The English should attack—and attack on horseback. This change of tactics at the right moment restored morale. After a bloody contest, victory was won, but its achievement had been endangered by imperfect control of men who were unaccustomed to battle discipline and longed to follow up an advantage even by dispersal.

Dispersal of a quite different kind played havoc with the great French army. It arose neither from military necessity nor, in our view, from lack of military courage. It was akin to desertion yet apparently without the usual motives for desertion.

If morale in a medieval army be held to have consisted principally in the consciousness of physical well-being, of military strength, of a just cause and of confidence in the leader, there are good grounds for believing French morale to have been high on the Sunday. The French numerical superiority is undisputed; their knights and men-at-arms must have been considered at least equal in valour and equipment to their opponents; their sufficiency of food and their good spirits are attested; and English depredations had given them just cause for hot indignation. King John's advisers summarized the situation for him: the English were few, wearied with travel and in a strange land, while the French were many, fresh, well fed and about to defend their own country.[23]

As for confidence in the leader, the medieval soldier attached less importance to this factor than does the modern and that for two reasons. Commanders were not chosen primarily for their gifts of leadership: they were almost invariably royal personages. Secondly, chivalry esteemed individual prowess so highly and was so enamoured of frontal attacks that it undervalued the arts of generalship. John was recognized as brave; he had experienced soldiers as marshals and consulted them about tactics; during the preceding twelve months he had had some successes in that both Edward III and Henry of Lancaster had retired or appeared to retire before him when he took the field. Of the nobles' confidence in his military capacity there is no direct evidence but they accepted his pay and came in great numbers to join him. With this qualification, the French army must be regarded as in good fighting form on the day before the battle.

Yet numbers of French knights as well as other ranks left the field without fighting. Among them was the Duke of Orleans 'and a great company with him'. There were also the king's sons. The impropriety and even the shamefulness of such conduct is noted by the chroniclers. 'There were many good knights and squires, though their masters departed from the field, yet they had rather a died than to have any reproach'. 'Both knights and squires fled away in shameful and cowardly fashion.'[24]

The phenomenon calls for explanation. We cannot agree that the one-day truce was disastrous to morale [25]—on one side only. That the French on that day fed well and were light-hearted, that some of them fraternized with the English, that the king would have preferred to fight immediately lest the prince should escape— these things made no material difference to the situation. Nor do we believe that the king's moral ascendancy over his army was seriously impaired by the brief delay. He held council with his marshals and the terms he communicated to the cardinal for transmission to the prince, showed great confidence in French power. Nothing in this could impair his prestige and, if French knights were impatient for battle, they knew by nightfall that the king also was impatient. The causes of decline in morale must be sought elsewhere.

Contemporary writers in mentioning the departure of these troops add ironic, regretful or abusive comment, but give no explanation.[26] Cautiously we put forward the view that the French direction of the battle was bound to have a depressing effect on the spirits of French knights and men-at-arms. The king's plan was to attack, not by the overwhelming weight of cavalry charges for which the French were well trained, but by a novel approach by dismounted horsemen, making their way on foot, under the burden of armour, across an area affording little or no cover, in order to use a form of combat for which they were not trained.

Before the plan was put into operation and before the king had reached a position from which he could take command of the situation, the marshals felt obliged to begin an action which, though right in aim and spectacular in execution, proved costly and ineffectual. The discouraging and even ominous start was followed by the planned frontal attack on foot, an operation utterly void of the exhilaration which would accompany a cavalry charge. That also was very costly. It was at this point that strong and encouraging leadership was needed, but the king was still far away with his reserve. Trained and equipped for equestrian warfare, nourished on ideals of knightly combat and yearning for glory, the French knight now found himself deprived of his trusted horse, reduced to the level of a foot soldier and required to engage in a struggle with mere archers. There could be no honour in such an engagement. It was not for this that he had hurried expectantly half way across France. Disappointed and disgruntled, he felt an impulse to withdraw from the distasteful scene. Circumstances increased his impulse. Others were already withdrawing—for what reasons he did not know. He gained his horse and joined them.

There were no doubt several other reasons for withdrawal from the battlefield. All armies contain a few cowards and the ultimate phase of the foreign mercenary is not self-sacrifice but survival. One important reason lay in the evacuation of the king's sons. Carried out by the king's command and under the protection of a strong escort, it could not fail to be interpreted as a pointer to the issue of the day: the king himself was not confident; he had already concluded that the battle was lost; the prudent course then was to withdraw.

It was, we suggest, such circumstances as these that account for the failure of morale in the French troops. Discipline was weak. The sense of seigneurial independence was strong. The combat was not suitable for chivalric heroes. Withdrawals continued till, in the last phase, they became a disordered rout. But in the earlier phases, the will to fight had not been sapped by fear. It had shrunk because the kind of fighting made so little appeal to the fighter, and the valiant king was not among his troops to set an example of valour and endurance.

But a study of terrain and tactics and a modern enquiry into morale cannot convey the experiences of the expeditionary force. Most of its members saw only a limited part of the field and limited aspects of the action. What they experienced was a furious clash of arms, full of colour, sound, animation, grim bloodshed, fallen horses and dead and wounded men. Imagination is needed to visualize the scenes as one episode followed another, and some of the chroniclers supply vivid touches for a picture.

For the general scene—'There might have been seen great nobleness of fair harness and rich armoury of banners and pennons.' There were 'banners and pennons unfurled to the wind whereon fine gold and azure shone, purple, gules and ermine'. 'They saw the French king's banner wave in the wind' and the Lord of Charny who bore it had also his own banner gules, three scutcheons silver. Louis of Recombes bore a silver shield, five roses gules, and there was Sir Eustace d'Aubrecicourt with his two hamedes gules on a field ermine, and many scores of knights each with his distinctive shield.[27]

The noise 'could be heard for miles' as 'the French fighting in companies, cried out, "Mountjoy! St. Denis", and the English shouted, "St. George! Guienne". Men on both sides in a thunderous roar shouted "St. George" or "St. Denis" and cried that victory would be theirs'. 'They sounded their trumpets, one giving answer to another, they made such a noise that the walls of Poitiers sounded with the echo'. Loud trumpets sounded and tabors and horns and clarions and 'clamour began and a right great shout was raised and the prince broke up the camp'. 'It was a wonderful and terrible thing to hear the mingled noise of the horses, the cries of the wounded, the sound of horns. . . .'[28]

Concerning the action, 'in the encountering you might see great lances couched and thrust on both sides; each one bore his part well . . .; plying the business of arms in such right knightly fashion that it was great marvel to behold; . . . (he) strives with all his might to acquit himself well'. The archers' efficiency is described: they 'shot so fast that the men of the King of France could not stay within their range'. 'They shot so thick that the

Frenchmen wist not on what side to take heed' and, as the French
cavalry advanced, they 'did slay and hurt horses and knights so
that the horses when they felt the sharp arrows, they would in no
wise go forward but drew aback and flang and took on so fiercely,
that many of them fell on their masters, so that for press they could
not rise again'. The Earl of Oxford . . . 'set the archers . . . commanding them to shoot at the hinder parts of the horses by means
whereof, the horses being galled and wounded, fell to tumbling
with them that sat on their backs or else turned back and ran
upon them that followed after, making greater slaughter upon
their own masters'.[29]

When the archers had shot all their arrows, they 'made haste to
draw them from poor wretches that were but half dead' and, at
another time, they were obliged to 'encounter with them that
were laden (covered) with armour'.[30]

The difficulties of the armour-clad knight who fell are mentioned: 'he was beaten down and could not be relieved' (set up-
right) . . . 'many a man was overthrown and he that was once
down could not be relieved', and the prince's strenuous activity
included 'raising the fallen'.[31]

'Our men carried those which were wounded of their camp and
laid them under bushes and hedges out of the way'. Audley
'was sore hurt in the body and in the visage. At last, at the end
of the battle, his four squires took and brought him out of the
field and laid him under a hedge for to refresh him; and they
unarmed him and bound up his wounds as well as they could'.[32]

Meanwhile Chandos remained at his vantage point, watching
the movements of banners and pennons and making his inferences till he could recommend an offensive. The rout began and
there are picturesque accounts of the chase for prisoners.[33]

That the chroniclers were consciously painting pictures is
true, but they are contemporary pictures based on impressions
drawn from men who took part in the battle.

An attempt to award honour to merit is limited by the circumstances of the Anglo-Gascon command and also by the
nature of the evidence. The prince acted as commander-in-
chief, but major decisions, as we have seen, were taken by, or at
any rate laid before, his council. The only evidence we have of
the meetings of this body comes from the prince's own pen and
he merely reports 'we took counsel' or 'it was agreed'. The
opening of negotiations through the cardinal had had the coun-

cil's approval; the first move on the day of the battle had been
'agreed'. (The prince adds 'and so forthwith it was done'. There
is some evidence that he would have preferred to avoid battle
and perhaps even expected to do so. The agreed plan was, however, executed.) For this part of the day's operations at least,
responsibility must be shared.

Concerning the direction of the battle during the rest of the
day, contemporaries are not helpful. The letter-writers give no
details of the engagement and the chroniclers are more interested
in valour than in generalship. One praises Warwick, another
Warwick and Suffolk, a third the Captal de Buch and so on. Such
differences in emphasis would be expected in narratives based on
the evidence of men who had seen different phases of the action.
From Chandos Herald and from Froissart, however, it is clear
that Chandos remained with the prince throughout the day and
Audley was with them for some time. Chandos indeed is depicted
as the prince's adviser.[34] Since their task was to fight a defensive
battle against heavy odds, prolonged endurance was called for.
That quality is implied rather than mentioned in the chronicles.

The portrait of the prince as painted by the chroniclers is, of
course, favourable. He is stated to have addressed his men.
According to the *Eulogium*, he told them that strength in battle
lay not so much in men and arms as in those who put their trust
in God. Froissart's report (he uses *oratio recta*) includes a similar
note: 'Victory lieth not in the multitude of people but whereas
God shall send it.' Their victory, he continued, would bring
very great honour, their defeat revenge. Let them do their duties.
Baker gives two very polished speeches (which he admits are not
ipsissima verba), the one addressed to a body of troops, the other
to the archers. The speeches include references to the valour of
the men's forbears and to his father's claim to the French throne.
Honour, love of country and desire for rich spoils, he said, moved
them to follow their fathers' steps. Let them carry out commands.
Victory would cement friendship. Death would lead to eternal
fame.[35]

In all three reports there is a reference to the disparity in
numbers between the opposing forces; and all three accounts
mention the effect of the speech on the men. Writers not uncommonly attribute speeches to generals and invent what they
believe to be suitable phrases. In view, however, of the three
independent accounts and of the similarity of sentiment, it is

likely that at least the prince did address his troops or their leaders and that his words helped to strengthen morale.

Later, when the decisive change was made and the order for the English to advance was given, the prince is described as joining heartily in the very heavy fighting till the day was won.[36]

Though the names of the commanders, the post of Chandos and the exploits of Audley and Berkeley have long been well known, little attention has been given to the parts played by other men during the battle. From the miscellaneous grants made by the prince during the following years, it is possible to gain a little knowledge, because some of them are accompanied by phrases comparable with modern citations for distinguished conduct. In a few instances the commendatory phrases are linked with specific duties. The remainder are standardized eulogies. They may be imperfect indications of distinction, but some deserve mention for the light they throw on the more personal aspect of the battle.

The prince's standard-bearer was William Shank [37] (and not Sir Walter de Wodeland as has been generally stated. Letters of protection had been issued for Wodeland but his presence at the battle cannot be substantiated from the records).

The following were 'appointed to attend on the prince's person': Sir Nigel Loring, Sir William Trussell, Sir Alan Cheyne, John de Sarnesfeld (a yeoman) and John del Haye (also a yeoman). Each of these five is rewarded for 'good service and the very great position he held at the battle of Poitiers'.[38]

Others also mentioned for 'the very great position (they) held at the battle of Poitiers' include Sir John Chandos, Sir Baldwin Botetourt, Sir Edmund Wauncey, Sir John Sully, Sir Roger Cotesford, Sir Stephen Cusington, Sir Thomas Felton, Sir Tiderick van Dale, and Henry de Berkhamstead (a servant of the prince).[39]

Another group are noted to have given 'good service in Gascony and especially at the battle of Poitiers'. They include Sir Daniel van Pesse, Sir Bernard van Zedeles, Sir Hans Trouer, Sir Robert Nevill, William St. Omer (the prince's yeoman), William de Holford (also the prince's yeoman), together with a considerable number of Cheshire men both leaders and archers: Sir John Danyel, Richard Mascy, Simon de Grimsditch, David de Thornlee, Randolf de Stoke, Nicholas Dounes, William Dounes, Robert Legh, John de Cotton, William de Thenewell,

William Davy, William de Stockport, Robert Bolt, Adam de Bostock, Roger de Honford, William Neuton, Sir John de Hide, Sir John Fitton and others.[40]

Still others are cited for 'good service at the battle of Poitiers'. They include some already quoted and John de Palington (the prince's servant), William Bechynton and Roger Simondson (Cheshire archers).[41]

The absence of Welsh names from the lists is no doubt due to the loss of the Register for North Wales.[42]

There is no comparable Register for Gascony, but among the payments made by the Constable of Bordeaux occurs an annuity granted by the prince to Gerald de Tartas, Lord of Porane 'for good service in Gascony and especially at the battle of Poitiers'.[43]

We have traced the names of members of the force who received honourable mention shortly after the battle. Six centuries later, we still acknowledge the courage, skill and endurance not only of the named, but also of the hundreds of unnamed men who withstood the heavy assaults of the French army.

That the moment the scales turned decisively, they felt the elation of victory and, in pursuit, drove home their advantage by killing hundreds of fleeing opponents was natural. That they also captured rather than killed many of them was entirely in accordance with the principles of their day. We turn, therefore, to the subject of prisoners.

The flight or even the orderly departure of opponents made a problem for the commander of the other side. At a time when warfare had a business aspect, ransoms were of even greater value than booty. Knights, men-at-arms and archers had hopes of turning victory to personal advantage by capturing prisoners. The hopes were, of course, well understood by the commanders, and opportunities were not refused, provided they were compatible with the safety of the army as a whole. A premature dispersal of fighting power was, however, a serious danger and commanders had repeatedly to insist that there should be no breaking of the ranks and pursuit of retiring opponents. A second danger lay in the attitude of mind induced in combatants by the desire for ransoms. The soldier's primary task was the prompt killing of his enemy. Capturing him and guarding him wasted time, blunted the edge of battle and therefore diminished military efficiency. There were occasions when commanders issued the order 'no quarter' not through bloodthirstiness, but as a necessary disciplinary measure.

The legal and moral aspects of the capture and ransoming of opponents in the 1350s, as described by Froissart,[44] may be summed up in three principles:

(1) Soldiers have a right to take prisoners and hold them to ransom.

(2) It is creditable to capture famous men and profitable to ransom them.

(3) But the greatest credit should be reserved for those who, in spite of great temptation to seek personal gain, continue to fight whenever fighting has to be done.

The French, it must be remembered, acknowledged and, when opportunity occurred, exercised the right as well as the English. Salisbury's father and Suffolk had in fact been captured by the French and ransomed.

Before the battle of Poitiers, the commanders on both sides had laid down their policies. King John, according to Chandos Herald, had given the clearest order that no mercy should be shown. 'Spare not to put them all to death,' he is reported as saying. There was, however, to be one exception: should the Prince of Wales be captured, he was to be brought alive to the king. Moreover, the Oriflamme was carried.[45]

For the Anglo-Gascon force, the prince—with the assent of his council—had made an ordinance which was duly proclaimed 'that no man should linger over his prisoner . . . but that each man should have the prisoner to whom he should first be pledged'.[46] The pledge was usually accompanied by the handing over of some part of the arms or equipment.

During the battle, as individuals and groups on the French side began to retire from the field, very many of the English force broke into pursuit with a view to capturing opponents. Froissart cites two instances in which the Frenchmen turned and made their pursuers prisoners, one being the Lord Berkeley who was wounded, carried off to Chatellerault, nursed for a fortnight, transported in a litter to Picardy and subsequently released on payment of a large sum.[47]

As the battle drew to an end and a general rout began, many of the French fled towards the protection of the walled city of Poitiers. Amid scenes of great slaughter outside the gates, many captures were made for, in this closing phase, capture not killing was the aim of the victors everywhere. 'There you might see',[48] says Chandos Herald, 'many a knight, many an archer, many a squire running in every direction to take prisoners on all sides', and Froissart says that some English archers had four, five or six prisoners.[49] Success attained embarrassing proportions.

The state of the field may be seen in a sworn declaration made by the Count of Dammartin relating the circumstances in which he had been taken. First, the prince's squire, John Trailly, captured him, took his bascinet and gauntlet and handed him over to the custody of a yeoman. The yeoman, however, left his prisoner. Then a Gascon 'captured' him, took an escutcheon of his coat armour and left him. Thirdly, a man belonging to Sir John Blankmouster 'captured' him and brought him to the Earl of Salisbury. In order that he might be saved, the Count gave his fealty to all three of his captors and, with the consent of the third, he gave it to the Earl of Salisbury also. In view of the prince's proclamation about not lingering over prisoners, the episode led to conflicting claims to the ownership of the Count's person.[50]

The circumstances in which the French king was taken are also partly known. John's splendid bravery and that of his closest associates in the final struggle are universally acknowledged. Among the crowd of men who surrounded and sought to capture him was Denis de Morbek, a knight of Artois, banished from France on account of a murder and retained in the English army. Thrusting himself forward by sheer strength, he called to John 'in good French'. John yielded and gave his right gauntlet to de Morbek. There followed a disgraceful scene in which the king was snatched from de Morbek. Ultimately he was rescued from the brawling company by Warwick and Cobham who brought him to the prince.[51] Another knight, however, Bernard de Troyes, a Gascon, was able to put forward so good a case that *he* had captured the king that the rightful claimant could not be determined. The dispute therefore, was referred to King Edward.[52]

Towards evening as knights, men-at-arms and archers returned from the fierce fighting under the walls of Poitiers, from Chauvigny and from all the countryside, bringing back their prisoners to the rallying point where the prince's banner floated over a bush, it became evident that the mass of prisoners was unmanageable for an army that was still moving. Accordingly, many of the less important men were promptly offered terms and those who gave their pledge to return with their ransoms before Christmas to Bordeaux, were released immediately. The terms offered are said to have been easy, the principle being that the payment of his ransom should not so impoverish a knight that he could not 'maintain his degree'.[53] The remainder were disarmed but well treated, for chivalry commended courtesy to knights of any nation and common prudence pointed to the value of maintaining the health of a man whom it was hoped to ransom.

It is not known whether Warwick, Suffolk, Oxford, Salisbury and Cobham had made direct captures, but that the practice extended to eminent and wealthy commanders no less than to the lower ranks is seen in the names subsequently listed. Bartholomew de Burghesh, the prince's friend and contemporary, had taken the Lord of Pompadour; the Captal de Buch had taken the Count Charles of Artois; Sir Edmund Wauncey and John de Kentwood had jointly taken the French king's son Philip.[54] Neither Chandos nor Audley, however, had engaged in the practice. The former, acting as the prince's chief of staff, remained with his master throughout the day [55] while the latter, a pattern of the perfect soldier, 'that day never took prisoners but always fought and went on his enemies'.[56]

The prince had no part in the chase but it would be wrong to regard him as loftily aloof from a practice which he tolerated for the sake of expediency. He had refused offers of large sums of money at Carcassonne and at Perigueux. After Poitiers he plunged deeply into the business of ransoms. Baker says that he bought all the prisoners from their lords [57] and Froissart that he bought from the Gascons the greater part of the noble French prisoners and paid ready money for them.[58] Probably neither statement is quite accurate but he acquired possession of a great number of prisoners. We shall return to the subject in a later chapter.

The flight of the French brought two further grounds for satisfaction. The French king and nobles had travelled in style and with ample supplies of food. Their riches and stores were promptly seized. In addition to ransoms, therefore, there were gold, silver, plate, jewels, rich harness and a great quantity of valuables.

Among the king's precious goods were a silver ship taken by some Cheshire archers, a crown and star, a Bible Hystoriau and a volume of Les Miracles de Notre Dame. The ship was bought by the prince; the crown and star he subsequently pledged to the Earl of Arundel. The Bible is in the British Museum and the other volume in the Bibliothèque Nationale.[59]

Finally there was food in abundance for the famished English army and its prisoners. For King John and the captured nobles the prince had a supper prepared, he himself acting as host and (ironically) feeding his guests with meats taken from their own supplies. Froissart paints a picture of perfect courtesy on the prince's part toward his royal captive. In a speech or in a conversation overheard, he is reported to have declared that the French king had that day surpassed all in valour and, by universal consent, won the prize and chaplet'.[60]

Froissart also takes the opportunity to depict the prince favourably in relation to his warrior friend, Audley, who, after attending on him, had gained leave to plunge into the battle and been seriously wounded. The prince noted his absence and, on discovering the cause, promised him a very substantial revenue for life. Audley, equally chivalrous, is reputed to have passed on the gift immediately to his squires and the prince to have appreciated such generosity of mind and spirit.[61]

Night fell on the deserted field and the prince's tent was pitched among the dead and dying. He is said to have slept little that night[62] but that may well have been true of the greater number of the men on both sides, for the day had brought about an amazing change in the prospects of the opposing armies. France had suffered a disastrous defeat. Against all probability the Anglo-Gascon force had gained a resounding victory. Froissart, narrator of so many battles, felt that Poitiers needed an introductory note. 'Oftentimes', he says, 'the adventures of amours and of war are more fortunate and marvellous than any man can think or wish'.[63] Villani speaks of 'the incredible victory' and continues, 'Fortune was favouring the English'.[64] Jean le Bel says, 'Fortune wished to favour one side and trample on the other'.[65] With more piety, an English chronicler attributed the victory to divine grace and not human valour; another used almost the same words and added that on the morrow, 'the English praised God for the marvellous works He had wrought in them'.[66] It would take a few hours to adjust minds to the new situation.

In the meanwhile, practical tasks called for attention, namely a survey of the battlefield and the identification of the noble dead, the compilation of a list of the prisoners, a decision on the policy to be adopted now that the army's movements were no longer

K

governed by the needs of flight or battle, and at an early date it would be desirable and indeed agreeable to send news of the victory to England.

We turn first to the news. No dispatch written at this date has survived. An entry in the Issues of the Pells records a payment to Geoffrey Hamelyn, 'groom of the prince's chamber coming from Gascony with the tunic and bascinet of the French king'.[67] At some point, therefore, Hamelyn was dispatched with interesting and convincing evidence to England, but the whole drama of his departure, journey and reception in London must be left to the imagination. (He may have been preceded by Thomas, the prince's messenger who reached England with letters from the prince not later than October 12th, but there is no indication of the date or contents of his letters: they may have been written when the negotiations broke down or even earlier.)[68] On October 10th, King Edward gave instructions for the publication of the news.[69]

Concerning the great decision of policy, we know nothing except that on the following day the army began to move southwards. Froissart alone attempts to interpret the thoughts of the leaders. No attack, he says, was made on the city of Poitiers or any other fortress, for they 'thought it a great deed' (*leur sambloit uns grans esplois*) if they could bring the French king, the prisoners and the riches safely to Bordeaux.[70] In the light of the information available to the prince's council on the night of September 19th, however, the decision taken must be regarded as sound. Victory alone might conceivably have been followed by a different policy, but victory plus the possession of the royal person presented a quite different situation. Diplomatically and financially regarded, the king and his fellow captives were (or seemed to be) an enormous asset. Militarily, however, they were a great liability. Devastating though the defeat had been, France had not lost all her royal family, all her nobles, knights, men-at-arms and archers. The king was still on French soil and quite near at hand. The proper course for the Order of the Star was to rescue the king; the proper course for the English leaders was to remove him—with a large guard. It would have served no purpose to divide the small army into two parts, sending one to Bordeaux with the captives and keeping the other in Poitou. Further reasons there may well have been, such as the weakening of the force after the casualties suffered in the battle, the complete exhaustion of the supply of arrows for

English bows or even the lack of the artillery and artillers requisite for sieges. The raiding force had not set out in order to fight
battles or conduct sieges, still less to subdue France. It had
achieved far more than its members even expected. Rightly it
returned to its base.

On the Tuesday the prisoners and the French dead were listed.
Of the prisoners there remains no official roll but there are
several (not identical) lists. Baker quotes the king, his son Philip,
the Archibishop of Sens and the names of thirty nobles. Other
sources point to a total of about 2,000 men-at-arms.[71] No doubt
very many of these were liberated, as we have seen, on oath.

The listing of the French dead receives the scantiest mention
in the chronicles. On the misty Sunday morning following the
battle of Crécy, Cobham and Stafford had gone out with three
heralds for this purpose and had spent the whole day on the task
before their report could be presented.[72] During the evening
following the battle of Najera, four knights and four heralds
surveyed the countryside in order to make a report on the dead,
the prisoners and whether King Henry were dead or alive.[73] Some
such arrangement must have been made for the operation to be
carried out at Maupertuis, for lists of French nobles who had
lost their lives were soon available. It may be that in the task of
identification, help was received from French heralds coming
from Poitiers for the same purpose and that the work continued
after the English army had departed. Knighton's brief reference
says that the dead were found 'spoiled and stripped'.[74]

No official roll has survived. Baker quotes the names of sixteen
nobles including the Duke of Bourbon, the Constable of France,
one of the marshals of France and the standard-bearer. From other
sources there are estimates of about 2,000 men-at-arms and 800
others.[75] Many of the nobles were buried in the Franciscan convent
at Poitiers and others in the Dominican church in the same city.
The body of de Charny who had borne the Oriflamme, was
afterwards transferred at the king's expense to Paris.

That English losses were high would be inferred from the
weight of the attacks. There remains, however, no contemporary
list of the famous and only two estimates of the total. These
amount to 40 and 60 and may be dismissed as valueless.[76]

Preceded by a large body of men-at-arms, the Anglo-Gascon
force with its booty and its prisoners moved southward, still

prepared for an attack by the enemy. The march to Bordeaux—
a distance of 170 to 180 miles—appears, however, to have been
uneventful. No resistance was met; no towns or fortresses were
attacked; there is no mention of the wanton ravaging which had
marked the earlier phases of the second *chevauchée*.

The route taken is known.[77] At noon on Tuesday (20th), the
prince left the battle area but travelled only a few miles to Les
Roches on the main road from Poitiers to Angoulême. Here he
spent the whole of Wednesday. This slow start may have been a
preparatory step intended to get the prisoners out of the way
while his commanders effected some reorganization in the force
for the lengthy march. From Thursday morning onwards, each
day's progress marks a long stage on the journey towards Bordeaux. The army spent a night at Couhé Verac (22nd) and at
Roffec (23rd), and continuing down the great trunk road, crossed
the Charente, then turned south-eastward through Morton
(24th) and reached La Rochefoucault (25th). The direction of
march turned a little westward and the force came to Villebois
la Valette (26th). Somewhere near here, part of the troops may
have gone to Blaye on the Gironde and been taken up the river
by boat, but the main force continued its march on 27th to St.
Aulay in the valley of the Dronne. Next day it crossed the river
and proceeded to St. Antonin on the Isle. That river was crossed
and on the 30th, the men reached St. Émilion where some of
them had been stationed in the winter. On October 1st, the Dordogne was crossed and on the following day, most of the army
marched into Bordeaux. The prince and the king, however, waited
at Libourne till preparations had been made for a formal entry
and for suitable accommodation within the city.

The news of the victory reached London on or before October
10th [78] and was conveyed to the king by John le Cok of Cherbourg, who a year later, received a gift of twenty-five marks
from the king for 'the pleasing intelligence which the said John
brought . . . of the capture of John, King of France and others of
the French nobility at Poytiers'.[79] I have not been able to trace
John le Cok of Cherbourg elsewhere and cannot think that a
message of such importance would be sent from Gascony by a
man who was neither a knight nor an officer of the prince. There
was, however, a clerk of the wardrobe called John Cok [80] and I
incline to think that Geoffrey Hamelyn (or Thomas the messenger), travel-stained and exhausted, reached Westminster with

the news; that the king was not in London at the time and that John le Cok galloped away to take the news to him.

The impact of the announcement on the king, the Council and the nation at large may perhaps be estimated by considering its relation to the information already in their possession. Every adult could remember some English successes in France during the preceding ten years. Concerning the prince's work in Gascony, it was known that the campaign of 1355 had encountered no serious opposition (and, if news of the recent campaign in August and early September had reached England, then it would be known that this campaign also was proceeding easily). Satisfactory news, therefore, would not be especially significant. A victory though gratifying, would not be—to them—surprising. But the capture of the King of France! and some scores of French nobles! Never in the course of English history had that happened. And it is noteworthy that even in the Issues of the Exchequer, just as the reward of John le Cok is not for news of Poitiers but for news of John's capture, so also when the Council sat for two days and expenses were subsequently paid, they were described as arising from the fact that members 'tarried at Westminster for two days at the time when news came of the capture of John, King of France'.[81]

The news was made known in letters to the archbishops and bishops requesting them to 'offer up thanksgivings and prayers for the king and the prince, for the further success of the war and the desired issue',[82] and the bishops' action may be traced in some of their registers.[83] Froissart refers to the joy in England when the news was received and adds that 'great solemnities were made in all churches and great fires and wakes throughout' the land.[84]

News of the victory resounded throughout western Europe. England, remote from the Mediterranean with its traditions of civilization, far less populous and less rich than France, relatively insignificant in the eyes of many Europeans, had inflicted a most humiliating disaster on her great neighbour. The vassal had defeated and captured the suzerain.

CHAPTER VI

AFTER THE RAIDS

J<small>UST</small> a year had passed since the Anglo-Gascon force set out on its first raid. Now, as the *vendange* was drawing to a close, the force returned from its second raid, enriched by booty, exhilarated by victory and full of expectations of fortunes to be derived from ransoms.

Local patriotism, human interest and business instinct combined in a long and enthusiastic welcome for the heroes. Gascon initiative had called in the English army; Gascon arms as well as English had won the victory; Gascon skill and pertinacity had filled the wagons with spoil. Guienne would not be swallowed into France. It would preserve its identity; it might be the nucleus of a great region, la Grande Aquitaine, with Bordeaux of course as its capital. Bordeaux was, and would continue to be, prosperous.

Processions, thanksgivings, prayers, festivities expressed the city's delight. The prince was lodged in one part of the abbey of St. Andrew and the king in another. They passed the winter in Bordeaux and, according to Froissart, there was mirth and revelry in the city till the following Lent, Englishman and Gascon alike pouring out the gold and silver they had gained and even spending the ransoms as they came in. Bordeaux was used to the entertainment of English troops. Notabilities arrived and departed. Messengers went to London, Avignon, to Paris. Presents were given and received. From some source, the prince acquired a lioness.[1]

Under the circumstances of the time, the guarding of the French king would be held to require the presence of a considerable armed body, but I have found no indication of the winter quarters and activities of the English troops. The surviving evidence relates to supplies, communications with England, negotiations for a truce and the departure of the army from Bordeaux with many prisoners.

The presence of English troops accentuated Gascony's normal deficiency of foodstuffs. In addition, therefore, to the usual cargoes of corn brought out by English merchants trading under export licences,[2] further supplies were sought. Four hundred quarters of wheat and oats were to be sent from Kingston upon Hull expressly for the prince's needs;[3] John de Palington was sent from Bordeaux to get as much hay and oats as possible in Cornwall and Devon, and the good men of Devon made a grant of two thousand quarters of oats for the prince's horses.[4] Moreover, large quantities of bows, arrows and bowstrings were ordered in Lincolnshire and sent out to Gascony in the *Saint Marie*.[5]

Money also was needed and John de Padbury, one of the regular nuncii, took a sum in gold from the king in February 1357. He travelled via Winchester, Exeter and Plymouth and delivered the specie to the prince at St. Andrew's abbey.[6]

The situation which had arisen in Gascony was of vital importance to Edward III and indeed to the English parliament and people. Some kind of communication, as we have seen, was sent to London immediately after the victory of Poitiers. At the end of October, Sir Nigel Loring and Sir Roger Cotesford took a message to the king from the prince which may well have been a dispatch comparable with the one he had forwarded in the preceding December.[7] Loring also bore a letter to the Mayor, Aldermen and Commonalty of London and Cotesford a letter for the Bishop of Worcester. Both of these letters have survived.[8] That addressed to the Londoners is similar in scope to the dispatch in which the prince described the first raid, but it differs in tone: there is not a word about devastation. The great battle receives only slight and impersonal treatment: 'God be praised for it, the enemy was discomfited and the king was taken and his son and a great number of other great people were both taken and slain'. For further information, the Londoners are directed to enquire of Loring. Geoffrey Hamelyn, as we have seen, was sent to London with the French king's tunic and bascinet, and Sir Baldwin Botetourt also went to England 'on the prince's business'. That other messages were sent there can be no doubt. A series of grants referring specifically to service at Poitiers are dated from London in November and the following months.[9] The king's measures for the assembly of ships and his arrangements for the reception of the French king show his awareness of impending needs.

Communication in the other direction would be equally important. As Loring and Cotesford returned to Bordeaux [10] after delivering their letters, they probably brought information and instructions. Indeed the purpose of sending such men was to gain a full exchange of opinion. Padbury also may have brought letters as well as gold.

It is very doubtful whether the Anglo-Gascon leaders as they returned to Bordeaux in the early autumn of 1356 had a clear plan of action for the immediate future. Their prompt departure from the battle area, the disciplined order they maintained along the route and the fact that they did not pause for rest, suggest that they expected to be attacked. There were good grounds for such an attitude. During the preceding November, Jean d'Armagnac had harassed the English withdrawal by repeated blows. Similar attacks would now be likely. Above all, it probably seemed unthinkable that the French nobles would allow their king and nobles to be carried into captivity without a quick counterstroke. As the days went by with no sign of serious French attacks, resort to negotiation grew more probable. Arms might give way to diplomacy.

The pope had never ceased to press the need of peace on the kings of France and England. From the beginning of May 1356, two cardinals Helie Talleyrand, Cardinal of Perigord and Nicholas, Cardinal of St. Vitalis had had the special duty of attempting to mediate between them. The pope had directed their activities and begged members of both nations to accept their proposals.[11] We have noted Talleyrand's efforts at Poitiers. Soon after the battle, he resumed the task with which he was charged. The English, however, had two serious grievances against him. In the first place, whatever the purity of his motives, the truce he had induced them to agree to had been advantageous to their enemies, for it enabled the French to have still greater forces arrayed in battle on the following day. Secondly, some of the cardinal's large entourage had fought on the French side. When, therefore, he sought a safe-conduct with a view to conferring with the prince, he was not *persona grata*. Some Gascon lords, however, induced the prince to grant him an interview and, after hearing the cardinal's statement of his position, the prince fell in with the pope's request. The cardinal was again regarded as trustworthy.[12] It is a mark of his skill or integrity that he gained the confidence of King John also.

Negotiations were bound to raise very wide questions, for to all the previous grounds of dispute had now been added the terms on which the French king might be released. 'The prince shall

have power under the king's great seal', the indenture of July
1355 ran, 'to make truces, long or short, and armistices, as he
shall think most profitable for the king. . . .'[13] In August 1356,
at the pope's request, the prince had been given additional powers
to treat with the French king and in December these powers were
confirmed.[14] They did not, however, cover the release of a captive
monarch.

Nor was the prince likely to exceed his powers. He continued
to act with the correctness which had marked his conduct from
the outset of the first raid. At every important step, he had made
clear that he had the assent of the lords who accompanied him
or that he was the instrument of his father's policy and could not
commit King Edward without prior consultation. To the French
king he had given a courteous assurance of his father's personal
friendliness, but he sent King Edward an account of the negotiations lest he should appear to be acting without his father's full
approval. And, when he had a serious difference with the Gascon
lords over the removal of the French king to England, it was his
father's will that he quoted as the justification for his proposed
action.

For King Edward the tide was flowing very favourably. The
Scots had been trounced. The Valois king was a prisoner. In
September, Philip of Navarre had done homage and entered into
an agreement to wage war in Normandy. In October, Henry,
Duke of Lancaster laid siege to Rennes in Brittany. If negotiations with John were resumed, Edward's juristic position would
remain unchanged—he had in fact authorized the prince to deal
with that—but the pressure he could exert on the Valois king
was now immeasurably increased. When the emperor offered his
services in the drawing up of a treaty of peace between the two
kings, Edward replied cordially that he wished for peace as he
always had done.[15] The old phrase, however, had now a new
meaning. Aware quite early of Talleyrand's intentions, he sent
William de Lynne, Dean of Chichester, to take part in the negotiations.[16] Lynne was a doctor of laws. So was John de Stretelee,
Constable of Bordeaux.[17] The good sense of the magnates was to
be reinforced by the skill of the trained officials. The prospects of
a settlement advantageous to the Plantagenet cause were very
bright. On the French side, the outlook was very dark. Crécy had
been a defeat. Poitiers was a major disaster. If the effects seem to
be out of proportion to the cause, it is because the structure on

which the blow fell was not soundly built. France had not yet evolved governmental and administrative machinery suited to her needs. In large measure, the king was the state: it was the king personally that the royal officers served; it was to the king personally that the lords were bound by homage. Yet his powers were very limited, his assured revenue small. In the hour of humiliation, responsibility for France's woes was attributed to this or that group or class, and reforms were demanded. Sectional leaders arose, discredited counsellors came forward, the evil genius of Charles of Navarre was ever close at hand. But of strong leaders capable of putting the national interest before all others, there were none.

The first problem of the young dauphin, Charles, now lieutenant of the captive king, was the war itself. Defeat had not terminated hostilities, but Charles had no reputation for valour or leadership, no personal ascendancy, no prestige of any kind. In the circumstances in which he found himself, there was no immediate prospect of his leading an army against the English. Recourse must, therefore, be had to negotiations. Indeed, his father was already taking the initiative.

John of Valois occupied a peculiar position. Edward III regarded himself as *de jure* King of France but he had had to negotiate with John as *de facto* ruler of that state. Since his capture, John was not even (unless by a fiction) *de facto* ruler. As the emperor put it, 'being in captivity, he has no power over himself'.[18] Nevertheless, it was with John that the negotiations were begun and the agreement which was at length reached, was an engagement between John and the prince.

The captive king enjoyed the utmost consideration in his confinement but his plight naturally roused widespread sympathy. Jean d'Armagnac sent him furniture, silver plate and provisions.[19] The Estates of Languedoc, hastily assembled at Toulouse in mid October, decided to make great sacrifices in order to equip and maintain troops for the war and decreed that while the king was a prisoner, jewels and costly raiment should not be worn, and balls and public festivities should not be held.[20] In Paris, the people voted subsidies to enable the dauphin to liberate the king. These were significant signs of national feeling. John, however, was opposed to further fighting. In a letter addressed to the merchants of Paris (and thereafter to the whole realm), he sought to dissuade them from continuing the struggle. The fortunes of war, he argued, were uncertain. Any attempt to rescue him would be easily frustrated. Let them, therefore, decide to make an honourable peace or his liberation would be impossible. It may be that the advice he tendered was sound, but the candid disclosure of his personal advantage as a ground for national action has reflected badly on his reputation.

The group of men appointed by the prince to confer with representatives of the French kingdom included the Earls of Warwick and Suffolk, Burghersh, Chandos, Cobham, Loring, Stafford, the Captal de Buch, the Lord of Pommiers, the sire of Montferrant, Stretelee and Lynne (doctors of law), Gilbert of Chatillon and William Burton.[21]

The French group included James of Bourbon and several nobles who were prisoners. They were described as representing the King of France and the Duke of Normandy, his eldest son.[22]

The proceedings were marked by an ironical feature: the mediators themselves were at variance. Before the negotiations started, Cardinal Nicholas incurred the pope's reproof for differing from Cardinal Talleyrand. Their tasks (and perhaps their temperaments) differed. Talleyrand, dealing with affairs at Bordeaux, was able to express hopes of a successful outcome. Nicholas, seeking to maintain contact with London and Paris, had to report depressing news. He also stated that he and his colleague rarely met and more rarely agreed. Fearing a breakdown in the negotiations, the pope insisted on concerted action.[23]

The scope of the negotiations does not appear to have been defined in advance. Three large problems presented themselves, namely the cessation of hostilities, the release of prisoners and the terms of peace. For the first a pattern already existed in the document which had defined the relations between the two kings and their respective peoples between 1347 and 1355. The second and third problems could not admit of quick solutions. Baker mentions rather obscurely a conference respecting a peace treaty, convened by the prince at the urgent request of the prisoners, and the pope makes reference to a final peace. There is evidence also in the Anonimalle Chronicle and in Froissart that efforts were made on the French side to settle the ransoms and secure the release of the French king, his son and the other prisoners.[24] But the only agreement which emerged was a truce.

The terms of the Truce of Bordeaux, March 23rd, 1357, are similar to those which were in operation between 1347 and 1355.

They extend to all the allies of both sides and mention specifically the rulers of Castile, Aragon, Portugal, Bohemia, Flanders,
Hainault, Scotland and other states. Both sides are to abstain
from fighting and from provocation. Sieges are to be raised.
People and merchants are to be free to come and go. There is
explicit reference to the siege of Rennes, to Philip of Navarre, to
prisoners who have not paid their promised ransoms and to a
qualification of the freedom of movement. Men on either side
who have been banished for reasons other than war are not free
to return to their own countries except barons of Guienne,
Gascony, Languedoc and the people of Flanders. These shall be
free to come and go whether banished or not. Arrangements are
made for the execution of the terms. The truce is to last till
Easter 1359.[25]

Thus the fighting ended. The active, military work of the
expeditionary force had ceased on the day it entered Bordeaux
in the previous autumn. The fruits of its labours were not yet
gathered but, in the persons of King John and his fellow prisoners,
the prince had assets of very great value which were to be used
in the fuller negotiations that were yet to come.

The fate of the prisoners remained for individual settlement.
The truce though technically an agreement between King John
and Prince Edward, was in effect an instrument of international
law. Its provisions included certain measures concerning the payment of ransoms. They could not fix the sums payable. Still less
could they foreshadow the periods which would elapse before
liberation of particular prisoners would be gained. It was necessary, therefore, to decide where the chief prisoners should stay
till the individual settlements had been reached. Commonly, the
more important prisoners spent years in comfortable captivity
and there were very well-known instances of French prisoners
being taken to England.[26] That John also would probably be
taken there must have been in the minds of all the better informed
men in the English and Gascon armies. Yet the announcement
that the prince was in fact arranging to take the king with him
when he sailed, provoked a serious disagreement between the
English and Gascon leaders.

In Froissart the episode is made dramatic. When everything
was ready for the prince's departure, the chronicler says, he held
a formal meeting at which, amid thanks for services rendered,
promises regarding the future and a statement concerning the

government of Gascony, he announced that he was about to take
John to England. The Gascon reply came instantaneously. With
courtesy but with great firmness, 'It is not our intention that you
should take the King of France from us,' they said. They had,
they argued, contributed largely to the king's capture and they
were powerful enough to guard him against any French force
which might attempt to rescue him. In reply, the prince explained
that he was carrying out his father's wishes; he appreciated their
services and they would be rewarded. These words, however,
did not satisfy the Gascon lords. Cobham and Chandos, therefore,
recommended that a large cash payment should be made for distribution among them. Sixty thousand florins were offered but
this sum had to be raised to one hundred thousand florins before
the Gascons would agree to the prince's plan.[27]

The story is in accord with Froissart's view of the Gascon
character. It is moreover substantially true, but it must be quali-
fied by the fact (which Froissart himself discloses much later) that
a dispute over the removal of the French king to England had
existed for four months.[28] Further, in extenuation of the Gascon
attitude, it must be allowed that while King Edward, the prince
and Denis de Morbek (or Bernard de Troyes) had legal or quasi-
legal rights to the large sums which (it was expected) would accrue
from ransoms or compensation, the Gascons had this moral right
that without their aid, the great prisoners would not have been
captured. Finally, by the end of March 1357, the prince had
made some handsome rewards to several of the English leaders.[29]
The Gascons also had served him well.

With the truce concluded, agreement about the departure of
the French king reached, and shipping assembled in the Garonne
for the return journey, the prince turned to the miscellaneous
arrangements incidental to the ending of his work in Gascony.
Some of his foreign helpers went to their homes: John Neufee
returned to Burgundy, John Gunsals, Benedict Lopes and Fer-
rand Martyn to Spain.[30] Deossent of Spain on the other hand and
several Almains were to accompany the prince to England.[31]
Some of the Gascon lords were given responsible posts in the
defence of their country.[32] Others (including the Captal de Buch,
Sir Aymery de Tarse and the Lord of Mussidan) were chosen to
go with the prince to London.[33] A large part of the English force
was to sail to England but the two leaders so often associated in
action, Chandos and Audley, were to remain behind.[34] Some of

the prisoners were sent to their homes.[35] Others—including the most famous—were taken to England.

In the meantime, preparations for the prince's return were being made in England. In December 1356, nine ships had been requisitioned—the purpose is not clearly stated—and in January 1357, Robert Ledrede had been appointed to command 'the fleet about to be sent to Gascony for the purpose of importing wine into England'.[36] That such a fleet might serve another purpose may have been in the king's mind. Some or all of the vessels were in fact used for bringing the English army home from Gascony. From the middle of February, clearer indications appear. On the 15th, two of the prince's serjeants are to make purveyance of hay, oats, litter and wheat.[37] On the 27th there is a reference to 'the great need of money in which the prince expects to be at his return to England'; the Chamberlain of Chester and the Receiver of Cornwall are to get all the money they can by Easter and also to have horses available for the prince.[38] In March, orders become quite specific. The Prince of Wales and John of France 'are shortly coming to Plymouth'. John Brocas and Thomas Durant, therefore are to obtain horses for mounts and for transport; the Sheriff of Devon is to make purveyance of victuals and carriage; the collectors of customs at Exeter are to provide Durant with ready money for his expenses.[39]

Though some of the ships used for the transport of the prince, his troops and the prisoners between Bordeaux and England were no doubt sent out expressly for that purpose, it is likely that others which chanced to be in the port, were pressed into service. No complete list [40] of the ships used is known to have survived, but the following were certainly used:

The *Clement* of Dartmouth
   ,, *Edward*
   ,, *Eleanor* of Dartmouth
   ,, *Espirit* of Bayonne
   ,, *George* of Sidmouth
   ,, *Gracedieu* of Hok
   ,, *John* (cog)
   ,, *Michael* of Hok
   ,, *Rode* cog of Bristol
   ,, *Saint Marie*
   ,, *Saint Marie* cog of Dartmouth

The *Saint Marie* cog of Polruan
  ,, *Saint Sauvourcog* of Fowey
  ,, *Thomas* (cog) of Dartmouth
  ,, *Welifare* of Hok
  ,, *Welifare* of Hok
and the following were probably also used:
The *Blaunche*
  ,, *Christofre*
  ,, *Jerusalem*
  ,, *Gabriel*
The fleet is stated to have left Bordeaux on April 11th.

For the voyage the *Saint Marie* was assigned to the King of France [41] and the prince sailed in the *Espirit* of Bayonne.[42] Some or all of the ships reached Plymouth by May 1st.[43] With his usual liberality, the prince rewarded the master and crew of the *Saint Marie*. To the master, William Pierres, he gave 20*l.*, to two men who had piloted the vessel he gave five marks apiece and to each of the hundred mariners one mark.[44]

At Plymouth, John Brocas was waiting with twelve horses from Windsor Park and twelve grooms. He had also brought a farrier and eight more horses and eight grooms belonging to the Bishop of Bath, the Abbot of Glastonbury, the Earl of Devon, the Rector of Crewkerne and the Abbot of Thorne.[45]

More than three weeks elapsed before the prince entered London. The apparent slowness of his movements may have been due to the lack of harbour facilities for unloading vessels at Plymouth, to the need for the travellers to refresh themselves and their horses after a longish period in confined quarters at sea, to the fact that many of the accompanying troops made the journey to London on foot and to the desire, on the part of the prince and King Edward, for adequate preparations to be made in London for a suitable reception. The route taken lay through Salisbury and Winchester. From Salisbury a messenger was sent forward to obtain and bring back to the prince quantities of sweetmeats.[46] On May 22nd, the prince received 200*l.* from the keeper of the wardrobe for his expenses in bringing the royal prisoners from Plymouth to London.[47]

The formal entry into the capital was made on Wednesday, May 24th. Never in its history had London seen such rejoicings and excitement. Great preparations had been made for an impressive occasion and wine was available in abundance and free for all who wished to drink. The mayor, aldermen and members of the guilds, mounted and newly apparelled, went out to meet the cavalcade at the head of which rode the prince, King John, his son Philip and thirteen of the most important prisoners. Then they turned about and led the long procession over London Bridge, through streets decorated with arms, armour and tapestries, past St. Paul's Churchyard where the Bishop of London and the clergy were stationed, and by way of Ludgate and Fleet Street to Westminster where the King of France entered the royal palace and met the King of England.

The expeditionary force had finished its labours. It remained for diplomacy to ensure that the victory it had won and the assets it had gained, were used to the best advantage. John and his fellow prisoners were suitably housed.[48] Cardinal Talleyrand came over to England and the work left unfinished at Bordeaux, was taken up in London.

That work was greatly complicated by John's strange position, for the opportunity of insisting on an immense ransom was too good to be missed. To the well-known Plantagenet claims—dynastic and territorial—were added rather ignoble financial demands. And, in order that King Edward's rights might be beyond dispute, King John's position was made manifest. The indenture of 1355 between Edward and his son had contained an important reservation: the King of France, if captured, was to be Edward's prisoner. John had acknowledged—perhaps conversationally rather than formally—that according to the laws of war, he was subject to the prince [49] and later, while still in France, he had given evidence that de Morbek was his captor.[50] It was, however, necessary to establish Edward's right in the royal prisoner. This was done in December 1357 by *litterae testimoniales* setting forth clearly that John had acknowledged the fact of his surrender to Denis de Morbek on the day of the battle of Poitiers; that Denis de Morbek had delivered John's person to the prince on that day and that Denis de Morbek had freely and unconditionally given to Edward all his rights in John.[51] Edward's legal and moral right to deal with John's ransom were now beyond dispute.

As the long negotiations, the further fighting and the ultimate settlement belong to the national history, we give here only a summary. John and Edward reached an agreement by which the French king would cede a great part of the Plantagenet claims to territory in France; these territories Edward would hold in full sovereignty and John would be released on his promise to pay a ransom of 4,000,000 gold crowns. These terms were, however, rejected by the dauphin and his advisers. In October 1359, therefore, war was resumed and in May 1360, by the Treaty of Bretigny, a settlement was reached. Edward abandoned his claim to the French throne and reduced John's ransom to 3,000,000 gold crowns, but Edward recovered the Agenais, Perigord, Quercy, Rouergue, the county of Bigorre, the Limousin, Sainttonge, Angoumois, Poitou, the counties of Montreuil, Ponthieu and Guines and he retained Calais. A first payment of 600,000 crowns was to be made at Calais within four months of John's arrival in that town. In June 1360, the two kings gave their assent to this treaty and in July, John reached Calais. The first payment was not delivered in full, but Edward was temporarily satisfied with 400,000 crowns. On October 24th, the definitive treaty of Calais was sealed and on the following day, John left Calais for his own country.[52]

It is in the light of this settlement that the work of the Black Prince's expedition must be judged. In the plans for the expedition, the Plantagenet cause was to be advanced by the recovery of lost territories, the recovery of lost allegiances and the engagement of new friends and additional forces. Very much had been achieved in all three directions, but the situation had become involved by John's anomalous status for, while John's assent was necessary to a settlement, the settlement to which he was prepared to assent was not acceptable to his people. Further fighting, therefore, had ensued. Nevertheless, 'the Treaty of Bretigny', as Delachenal wrote, 'was the direct consequence of the capture of John II'.[53] The territorial (as well as the financial) gains embodied in that treaty may, therefore, be attributed in large part to the prince's expedition of 1355–7. King Edward gave up his claim to the French throne, but he now held in full sovereignty the whole of the duchy of Aquitaine, the county of Ponthieu and the recent conquest, Calais. If the settlement did not represent the full Plantagenet dream, it was nevertheless a very great achievement.

CHAPTER VII

RANSOMS, REWARDS AND PARDONS

THE exhilaration of adventure, the companionship of fellow men, the distinction gained by skill, bravery and endurance —these the members of the expedition had known. There were also material or quasi-material rewards. Ransoms and gifts or pardons for services rendered were not new in English history but their importance was increased by two circumstances: no previous expedition had brought back so many rich prisoners; the spirit of the age combined chivalrous ideals with economic motives. Our knight

> loved chyvalrie,
> Trouth and honour, fredom and curtesie.
> Ful worthi was he in his Lordes warre,
> And thereto had he riden, noman farre. . . .

It was, however, expedient to ensure that service did not go unrewarded, for

> It becometh a king   who keepeth his realm,
> To give Meed to men   who humbly serve him,
> To aliens, to all men,   to honour them with gifts,
> Meed maketh him loved,   Meed maketh him a man.

Adventure and meed went hand in hand and, when the prospect of ransoms was added, personal and national gain coincided —or so it seemed—for ransoms brought money into the country. It could be argued that war was profitable.

The loot gathered on the marches had been taken to Bordeaux where no doubt much of it was disposed of or lost as easily and as quickly as it had been gained. The prisoners, however, remained in the victors' hands or, if they had been released, they were under oath to return. From them riches were to be had. Some had paid their ransoms in France. Others—and they were the richer ones—were brought to England and held captive for months and even for years.

The circumstances of their captivity will become clearer if we first give a broad outline.

The current view of the captor's right is expressed by Froissart thus: 'That day whosoever took any prisoner, he was clear his, and might quit or ransom him at pleasure.' Froissart also provided two little dramas of the capture of wounded Englishmen in which the decisive words are as follows:

(1) 'Ye shall be my prisoner . . . and I shall see that you be healed of your hurt.'

'I am content to be your prisoner for ye have by law of arms won me.'

Then he sware to be his prisoner, rescue or no rescue.

(2) 'Yield you, rescue or no rescue, or else I shall slay you.'

The Englishman yielded and went with him.[1]

The captor's right and the prisoner's obligation to pay an agreed sum of money before release are universally recognized, but the two men do not necessarily proceed to negotiate, for the captor may be a man of lowly status and the captive a noble (perhaps wounded or exhausted). The captive may be handed over for a consideration to a more eminent person. In a short time, the French nobles come to be the property of English nobles or knights.

Now a prisoner may have surrendered quite voluntarily, almost choosing his captor, or he may have given in only under threat of death. He may be the captive of one man or of a group of men who regard themselves as legally entitled to equal shares in his ransom. He may subsequently be purchased by one man or by a group. Members of the group may sell their individual shares of the prisoner's ransom.

The Truce of Bordeaux provides that French prisoners, unless they have just cause for not being kept captive, shall go to England with their masters. To England, therefore, many go. Chivalry and good sense ensure that the prisoner is kept in good health and he may be invited to jousts and festive occasions in England, but there may be some hard bargaining over the sum for which he is to be released. Once agreement has been reached, a document is prepared setting out the sum, the currency in which it is to be paid and (since the currencies of both England and France have undergone frequent changes) the rate of exchange or the actual coins. Provision may also be made for the payment to be made by instalments at fixed dates.

But it is not possible for a French noble resident in England to guarantee the delivery in England of a large sum of money without first considering the condition of his estates in France.

It may be necessary for him to pledge his property or sell an estate or raise a loan from an Italian banker. Either therefore, he must be allowed to go to France to conduct the business himself or an agent must come over from France to confer with him and receive authority to act on his behalf. Accordingly, there is much coming and going between England and France in the second half of 1357 and in 1358.

When the sum demanded has been paid, the prisoner is released—provided there are no political complications. If, however, he is a member of a ruling house, his captivity may be prolonged. By 1357 when the negotiations over the important French prisoners began, David, King of Scotland, had spent eleven years as a prisoner in England and Charles of Blois had spent ten.

We turn now to King Edward and his royal prisoner. The transfer of 400,000 crowns as a first instalment of King John's ransom was, as we have seen, effected in October 1360. According to the treaty, the money was to be paid in French gold crowns two of which equalled in value one English noble, the noble being worth six shillings and eightpence. It was intended that the huge quantity of specie which would gradually be received should be stored, reminted or spent as occasion demanded and the king decided. Further instalments were received in 1361–3. The coins used were of various moneys of different dates and different degrees of fineness. For some of the deliveries, detailed statements still exist showing the contents of each bag and its value in English currency of that date.[2]

The French experienced very great difficulty in raising the sums requisite for the regular payment of instalments. John, therefore, as a good knight, decided to go back to England. In January 1364, he returned and on April 8th of that year he died in England. Payments, however, continued to be made for some years after his death. The total sum received in England has been studied,[3] but a just statement would need longer and more complex treatment than is appropriate in this work.

King Edward's claim had been confined to the person of the French king. Concerning other prisoners who might be taken, the indenture stated that, 'the prince shall have his will of them'. The prince, therefore, was at liberty to decide what fraction, if any, of the ransoms gained by men serving under his command, he should claim for himself. Such a claim would diminish the captors' rights, but it had been, and continued to be, usual for the king to demand a share—usually a third—of the ransoms.[4] The fraction might have been settled by custom or by what later ages would have called 'the state of the market' since the prospects of ransoms would affect recruitment. Campaigning was less profitable in Scotland than in France.

It is unfortunate that the evidence bearing on the fraction claimed by the prince during the campaigns of 1355 and 1356 is very slight. Two indentures of 1347 between the prince on the one hand and two of his knights on the other, contain the provision 'If he take a prisoner, he shall have a half of his ransom'.[5] And, in the only clear references I know—there are two—relating to the expedition of 1355-7, the same fraction is cited. In the one (an order following an allegation of concealment of a prisoner), it is laid down that 'the prince ought to have a moiety of the ransoms of all prisoners taken by men in his following'. In the other, a knight is reminded that a moiety of the sum he had received for a prisoner, belongs to the prince.[6] These are clear enough, and the prince no doubt insisted on his right wherever it was practicable. I have not, however, been able to trace evidence that moieties of ransoms were in fact generally paid to the prince.

But the question of a fractional sharing of ransoms did not arise when the prince bought prisoners himself. That the prices paid were broadly related to the supposed wealth of the prisoners is natural, but they are not definite fractions of anticipated ransoms, for, in the first place, the word used in the documents is 'bought' (without any qualification), and secondly, the prisoner might be resold (as he usually was, to the king)—again without any note of future ransom value.

In contemporary records, however, the transactions appear to fall into two classes. On the one hand, the prince appears as a dealer who buys for himself. He acquired Philip, the French king's son, the Count of Sancerre and the Lord of Craon and sold them in one group to the king. On the other, he plays the part of an agent buying on behalf of the king. In this second role, he is described as having undertaken to pay given sums to the vendors for certain prisoners whom he had bought 'for the king's use'.[7] It is likely that the distinction of roles was not apparent at the beginning of the transactions but arose subsequently owing to the state of the princes' finances. These, it will be remembered, were in an embarrassed state when he left England in 1355. Whether the resources on which he could draw in Gascony were sufficient for the payment of his troops, for his own extravagances and, in addition, for the purchase of eminent prisoners and even for the buying of Gascon assent to the removal of King John to England —these things fall outside our immediate purview. Apparently the prince tried to buy the greater part of the prisoners who accompanied the Anglo-Gascon army back to Bordeaux. To achieve this end, he was obliged to undertake to pay large sums on fixed dates, but it became impossible for him to fulfil some of his obligations. The king, therefore, took over these obligations, paid the unpaid balances of the agreed sums direct (but by instalments) to the vendors and, in these cases, the prince is described as having bought the prisoners for the king.

Thus some of the prince's purchases were transferred to the king. Others, like Prince Philip, he paid for himself and sold to the king. Moreover, the king bought noble prisoners or shares in prisoners not only from the prince but also from English and Gascon knights. Ultimately, by one channel or another, nearly all the noble prisoners mentioned in the Treaty of Bretigny as having been taken at the battle of Poitiers, became the king's property. It was under his direction that their ransoms were negotiated. For a time, he used the services of the Earl of Warwick as his negotiator and authorized the drafting of documents embodying the sums agreed between Warwick and the prisoners.[8]

If the king's financial interest in the prisoners was great, the prince's interest also was very considerable. I have not found evidence that he or an agent acting on his behalf, negotiated ransoms, but the very large sum he received for the three prisoners mentioned above (20,000*l*.) suggests that his transactions were not without profit. To such gains must be added his fractional share in the ransoms obtained by his followers. His receipts from this source cannot be traced but, in the aggregate, they may have been large. His share (it is not clear whether it is a moiety or not) of the ransom of the Count of Dammartin was 1,000*l*.[9]

The gains derived from prisoners by other members of the expeditionary force fall into two classes, namely ransoms directly negotiated and profits from the sale of captives. The Earl of Warwick ransomed the Archbishop of Sens for 48,000 crowns.[10] The Earl of Salisbury appears to have received 2,000*l*. for the Count of Dammartin.[11] For the most part, however, the figures

of privately negotiated ransoms cannot be traced. Some of the
sums received for sales on the other hand, are recorded and will
be quoted later. It is noteworthy that Audley and Chandos,
models of rectitude during the battle, acquired shares in a prisoner
afterwards. There is a good deal of evidence of prisoners or their
agents crossing from England to France in order to raise money.[12]
For these men, no less than for the regent Charles, the task proved
very difficult. Polite tradition held that ransoms should not be
ruinous. In practice, however, the sums demanded were large and
the alternative to payment was an indefinitely prolonged captivity. Moisant cites instances of men who were driven to the
expedient of freeing serfs in order to raise money and the archives
of Poitou afford examples of other expedients.[13]

A broad review of the riches gained by the victors from ransoms must take into account the large number of deals effected
without any mention in the Black Prince's Register or any state
paper. Of these our evidence is scanty, but a few interesting
examples survive. The Lord Berkeley who was taken prisoner by
the French, appears to have gained his freedom by the payment
of a large ransom and then to have engaged in the ransom business himself. His great grandson told Leland that Beverstone (in
Gloucestershire) had been built with the ransoms of Poitiers
prisoners.[14] A second example is mentioned by Froissart. One
day in 1388, at an hostelry in Orthez, he met a fellow called the
Bascot of Mauleon, who was travelling in very considerable style
and who willingly told the chronicler about his adventures.
'The first time that I bare armour', he said, 'was under the Captal
de Buch at the battle of Poitiers and, as it was my hap, I had that
day three prisoners, a knight, and two squires of whom I had one
with another [three thousand] francs'.[15]

A third example is found in the records of the city of London.
Thomas de Vaudenay, a knight of Burgundy sent his ransom to
William de Welesby, an English knight, by the hands of a merchant of Lucca, Turel Guascoin. The ransom (300 golden florins
of Florence, a goblet with a covercle of silver and a ring of gold
without stone) was handed over to Simon of Worsted, a citizen
of London, acting on Welesby's behalf and formally acknowledged by Simon in the presence of the Mayor of London on
Christmas Eve, 1356.[16]

The periods during which French prisoners remained captive
varied greatly. Among those who secured early release was Jean

le Maingre, called Boucicaut. On June 1st, 1357, letters of protection were issued in order that his messenger might go to
Poitou and Saintonge. His ransom must have been paid with
relative speed for in, or before May 1358, he was appointed to an
office in France and shortly became Marshal of France in succes-
sion to Jean de Clermont.[17] Other prisoners were less fortunate.
King John and his large staff remained in England till July 1360.
The Count of Dammartin did not gain his release till February
1361.[18] The last instalment of the ransom of James of Bourbon
was paid in January 1362; that of the Archbishop of Sens at
Easter, 1362.[19] Moreover, a number of the prisoners had to
remain in England or return to England in accordance with the
terms of the Treaty of Bretigny.[20]

We now present in summary form examples of the transactions
in which the king, the prince and others engaged.

The prince acquired:
James of Bourbon from the Captal de Buch and others for
    25,000 crowns to be paid in money of Bordeaux.[21]
Philip, the son of King John, from John de Kentwood and Sir
    Edmund Wauncey for 4,000 marks.[22]
The Count of Auvergne from Deossent of Spain for 5,000 old
    crowns.[23]
A prisoner (unnamed) held by Sir James Audley, Sir John
    Chandos and Sir Robert Nevill for 565*l*. 12*s*. 6*d*.[24]
A prisoner (unnamed) from Hugh de Colsweynsok and Randolph
    d'Okeston for 20 florins of the leopard.[25]
The Count of Vendome from the Lord of Capene (3,000 florins).[26]
The Count of Joigny from Arnold Raymond (1,500 florins).[27]
The Lord of Dirval from the Captal de Buch and others.[28]
The Count of Audrehem.[29]

The king acquired prisoners:
1. By reserving his right to 'the head (*chief*) of the war', that is
   King John.
2. By purchase from the Prince of Wales, for example—
   Philip, son of King John ⎫
   the Count of Sancerre   ⎬ for 20,000*l*.[30]
   the Lord of Craon   ⎭
3. By transfer from the Prince of Wales, for example—James of

Bourbon, the Count of Vendome, the Count of Audrehem, the Count of Joigny, the Lord of Dirval.[31]

4. By purchase from others, for example—

The Count of Auxerre (a share in) from the Earl of Suffolk for 3,000 old florins.[32]

The Lord Daubigny from Sir John Wengfeld for 2,500 marks.[33]

The Count of Longueville (a share in) from Sir Reginald Cobham for 6,500 old florins.[34]

The 'Archbishop' of Le Mans (a share in) from Robert de Clynton for 1,000*l*.[35]

Various prisoners from the Captal de Buch, the Lord Montferrand and the Vicomte d'Urtria for 'great sums'.[36]

The Count of Eu from Elie de Pommiers for 10,000 florins.[37]

Among other prisoners, the following may be mentioned:

Boucicaut (the king); Herpin de Saint Sauveur and Simon de Joy (Denis de Morbek); the Lord of Magnalers (Thomas de Walkfare); Jean de Chirlieu (Richard de Berwick); Jean de Melun, Count of Tancarville (Thomas de Bronne); Florimond de Soully (Rees ap Griffiths); Guichard Dolfyn (Walter de Daldeby); Jean Rocourt (Ralph Shelton); Robert Faveroll (Thomas Chaundler); Jean de Corbauton (Roger de Warre); Peter de Craon (Bernard van Zedeles); Theobald Viapre and Walter Felonyes (John Dymmok).[38]

The full extent of the business in ransoms cannot be clearly defined. French sources provide very little relevant material. Only a small part of the prisoners were brought to England. There are statements on the French side which cannot be checked in English sources and traditions (like that of Beverstone) which cannot be verified. There were transactions in France before the army left Bordeaux which were not recorded in English official documents. The very size of the prince's fractional share would lead to private dealings. Finally, as we have shown, vendors of prisoners were not necessarily their captors. A French noble might have changed hands several times before his sale to king Edward resulted in his being mentioned in a document likely to survive. The evidence is, however, sufficient to show that the number and wealth of the prisoners captured at Poitiers led to much business in ransoms, to the transfer to England of large quantities of French specie, to the enrichment of many members of the expeditionary force and to great hardship for the more eminent of their prisoners.

Ransoms were not necessarily the fruit of prowess or even of anything more than trading enterprise. Rewards might, however, be honourably gained by men who followed the prince. 'Good service in Gascony', 'good service . . . especially at the battle of Poitiers' was recognized in a series of grants of money, annuities, and offices, the more valuable of which are set out on the following pages.

A good deal of biographical information would be needed for a full interpretation of these grants. Only a few observations will be made here. Not only was it the prince's nature to be lavish with gifts but also the spirit of the age made it politic 'to give meed to men who humbly serve him . . . to honour them with gifts'. Almost all the men whom the prince rewarded were already well known to him. They were in fact members of his staff and some of them would, no doubt, sooner or later have been given appropriate revenues to enable them to maintain their style as members of his entourage. A few of the gifts were promised on the battlefield of Poitiers; some of the grants were made a little later while the army was in France, others after the return to England. Further, though for the sake of brevity and clearness we are obliged to describe most of these rewards simply as annuities, many of them were granted (as was usual) 'until the prince shall have provided him with an equivalent of land and rent elsewhere'. The large grants made to Audley and Chandos are significant: the grants of identical annuities in France provide one more association for these two men, but they are probably explained by the fact that at the time the grants were made, April 1357, the two leaders were about to remain for duty in France.[39]

Recipient	The prince's	Reward	Reference in B.P.R. or C.C.A.
Audley, Sir James	bachelor	Annuity 400*l.* Annuity 600 gold crowns (from Mirmande, Gascony)	II, 105; IV, 291; IV, 359
Baskerville, Sir Richard	—	Gift 100 marks	IV, 403
Berkamstead, Henry de	yeoman	Office and rents	IV, 194, 196, 224, 225

Recipient	The prince's	Reward	Reference in B.P.R. or C.C.A.
Blakwater, William	clerk	Gift 20*l.*	IV, 208
Bond, Nicholas	yeoman	Annuity 50 marks (later manors of Kennington and Vauxhall)	IV, 197, 360
Botetourt, Sir William	bachelor	Grant for life of manor of Newport (Essex) Annuity 40*l.* Gift 100*l.*	IV, 190, 215, 252
Chandos, Sir John	bachelor	Issues of Kirkton (Lincolnshire) of Drakelow (Cheshire) Annuity 40*l.* Annuity 600 gold crowns (from Mirmande, Gascony)	IV, 193, 210, 223; III, 231, 267; IV, 359
Cheyne, Alan	yeoman	Annuity 40*l.*	C.C.A., 242, 253, 270
Cotesford, Sir Roger	bachelor	Annuity 40 marks	IV, 196
Cusington, Sir Stephen	bachelor	Earlier annuity increased to 100*l.* also annuity 40*l.*	IV, 178-9, 555
Dale, Sir Tiderick van	bachelor	Annuity 200 marks	IV, 207, 218
Dokeseye, Richard de	baker	Annuity 10 marks	C.C.A., 243, 253, 270
Felton, Sir Thomas de	bachelor	Annuity 40*l.*	IV, 207
Harpenden, Wm. de	yeoman	Annuity 40 marks	IV, 203
Hay, John del	yeoman	Annuity 20*l.*	IV, 209
Ilegh, Sir Richard de	bachelor	Gift 100 marks	IV, 289
Lenche, William	porter	Issues of Saltash ferry	II, 98
Leominster, Richard	(friar preacher)	Annuity 20*l.*	IV, 255
Loring, Sir Nigel	chamberlain	Annuity 83*l.* 6*s.* 8*d.*	IV, 206; II, 136
Loterell, Sir Andrew	—	Gift 20*l.*	IV, 251
Moigne, Sir William	bachelor	Gift 100 marks	IV, 284
Nevill, Sir Robert	bachelor	Annuity 100 marks	III, 306; IV, 219, 308
Palington, John de	servant	Some lands for life	IV, 193
Pesse, Sir Daniel van	bachelor	Annuity 100 marks	IV, 234

Recipient	The prince's	Reward	Reference in B.P.R. or C.C.A.
Plays, Sir Richard de	—	Gift, 250 marks (or 1,000 crowns?)	IV, 289, 388
Punchardon, Richard	yeoman	Annuity, 40 marks	IV, 307
Reppes, John de	—	Gift 100 marks	IV, 283
Rode, John de	—	Gift 20*l.*	IV, 252
St. Omer, William de	yeoman	Manor of Wisley for life	IV, 191
Sandwich, Thomas de	yeoman	Extension of lease	IV, 198
Sarnesfeld, John de	yeoman	Annuity 50 marks	C.C.A., 243, 253, 270
Shank, William	yeoman	Annuity 40 marks	IV, 203
Stafford, Sir Richard	bachelor	Gift 500 marks	IV, 202, 232
Sully, Sir John	bachelor	Annuity 40 marks	II, 99
Trouer, Sir Hans	bachelor	Annuity 100 marks	IV, 236
Trussell, Sir William	bachelor	Annuity 60 marks and later annuity of 40*l.*	IV, 261–2; III, 461
Wauncey, Sir William	bachelor	Annuity 20*l.*	IV, 198
Walkfare, Sir Thomas	bachelor	Gift 100 marks	IV, 308, 388
Zedeles, Sir Bernard van	bachelor	Annuity 100 marks	IV, 234

In comparison with the rewards given to members of the prince's staff, those made to the Cheshire archers are of trifling value. Yet they are interesting. For a few of the newly enriched knights and yeomen, Cheshire produced revenue. For the archers, Cheshire was home. Some weeks after the end of the campaign, when it became evident that they would soon take ship for England, they asked their boons. The boons are personal, local and quite modest. Many are granted while the men are still in Gascony, others immediately after they reach England, a few on the occasion of the prince's visit to his earldom in 1358. There are grants of pasture for six, eight, twelve great beasts in one or other of the Cheshire forests, grants of turbary,[40] and gifts of two three, four, five oaks [41] fit for timber 'for the repair of their houses' from the prince's woods (especially at Peckforton). There are offices of no great eminence but desirable to men who expect to live their lives near their homes: to be hayward of the prince's manor of Frodsham, keepers of his parks at Macclesfield, at Peckforton and at Loitcoit, serjeant of the hundred of Bucklow, seller of felons' goods, and to hold the avowries of Cheshire.[42] And there is freedom to trade in the town of Middlewich.[43] One former soldier reports a dispute between himself and the prince's officers as to whether a creature taken on his soil on the Mersey's bank was a porpoise (which would be his own property) or a grampus (which would belong to the prince). The officials are directed to do the right to the soldier—'the more so because of the good position he held at the battle of Poitiers'.[44] Finally, half a dozen men gain exemption for life from being put on assizes or juries in the county of Chester.[45]

These minor rewards are made in the same terms as those made to the knights, with due acknowledgment of services rendered in Gascony but, by the beginning of September 1357, the prince and his council are so occupied with other business that they have 'to a great extent forgotten' what they have granted. Some men have asked for further rewards of the same kind. The lieutenant of the justice of Chester is directed, therefore, that if 'double warrants on behalf of one man and for the same kind of thing, whether trees or anything else' should reach him, the second is to be disregarded.[46]

Finally, there are rewards of no direct material value but desirable or even indispensable to men who would live in peace, namely pardons for felonies committed. The Patent Rolls of the period abound in instances of pardons granted in consideration of service done in Brittany, in Scotland and in Gascony. Usually the crime is specified and the pardon is said to be granted at the asking, or on the testimony, of the leader of the company in which the grantee has served. Many members of the expeditionary force received such pardons.

For the Cheshire men, the grants of pardon are recorded concurrently with grants of rewards. Both are boons conferred for service, and pardons are given with as much graciousness as the administrative machinery permits. The justice and chamberlain are directed to execute all warrants that have reached them or shall reach them under the seal used in Gascony as if they were made under the seal used in England, and the Cheshire men who have served in the prince's company in Gascony are to obtain their charters of pardon 'quit of the fee of the seal pertaining to the prince'.[47] Three men are pardoned for murder.[48] There are a few other specific breaches of the peace, but the greater number of the charters are couched in general terms—'pardon of all felonies and trespasses committed by him in the county of Chester prior to' a given date which varies between December 1356 and May 8th, 1357.[49]

Outside Cheshire, about one hundred and twenty pardons are granted. Here the king is of course the grantor and the general formula runs: 'Pardon at the asking of the king's son, Edward, Prince of Wales, and for good service to the king and the prince done by X. Y. of Z in the prince's company in Gascony, to him for the (death of, rape of, theft of —— belonging to A. B.), whereof he is indicted or appealed and of any consequent outlawry.'[50] Almost all the pardons are for murder and, in the great majority of the documents, the words 'killed before 20th September in the thirtieth year' are inserted after the name of the victim. The grants begin before the troops return to England. Very many of them are dated in July 1357 but the issues continue through much of 1358.[51] An analysis of the places mentioned shows that south of the Tees there is scarcely an English county from which at least one murderer had not joined the expedition.

To sum up, payment at the agreed rate was by no means the only return for service with the prince in Gascony. In the technical language of the period, the 'advantages of war'[52] covered certain material gains arising from military operations—gains which the king might allocate at his pleasure. In a non-technical sense, the advantages of the campaigns of 1355 and 1356 fall broadly into four groups: a share in the loot (valuables, jewels, cash), a share in the ransoms (paid in France or in England) or the sale of prisoners, a pardon for felonies, a material reward (gift, annuity, office or right). There can have been few members of the expeditionary force who had not 'had profit' from at least two of these sources. Some Cheshire men may have benefited from all four.

It is not practicable to follow the fortunes of the Gascons in such detail, but they were not without advantage. Their territory had been made safe. They had had their shares of the loot and the ransoms. They had received a large sum to conciliate them for the transfer of King John to England and definite figures are available for some of their transactions and rewards. The Captal de Buch and a group of Gascons, for example, brought off a major deal in the sale of James of Bourbon for 25,000 crowns.[53] The Captal and the Lord of Mussidan sold the Lord of Dirval for

3,000 florins.[54] The sums paid in gifts to Sir Amanieu de Pomers, Sir John de Pomers, Sir Petiton de Curton, the Lord of Lesparre, Sir Aymeric de Tastes, and Sir Gerard de Tartas are recorded in the Prince's Register [55] and a series of receipts in the Exchequer of Account [56] shows that the following had pensions:—Amanieu de Monte Pesato, Sir Aymeric de Tastes, Sir Amanieu de Pomers, Raymond de Pelagria, Arnold de Renynhan, Bertrand Frank, Sir John de Pomers and the Soldan de Trau. The pension granted to Sir Gerard de Tartas has already been mentioned.[57]

CHAPTER VIII

EPILOGUE

IT would have been gratifying to have been able to describe the dispersal of the expeditionary force as we described its assembly. Unfortunately, that is impossible. The creation of such a force led to a much greater deposit of documents than did its disbandment. For the latter no leaders needed to be appointed, no arrangements devised: it was a mere melting away. From what points, at what dates and by which routes the various groups left the army I cannot say. The prince's staff went to London. I believe that the earls and a large part of the army also went to London and took part in the procession through the city before leaving for their homes.

Some of the foreign knights remained in England for more than a year. One of them, Zedeles, obtained from the prince a handsome testimonial alluding particularly to his honesty in respect of wages and prisoners. In 1358 he and others returned to their homes in Flanders, the Empire, Spain and Gascony.[1]

Early in the summer of 1357, the Cheshire men are back in their county and dozens of tiny items of administrative business, severally unimportant but collectively significant, enable us to trace minor and distant effects of membership of the expedition. For many months orders are received which afford the returned archer some little gain. There are the grants of pasturage or turbary or timber or offices or privileges of trading or exemption from burdensome duties or pardons for crimes committed.[2] Naturally other archers ask for similar rewards.[3] There is also a settling of accounts: the archers who had picked up King John's silver ship among the spoils of the battle receive their moiety of its value;[4] a man who sold the prince a horse four days before the battle receives payment in Cheshire;[5] a soldier wounded in Gascony and left behind, at last reaches Cheshire and receives a cash present;[6] two leaders who had been overpaid have to return the excess payments.[7] And there is the sadder side: a woman whose husband had been killed in the battle, complains that she cannot get possession of her husband's money;[8] two men accused of taking a prisoner and failing to give the prince his share of the ransom, are thrown into prison. Later the accusation is found to be unjust.[9]

Memories of the two great *chevauchées* and of the battle of Poitiers are still fresh when the curtain rises on another expedition, for in 1359, the king decides to strike another blow at France. This time the king himself and the Duke of Lancaster share in the command. With them are the prince and many of the knights and men whose movements we have followed in this study. Warwick and Salisbury, Audley and Chandos, Cobham and Burghersh, Stafford and Cheyne are members of the expedition. So are the Cheshire leaders who went overseas in 1355. And as they march down to the port—it is Sandwich this time—among the archers are several of the men who had accompanied them in Gascony in 1355–7.[10]

SOURCES AND BIBLIOGRAPHY

ORIGINAL AUTHORITIES

I. UNPUBLISHED

At the Public Record Office

The principal sources are :
Exchequer, Accounts Various
Gascon Rolls (and French Rolls)
Issue Rolls
The Account of John de Stretelee in Pipe Roll, 36 Edward III

At the Duchy of Cornwall Office

The Journal of John Henxteworth

A broad account of the contents of this MS. will be found on pages 81–2.

II. PUBLISHED

Official Records:
Archives Historiques du Poitou, XVII, Poitiers, 1886, XLVI, 1928.
Calendar of Close Rolls.
    ,,   ,, *Inquisitions, Miscellaneous.*
    ,,   ,, *Patent Rolls.*
    ,,   ,, *Papal Letters.*
Cheshire Chamberlains' Accounts, ed. Stewart-Brown, R., The Record Society, 1910.
Flintshire Ministers' Accounts, ed. Evans, D. L., Flintshire Historical Society, 1929.
Pell Records, ed. Devon, F., London, 1837.
Register of the Black Prince, 4 parts, London, 1930–3.
Rolles Gascons, Catalogue des, ed. Carte, T., London, 1743.
Rymer's Foedera, Record Commissioners, London, 1816–19.
Chronicles:
A. *Anonimalle Chronicle*, ed. Galbraith, V. H., Manchester, 1927.
   Anonymi Cantuarensis, ed. Tait, J., Manchester, 1914.
   Avesbury, Robert, Chronica Adae Murimuth et Roberti de Avesbury, ed. Thompson, E. M., London, 1889.
   Baker, Galfridi le, ed. Maunde Thompson, E., Oxford, 1889.
   Chandos Herald (*Life of the Black Prince*), ed. Pope, M. K., and Lodge, E. C., Oxford, 1910.
   Eulogium Historiarum, ed. Haydon, F. S., London, 1863.
   Knighton, Henrici, Chronicon, ed. Lumby, J. R., London, 1895.
   Reading, Johannis de, ed. Tait, J., Manchester, 1914.
   Scalacronica, ed. Maxwell, H., Glasgow, 1907.

Walsingham, Thomas, Chronica Monasterii, S. Albani, ed. Riley, H. T., London, 1863–4.

B. *le Bel, Jean,* ed. Viard, J., and Duprez, E., Paris, 1905.

Chronique Normande du XIVe siecle, ed. Molinier, A. and E., Paris, 1882.

Chronique des Quatre Premiers Valois, ed. Luce, S., Paris, 1862.

Chronique des Règnes de Jean II et de Charles V, ed. Delachenal, R., Paris, 1910.

Froissart, Jean, Œuvres, ed. Lettenhove, K. de, Brussels, 1876.

Froissart, J., ed. Macaulay, G. C., London, 1924.

Lescot, Richard, ed. Lemoire, J., Paris, 1896.

Textes et Documents d'Histoire, ed. Calmette, Joseph, Paris, 1937.

OTHER WORKS
MILITARY

AUDINET, E. *Les Lois et Coutumes de la Guerre à l'Epoque de la Guerre de Cent Ans* (Mémoires de la Société des Antiquaires de l'Ouest, t. IX), Poitiers, 1917.

BELLOC, H. *Crécy,* London, 1912.

—— *Poitiers,* London, 1913.

BURNE, A. H. *The Battle of Poitiers* in E.H.R., LIII, 1938.

—— *The Crécy War,* London, 1955.

DENIFLE, H. S. *La Désolation des Eglises, Monastères et Hôpitaux en France,* Paris, 1897–9.

GALBRAITH, V. H. *The Battle of Poitiers* in E.H.R., LIV, 1939.

GLENISON, J. *Quelques lettres de défi du XIVe siècle* in Bibliothèque de l'Ecole des Chartes, CVII, Paris, 1948–9.

HAY, D. *The Division of the Spoils of War in Fourteenth-Century England,* R. H. S. Transactions, 5th series, Vol. 4, London, 1954.

LEWIS, N. B. *The Organization of Indentured Retinues in Fourteenth-Century England* in R.H.S. Transactions, 4th series, XXVII, 1945.

LOT, F. *L'Art militaire et les armées,* Paris, 1946.

NYS, E. *Les Origines du Droit International,* Paris, 1894.

OMAN, C. *A History of the Art of War in the Middle Ages,* London, 1924.

PRINCE, A. E. *The Indenture System under Edward III* in 'Historical Essays in honour of James Tait,' Manchester, 1933.

—— *The Payment of Army Wages in Edward III's Reign* in Speculum XIX, 1944.

—— *The Importance of the Campaign of 1327* in E.H.R., L, 1935.

—— *The Strength of English Armies in the Reign of Edward III* in E.H.R., XLVI, 1931.

—— *The Army and Navy* in 'The English Government at Work,' Cambridge, Massachusetts, 1940.

RAMSAY, J. H. *The Strength of English Armies in the Middle Ages* in E.H.R., XXIX, 1914.

THOMPSON, A. H. 'The Art of War to 1400' in *C. Med. H.,* VI.

TOURNEUR-AUMONT, J. M. *La Bataille de Poitiers (1356),* Paris, 1940.

TOUT, T. F. 'Medieval and Modern Warfare' in *Bulletin of the John Rylands Library, Vol. 5,* Manchester, 1919.

LOCAL

BEMONT, C. *La Guyenne sous la domination anglaise*, London, 1921.
BOUTRUCHE, R. *La Crise d'une Société*, Paris, 1947.
BREUILS, A. *Histoire de Nogaro* in *Bulletin de la société archéologique du Gers*, 1915–16, Auch, 1915.
DARMAILLACQ, B. *Le Prince Noir contre le comte d'Armagnac* in *Revue de Gascogne*, N.S. t. 14, 1914.
DEVIC, C., and VAISSETE, J. *Histoire Générale de Languedoc*, IX, Toulouse, 1885.
FEDIE, L. *Histoire de Carcassonne*, Carcassonne, N. D.
JEANJEAN, J. F. *La Guerre de Cent Ans en Pays Audois*, Carcassonne, 1946.
LODGE, E. C. *Gascony under English Rule*, London, 1926.
—— *The Constables of Bordeaux in the Reign of Edward III* in E.H.R., L, 1935.
—— *The Relations between England and Gascony, 1154–1453*, in *History*, September 1934.
MICHEL, F. *Histoire du Commerce et de la Navigation à Bordeaux*, Bordeaux, 1867.
MOISANT, J. *Le Prince Noir en Aquitaine*, Paris, 1894.
MULLOT, H., and POUX, J. *L'itinéraire du Prince Noir à travers les pays de l'Aude* in *Annales du Midi*, t. 21, Toulouse, 1907.
RAMET, H. *Histoire de Toulouse*, Toulouse, N. D.
ROSCHACH, M. E. *Les quatre journées du Prince Noir dans la viguerie de Toulouse.* Mémoires de l'Académie des Sciences de Toulouse, Xe série, t. V, Toulouse, 1906.
DE SANTI, M. L. *L'expédition du Prince Noir en 1355.* Mémoires de l'Académie des Sciences de Toulouse, Xe série, t. V, Toulouse, 1906.

BIOGRAPHICAL

There is no satisfactory biography of the Black Prince.
BREUILS, A. *Jean Ier, Comte d'Armagnac*, Revue des Questions Historiques, LIX, Paris, 1896.
JAMES, G. P. R. *A History of the Life of Edward the Black Prince*, London, 1839.
PATTISON, R. P. DUNN. *The Black Prince*, London, N. D.

GENERAL

ARENHOLD, L. 'Ships earlier than 1500' in *The Mariners' Mirror*, Vol. I.
BELLOC, H. *A History of England*, Vol. III, London, 1928.
BELTZ, G. F. *Memorials of the Order of the Garter*, London, 1841.
BRINDLEY, H. H. 'Medieval Ships' in *The Mariners' Mirror*, Vols. II and III.
BROOME, D. M. The Ransom of John II, in *Camden Miscellany XIV*, 1926.

CAPES, W. W. *A History of the English Church in the fourteenth century*, London, 1909.

COVILLE, A. 'France. The Hundred Years War' in *C.Med.H.*, VII.

CLOWES, W. L. *The Royal Navy*, London, 1897.

CUTTINO, G. P. *English Diplomatic Administration*, Oxford, 1940.

DARBY, H. C. *Historical Geography of England before 1830*, Cambridge, 1936.

DAWSON, C. *Medieval Essays*, London, 1953.

DELACHENAL, R. *Histoire de Charles V*, Paris, 1909.

DELISLE, M. 'Les Miracles de Notre Dame' in *Comptes Rendus des Séances de l'Académie des Inscriptions*, Paris, 1867.

DEPREZ, E. *Les Préliminaires de la Guerre de Cent Ans*, Paris, 1902.

EVANS, D. L. *Some Notes on the History of the Principality of Wales in the Time of the Black Prince* in Cymmrodorion Society, Transactions, 1925.

FUNCK-BRENTANO, F. *Le Moyen Age*, Paris, 1922.

GOLLANCZ, I. *Ich Dene*, London, 1921.

GROSJEAN, G. *Le Sentiment National dans la Guerre de Cent Ans*, Paris, 1927.

GRUBER, J. *The Peace Negotiations of the Avignon Popes*. Catholic Historical Review, Vol. 19, 1933–4.

HANOTAUX, G. *Histoire de France*, t. III, Paris, N. D.

HEWITT, H. J. *Medieval Cheshire*, Manchester, 1929.

LAVISSE, E. *Histoire de France*, Paris, 1902.

LONGMAN, W. A. *History of the Life and Times of Edward III*, London, 1869.

MACKINNON, J. *History of Edward III*, London, 1900.

MATHEW, G. *Ideals of Knighthood in Late Fourteenth-Century England* in 'Studies in Medieval History presented to F. M. Powicke', Oxford, 1948.

MOLLET, G. *Innocent VI et les Tentatives de Paix entre la France et l'Angleterre*, 1353–55, in Revue d'Histoire Ecclésiastique, Louvain, 1909.

PERROY, E. *The Hundred Years War*, London, 1951.

POSTAN, M. 'The Trade of Medieval Europe' in *Cambridge Economic History*, II, Cambridge, 1952.

RILEY, H. T., Memorials of London and London Life, London, 1868.

SHARP, MARGARET. A Jodrell Deed and the Seals of the Black Prince in *Bulletin of the John Rylands Library*, Vol. 7, 1922.

—— The Central Administrative System of the Black Prince in Tout, T. F. *Chapters in Medieval Administrative History*, Vol. V, Manchester, 1930.

—— The Administrative Chancery of the Black Prince in *Essays in Medieval History presented to Thomas Frederick Tout*, Manchester, 1925.

TESSIER, G. *Une Cour Seigneuriale au XIVe Siècle* in Bulletin de la Sociètè de l'Histoire de France, Année 1941, Paris, 1942.

TOUT, T. F. *Political History of England, 1216–1377*, London, 1905.

UNWIN, G. *Finance and Trade under Edward III*, Manchester, 1918.

WILLARD, J. F., and MORRIS, W. A. *The English Government at Work, 1327–1336*, Cambridge, Massachusetts, 1940.

WILKINSON, B. *Constitutional History of Medieval England, 1216–1399*, London, 1952.

WROTTESLEY, G. *Crécy and Calais*, London, 1898.

ABBREVIATIONS USED IN THE NOTES

MS

Henxteworth   The Journal of John Henxteworth,

PRINTED WORKS

Audinet	Audinet, E. *Les Lois et Coutumes de la Guerre à l'Epoque de la Guerre de Cent Ans.*
Avesbury	Avesbury. *Chronica.*
B.P.R.	*Black Prince's Register.* The Register of Edward the Black Prince, 4 parts.
Baker	*Chronicon Galfridi le Baker de Swynebroke*, ed. Thompson, E. Maunde.
Boutruche	Boutruche, R. *La Crise d'une Société.*
Breuils	Breuils, A. *Jean Ier, Comte d'Armagnac*, Revue des Questions Historiques, LIX.
C.C.A.	*Cheshire Chamberlains' Accounts*, ed. Stewart-Brown, R., The Record Society.
C.C.R.	*Calendar of Close Rolls.*
C.P.R.	*Calendar of Patent Rolls.*
C. Pap. Lett.	*Calendar of Papal Letters.*
Chandos Herald	*Life of the Black Prince*, ed. Pope, M. K., and Lodge, E. C.
Delachenal	Delachenal, R. *Histoire de Charles V.*
Eulogium	*Eulogium Historiarum*, ed. Haydon, F. S.
Evans	Evans, D. L. *Some Notes on the History of the Principality of Wales in the Times of the Black Prince (1343–76).*
Froissart	Froissart, J. *Œuvres*, ed. Lettenhove, K. de
Froissart (Macaulay)	*The Chronicles of Froissart*, ed. Macaulay, G. C.
Hay	Hay, D. *The Division of the Spoils of War in Fourteenth-Century England.*
Henxteworth	*Vide supra.*
Hewitt	Hewitt, H. J. *Medieval Cheshire.*
Jeanjean	Jeanjean, J. F. *La Guerre de Cent Ans en Pays Audois.*
Mathew, G.	Mathew, G. *Ideals of Knighthood in Late Fourteenth-Century England.*
Moisant	Moisant, J. *Le Prince Noir en Aquitaine.*
Nys	Nys, E. *Les Origines du Droit International.*
Oman	Oman, C. *A History of the Art of War in the Middle Ages.*

Perroy   Perroy, E. *The Hundred Years War.*
Rymer   *Foedera,* ed. Rymer.
Tourneur-Aumont   Tourneur-Aumont, J. M. *La Bataille de Poitiers,*
                    1356.

NOTES AND REFERENCES

CHAPTER I: THE BACKGROUND

1. *C.C.R.*, 1354–60, 112.
2. *C. Pap. Lett.*, 560.
3. *Rymer*, III, i, 297.
4. *Ibid.*, III, i, 297. There is some obscurity about the dates. See *C.P.R.*, 1354–8, 22, where John de Chiverston is called Seneschal of Gascony in March 1354.
5. *Avesbury*, 424; *C.P.R.*, 1354–8, 203.
6. *Rymer*, III, i, 298, 299, 302. Prince, A. E., *The Payment of Army Wages in Edward III's Reign*, Speculum XIX (1914), 156; Issue Roll, 31 Ed. III, in 29.
7. *C.C.R.*, 1354–60, 210.
8. *Boutruche*, 130–3.
9. See for example Gascon Rolls 66/68 in 6.
10. *Boutruche*, 196–7.
11. *Ibid.*, 197.
12. *Ibid.*, 198, 202.
13. *Breuils*, 48.
14. *Ibid.*, 48.
15. *Ibid.*, 48–9.
16. *Ibid.*, 51.
17. This result was achieved: *valde confortavit fideles de Vasconia*. Baker, 128.
18. Bagehot, W., *The English Constitution*, Oxford, 1933, 28.
19. For example, those at Eltham, *B.P.R.*, IV, 124.
20. *Ibid.*, IV, 124
21. *Ibid.*, IV, 72, 73. The date is not later than 1352.
22. *Ibid.*, IV, 124. Had the colours been reversed, we should have had a clue to the appellation Black Prince.
23. *Ibid.*, IV, 70–1; 67–8.
24. *Froissart*, VII, 227, 213. The term was of course a very great compliment, but it was used also of others, e.g. of Sir John Chandos, *ibid*, VII, 458, and of the prince's army as it embarked at Plymouth, *Chandos Herald*, line 611. In a 'rédaction' written after the prince's death, Froissart said 'che fu en son vivant le plus honnouré prinche du monde', XVII, 355.
25. *Op. cit.*, 177.
26. Mathew, G., 'Ideals of Knighthood in late Fourteenth-Century England' in *Studies in Medieval History presented to Frederick Maurice Powicke*, Oxford, 1948.
27. His conduct at Limoges is well known, but several episodes in the first raid reveal the same trait. *Vide infra*, p. 57. *Froissart*, V, 454, says he was 'courageous and cruel as a lion' (Comme uns lyon fels et crueus) at the battle of Poitiers, and *cf.* le prince estoit cruels en son air. *Ibid.*, VII, 46. His father showed the same indifference in the well-known incidents at Caen and at Calais.
28. *B.P.R.*, IV, 86–90, 66–7, 157–68.
29. *Ibid.*, IV, 161, 74–5.
30. *Ibid.*, IV, 76, 151.
31. *Chandos Herald*, lines 531–2, 536–46.

32. *B.P.R.*, II., 77.
33. *Jus militare, Jus belli.* Baker, 86, 96, 154, *Droit d'armes.* Audinet, lxxii, xc.
34. *Froissart*, V, 435.
35. The division of the spoils is discussed at length in Hay, *op cit.* This is a valuable but, in my view, not a final treatment of the subject. *Vide infra,* pp. 154–5.
36. *B.P.R.*, IV, 145.
37. Mathew, G., *op. cit.*, 358.
38. 'Long processions with uncertain objectives' (Thompson, A. H., *op. cit.*, 798); 'the fitful purposelessness of many medieval campaigns'. (Tout, *Medieval and Modern Warfare*, 24.) 'He was not so much sluggish as without plan' (Belloc, H., *Crécy*).

CHAPTER II: THE PREPARATIONS

1. *C.C.R.*, 1354–60, 210.
2. *Ibid.*, 209.
3. *Ibid.*, 190.
4. *Ibid.*, 134.
5. *Ibid.*, 134.
6. *Ibid.*, 214–5.
7. *Ibid.*, 214–5.
8. Hewitt, 146, 156, 171; Stewart-Browne, R., The Avowries of Cheshire in *E.H.R.*, XXIX, 41.
9. *Hewitt*, 157–60.
10. *B.P.R.*, III, 173.
11. *Hewitt*, 84–8.
12. *Evans*, 48–51. See also Wrottesley, *Crécy and Calais*, London, 1898.
13. *B.P.R.*, I, 52, 55; Rymer, III, i, 67; Gascon Rolls (French Rolls), 30 Ed. III, m. 11.
14. *Evans*, 56–7, 106: *B.P.R.*, I, 13–15, 49, 50, 68, 80; *Flintshire Ministers' Accounts*, lv, lvi, 4, 56.
15. *Evans*, 57.
16. *B.P.R.*, I, 14–15, 80.
17. *Flintshire Min. Accts.*, 4.
18. *B.P.R.*, III, 201, 204; *C.C.A.*, 167, 219. The translator has obviously mistaken arrow for archer.
19. *Evans*, 52; *B.P.R.*, I, 13, 14, 68, 80.
20. *Evans*, 52, 53.
21. *Hewitt*, 15–19.
22. *B.P.R.*, III, 204.
23. *Ibid.*, 205.
24. *Ibid.*, 204.
25. *Ibid.*, 491.
26. *Ibid.*, 204.
27. *Ibid.*, 491.
28. *Ibid.*, 204, 491.
29. *Ibid.*, 491.
30. *Ibid.*, 204.
31. *Ibid.*, 204.
32. *Ibid.*, 204.
33. *Ibid.*, 491.
34. *Ibid.*, 204.
35. *Ibid.*, 491.
36. *Ibid.*, 200, 202.

37. *B.P.R.*, III, 200.
38. *Ibid.*, 212.
39. See the Gough map published by the Bodleian Libary.
40. See Darby, *Historical Geography of England before 1830*, p. 260.
41. *B.P.R.*, III, 204; *C.C.A.*, 228.
42. *B.P.R.*, III, 205.
43. *Ibid.*, 207.
44. *Ibid.*, 211.
45. *Ibid.*, 214.
46. *Ibid.*, 215.
47. *Ibid.*, 214.
48. *C.C.R.*, 1354–60, 21–2.
49. *B.P.R.*, I, 83, 127, 128, 129.
50. *B.P.R.*, II, 45–6.
51. *Vide infra, pp.* 23, 160–2.
52. *B.P.R.*, IV, 143–4.
53. Pipe Roll, 29 Ed. III, m. 7.
54. *B.P.R.*, IV, 144, Prince, A. E., 'The Payment of Army Wages in Edward III's Reign', *Speculum*, XIX, 1944, pp. 155–6; and *vide infra*, p.24.
55. Pipe Roll, 29 Ed. III, m. 7.
56. *Avesbury*, 424.
57. Knighton, II, 79.
58. Walsingham, I, 279.
59. *B.P.R.*, IV, 143–4.
60. Prince, A. E. 'The Strength of English Armies in the Reign of Edward III', *E.H.R.*, XLVI, 1931, 355–66. The writer also discusses Sir James Ramsay's estimate.
61 *Vide infra*, pp. 160–165.
62. *B.P.R.*, III, 215–16.
63. *C.P.R.*, 1354–8, 241.
64. For example, the men from Kingston upon Hull and Swinefleet to whom pardons were granted, *C.P.R.*, 1354–8, 560, 592.
65. These may have joined at Bordeaux. *Vide infra*, p. 44.
66. There are of course no comparative statistics. *Vide infra*, pp. 163–4, 196.
67. *Vide infra*, p. 23.
68. Prince, A. E., *The Strength of English Armies*, 366, n. 3.
69. Concerning the languages used in medieval England, see Legge, M.D., 'Anglo-Norman and the Historian' in *History*, December 1941, 163–175; Wilson, R. M., 'English and French in England, 1100–1300' in *History*, March 1943, 37–59; Suggett, H., *The Use of French in England in the later Middle Ages* in R. H. S. Transactions, 4th series, Vol. XXX. The greater part of the Black Prince's Register is in French.
70. *Rymer*, III, i, 297.
71. *Froissart* (Macaulay) 83, 113.
72. See *D.N.B.* (Ufford, Robert de).
73. See *D.N.B.* There is now material for a longer article.
74. See *D.N.B.* Also Evans, 33.
75. See *D.N.B.*; *B.P.R.*, III, 122–3; *C.C.A.*, 207, 214.
76. All the names cited in this and the following paragraph are found in *B.P.R.*, II, III, or IV. Most of them occur also in Henxteworth's journal.
77. *B.P.R.*, IV, 167, 228; *Rymer*, Appendix E, 16.
78. *Chandos Herald*, lines 573–6, and *vide infra*, pp. 81, 129.
79. *B.P.R.*, III, 208, 211, 212, 214. *Rymer*, Appendix E, 15–17.
80. *B.P.R.*, III, 213, and see *ibid.*, 207, 210–12, 214, and *B.P.R.*, IV, 142.
81. *B.P.R.*, III, 209–10.

82. *B.P.R.*, III, 207, 210, 211.
83. *B.P.R.*, IV, 166–7.
84. *Ibid.*, 166.
85. *Ibid.*, 134.
86. Issue Roll, 31 Ed. III, m. 29.
87. *B.P.R.*, IV, 139, 143.
88. *Ibid.*, 143.
89. *C.P.R.*, 1354–8, 251.
90. *Ibid.*, 255.
91. *B.P.R.*, IV, 157–68; 159, 160, 161; 167, 168.
92. *C.P.R.*, 1354–8, 264. When the prince went abroad in 1359, the period was raised to four years. *C.P.R.*, 1358–61, 268.
93. *B.P.R.*, IV, 143.
94. *B.P.R.*, III, 493.
95. *Ibid.*, 493.
96. *Ibid.*, 214, 215.
97. *Ibid.*, 215.
98. *B.P.R.*, IV, 141, 150.
99. Hoskins, W. G., *Devon*, 61.
100. *Ibid.*, 201.
101. *B.P.R.*, II, 77.
102. *Ibid.*, 78.
103. *Ibid.*, 83, 86.
104. *Ibid.*, 86.
105. *Ibid.*, 103, 107, 116, 141.
106. *Ibid.*, 80–88; III, 212–16.
107. *Ibid.*, IV, 157–68.
108. *Ibid.*, IV, 143–5.
109. *Ibid.*, 144.
110. Namely (i) the indenture quoted above (*B.P.R.*, IV, 143–5), (ii) four documents in Gascon Rolls, 29 Ed. III, m. 6.
111. Breuils, *Jean d'Armagnac*, 48.
112. Gascon Rolls, 29 Ed. III, m. 6.
113. *Ibid.*, m. 6.
114. *Ibid.*, m. 5.
115. *B.P.R.*, IV, 144.
116. Exchequer (Q.R.) Accounts E 101/26/35.
117. *C.C.A.*, 273.
118. *C.C.R.*, 1354–8, 244.
119. *C.P.R.*, 1358–61, 323.
120. Pipe Roll, 30 Ed. III, m. 42.
121. *Froissart*, II, 134, 145.
122. *Ibid.*, V, 257.
123. *Ibid.*; Rickert, E., *Chaucer's World* (London, 1950), 289; *B.P.R.*, IV, 13.
124. *Cambridge Economic History*, I, 461; Willard, J. F., and Morris, W. A., *The English Government at Work*, I, 417; *Lists and Indexes* (P.R.O.), XXV; *C.C.R.*, 1354–60, 446, 559; *C.P.R.*, 1354–8, 58, 111, 112, 285.
125. *B.P.R.*, III, 363; IV, 176, 290, 330, 484, 514, 530, 560. *Hewitt*, 56–8.
126. Willard and Morris, *op cit.*, 337–8, 353; *C.C.R.*, 1354–8, 22.
127. Some instance arising from the expedition of 1355–7 may be found in *B.P.R.*, II, 155; III, 332; IV, 253–4, 329, 384. In a pathetic letter of 1358, Sir William Trussell gives a list of six horses lost in military service and begs for payment. Cott MS., Caligula D III, 30.

128. e.g. Pipe Roll, 30 Ed. III, m. 7 (Colchester), Exchequer Accounts E 101/508, No. 19 (Dover).

129. *C.C.R.*, 1354–60, 111.

130. *B.P.R.*, IV, 143–5.

131. *Vide supra.*

132. *B.P.R.*, 152, 164.

133. *Rymer*, III, i, 310. Deyncourt's account shows that he went to Plymouth. It does not mention Southampton. Issue Roll, 30 Ed. III, Mich.), m. 24.

134. *B.P.R.*, IV, 144.

135. Quennell, M. and C. H., *A History of Everyday Things*, 3rd edition, London, 1950, I, 135.

136. Contemporary representations of English ships may be seen in (i) the gold nobles of Edward III, (ii) Pedrick, G., *Borough Seals of the Gothic Period*, London, 1904. It is, however, now recognized that these representations are 'distorted and conventionalized. . . .' See Clowes, G. S. Laird, *Sailing Ships*, London, 1932, p. 10, and Robinson, G., 'The Medieval Artist' in *The Mariners' Mirror*, III, 353. A better approach lies in following the evolution of the vessel. See the sketches in Quennell, *op. cit.*, I, 135, and Davies, H. W. C., *Medieval England*, 253–4.

137. The navy of the period is broadly treated by Prince, A. E., in *The English Government at Work*, I, 376–91.

138. *B.P.R.*, II, 77.

139. *Rymer*, III (i), 235, 236, 274.

140. *Rymer*, III, i, 299.

141. French Rolls, 29 Ed. III, m. 12.

142. Gascon Rolls, 29 Ed. III, m. 16.

143. Exchequer, Various Accounts, 29 Ed. III (E 101/26/37).

144. Pipe Roll, 29 Ed. III, m. 6.

145. *Rymer*, III, i, 299.

146. Gascon Rolls, 29 Ed. III, m. 5.

147. *B.P.R.*, IV, 143.

148. *Ibid*, IV, 166; Henxteworth, 2.

149. French Rolls, 29 Ed. III, m. 12.

150. Exchequer, Various Accounts, 29 Ed. III, m. 3.

151. French Rolls, 29 Ed. III, m. 12.

152. *Ibid.*, mm. 9, 12.

153. *C.P.R.*, 1354–8, 221.

154. Gascon Rolls, 29 Ed. III, m. 11. Longman, *Edward III*, Vol. I, 364, appears to be in error. He says that thousands of hurdles or fascines were ordered . . . for crossing swamps, protecting bowmen and covering movable towers. Here (and in all similar entries of the period) the hurdles are clearly stated to be *pro eskippamento equorum*. The account of the Sheriff of Cornwall reveals the expenses involved in the execution of the order: timber and nails for the gangways together with the cost of carriage amounted to 8*l.* 8*s.* 6*d.* For the hurdles, the expenses (including the wages of two men who brought them to Plymouth) were 57*l.* 3*s.* 6*d.* Pipe Roll, 30 Ed. III, m. 6.

155. *Avesbury*, 425; *Baker*, 125.

156. *B.P.R.*, III, 493.

157. *Avesbury*, 425–6, and see *Baker*, 290–1.

158. *B.P.R.*, III, 493.

159. *Vide supra*, p. 33.

160. *B.P.R.*, III, 493.

161. *B.P.R.*, IV, 143; Gascon Rolls, 29 Ed. III, m. 5. A sum was paid to

some mariners of Spain and Bayonne who stayed in the port of Southampton forty days awaiting the passage of the prince and the magnates. Issue Roll, 31 Ed. III, m. 11.

162. *Chandos Herald,* lines 611–14.

163. Exchequer, Various Accounts, E 101/26/34, and Pipe Roll, 29 Ed. III, m. 5.

164. Pipe Roll, 29 Ed. III, m. 6.

165. B.P.R., IV, 166; Henxteworth, 2.

166. *List A.* Exchequer, Various Accounts, E 101/26/37. *List B.* Gascon Roll, 29 Ed. III, m. 11. *List C. Rymer,* Appendix E, 13–14. List D. B.P.R., IV, 143.

167. Issue Roll, 30 Ed. III, m. 24. Their account of one such visit to Southampton in July (Exchequer, Various Accounts, E 101/26/38) supplies abundant details of masters and crew of no less than ninety-three vessels from east-coast ports. Unfortunately it makes no reference to the mission for which these vessels were assembled. I have felt obliged, therefore, to omit from my table what might have been a valuable List E. It includes two of the ships mentioned in List B, but conjecture about this large body of shipping would lead us far from our main theme.

168. Henxteworth, 4.

169. *Ibid.,* 2; B.P.R., IV, 166.

CHAPTER III: THE FIRST RAID

1. For a general picture of Bordeaux and the surrounding region in the fourteenth century, see *Boutruche,* 154–61 *et passim.*

2. *Ibid.,* 15–19 *et passim.*

3. *Ibid.,* 35 n. 2.

4. B.P.R., IV, 143–5; Gascon Rolls, 29 Ed. III, m. 6.

5. There is a short biography of John de Grailly in *La Grande Encyclopédie.*

6. The sources contain no statement of the number of Gascon and Bearnais troops employed. Guesses or inferences may be found in Ramsay, 386, 387, 393, and in Lot F., *L'Art militaire et les armées,* Vol. I, 352.

7. *Baker,* 128; Avesbury 437. *Froissart* (V, 344) omits reference to Armagnac but says that the leaders gave their views one by one that they should proceed towards Toulouse.

8. There is a short biography of Gaston Phoebus, Comte de Foix, by Molinier in *La Grande Encyclopédie* and the notes by de Santi (*op. cit.*) are valuable.

9. *Baker,* 128, 135, 138.

10. *Chevauchée:* see article in *La Grande Encyclopédie* and cf. 'Tous ceuls . . . qui doivent host et chevauchie', *Archives historiques de Poitou,* XVII, 205.

11. The quotations in this paragraph are from *Froissart,* IV, 412, 413, except the passage 'in a host such as the King of England was leading . . .' which the translator or editor has significantly omitted. This passage occurs in *Froissart,* IV, 413.

12. 'et ne desiroient cil chevalier et chil saudoyer de par le roi de France aultre cose fors que il peussent courir en Haynau pour pillier et gaegnier et pour le pays mettre en guerre . . . Si entrerent li Francois dedens et trouverent les gens, hommes et femmes en leurs hostels; si les prisent à leur volenté, et tout le leur, or et argent, draps et jouiaus et leurs bestes; et puis bouterent le feu en le ville et le ardirent si nettement que rien y demora fors les parois.' *Froissart,* III, 89. More succint descriptions of attacks on English territory occur in letters from the Seneschal of Gascony to the Constable of Bordeaux with reference to John de Claremont, Marshal of France 'qui cum magno

numero hominum armatorum equitaverat hostili more vexillis displicatis damnificando terram domini Regis'. Ancient Correspondence, LXVIII, 32 and 33 (November 1354). See also *Baker*, 125, 126.

13. *Baker*, 86, 87, 97; Eulogium, III, 211, 212; *Froissart*, V, 119, 121.
14. Hemingburgh (Chronicon), II, 422.
15. Exchequer (K.R.) Accounts, E 101/68/4, m. 72.
16. *Vide supra*, pp. 10–12.
17. Henxteworth, 1.
18. *Ibid.*, 1.
19. *Chandos Herald*, line 641 and *vide infra* note 25.
20. Henxteworth, 6. St. Macaire and Langon are on opposite sides of the river at the limit of tidal water.
21. *Ibid.* 1–4.
22. *Ibid.*, 8, 10.
23. *Ibid.*, 1.
24. *Baker*, 128; *Froissart*, V, 344.
25. *Baker*, 128. For the modern explanation of the loss in the following lines I am indebted to Mr. P. M. Bennett, M.R.C.V.S.
26. Henxteworth, 9.
27. *Baker*, 129.
28. *Ibid.*, 129.
29. *Ibid.*, 130. Froissart omits the devastation of Armagnac. He appears to hold that the prince followed a different route, crossing the Garonne at Port Sainte Marie (V, 344).
30. *Ibid.*, 129. (Edward III similarly had had his night quarters outside towns.) There was a pavilioner and a pavilioner-carpenter. Henxteworth, 8, 11.
31. *Ibid.*, 130. Breuils says that Jean d'Armagnac had ordered people to go to cities and castles taking food and valuables with them. *Histoire de Nogaro* (Société Arch. de Gers, XVI année), p. 110.
32. *Ibid.*, 130.
33. *Froissart*, V, 344.
34. *Baker*, 130.
35. *Avesbury*, 437.
36. *Ibid.*, 440 Breuils (p. 55 and 55 n. 3) mentions a document containing a list of 'villes, lieux et chateaux ravagés par le Prince Noir en 1355'. He says the list contains about 500 names (of which he supplies 19) and that the document is among the Gascon Rolls. If this document could be found, it might prove of very great value. Unfortunately, even the officials at the Public Record Office cannot trace it.
37. *Breuils* (*Jean Ier, Comte d'Armagnac*, 56) holds that Jean d'Armagnac, anticipating that the prince would march on Toulouse, had gone to Agen to stop him and that the prince, fearing to meet Jean, had changed his route. Here, as elsewhere, Breuils is unconvincing.
38. *Baker*, 130.
39. *Ibid.*, 130–1.
40. *Ibid.*, 131.
41. *Avesbury*, 440.
42. *Ibid.*, 437.
43. *Baker*, 131.
44. *Avesbury*, 440.
45. *Baker*, 131.
46. *Ibid.* The prince's movements are discussed at length by the local historians Mullot et Poux and Roschach.
47. *Froissart*, V. 345.

48. *Avesbury*, 437.
49. *Baker*, 131; *Avesbury*, 437.
50. *Froissart*, V, 346.
51. *Baker*, 131.
52. *Ibid.*, 132. Baker here makes specific reference to the Gascon and Bearnais troops.
53. *Baker*, 132; *Froissart*, V, 347, 'ou il li faisoient mescheif dou corps se il ne se voloit ranconner.' The itinerary of the Anglo-Gascon force is treated in detail from this point to Narbonne and back to Belpech (November 16th) by the local historian, Jeanjean, who also supplies a useful map.
54. *Baker*, 132.
55. *Avesbury*, 438.
56. *Ibid.*, 438; *Baker*, 132–3.
57. *Froissart*, V, 347.
58. *Baker*, 132.
59. *Ibid.*, 133; *Jeanjean*, 31–2. At Perigueux also there was a proposal that a town should be spared in return for a cash payment. *Vide infra*, p. 89. The prince's attitude was consistent.
60. *Froissart*, V, 349.
61. *Baker*, 133.
62. *Ibid.*, 133–4; *Jeanjean*, 38.
63. *Avesbury*, 438.
64. *Ibid.*, 438.
65. *Ibid.*, 438.
66. I have followed the route worked out by Jeanjean.
67. *Baker*, 135; Henxteworth, 11.
68. *Baker*, 135.
69. *Froissart* (Macaulay) 23; *Froissart*, V, 15.
70. Henxteworth, 9.
71. *Ibid.*, 11. (Payment, however, appears to have been made on the day his work was completed at Mezin. *Vide infra*.)
72. *Baker*, 136.
73. *Ibid.*, 137, 138.
74. *Ibid.*, 137.
75. *Ibid.*, 136–7; *Avesbury*, 438–9.
76. *Avesbury*, 439.
77. *Baker*, 137–8.
78. *Ibid.*, 137.
79. Henxteworth, 12.
80. *Froissart*, V, 353.
81. Mentioned in Bibliography, p. 170.
82. *Devic et Vaissete*, IX, 651 (note 2), 652 notes.
83. *Ibid.*, IX, 651, 652 notes; Tourneur-Aumont, J. M., *La Bataille de Poitiers, 1356, passim; Breuils*, 58 n. 3. *Denifle*, II, 86, 93.
84. *Froissart*, IV, 421, 427.
85. *Perroy*, 138.
86. *Avesbury*, 437.
87. *Ibid.*, 443.
88. *Jeanjean*, 54.
89. *Ibid*, 50–53.
90. *Froissart*, IV, 430.
91. *Baker*, 130.
92. *Froissart*, V, 346, 347.
93. *Ibid.*, V, 346.
94. *Ibid.*, V, 345.

95. *Froissart*, V, 346.

96. *Jeanjean*, 53.

97. *Avesbury*, 445.

98. Breuils' work is the only detailed study of Jean d'Armagnac that I know. It is sympathetic rather than critical. The date of Jean's birth is variously given as 1311 and 1318.

99. *Jeanjean*, 16.

100. Vaissete felt there were grounds for suspecting that the French generals were in league with the English; de Rozoi thought they were traitors or cowards; de Santi considered Jean a good soldier, a prudent general and a loyal friend of France; Breuils defends Jean wherever possible but acknowledges that the reasons for some of his acts are not known; Jeanjean's conclusion is that perhaps we shall never know the reasons why Jean d'Armagnac refused to come to grips with the prince.

101. *Froissart*, V, 345.

CHAPTER IV: BETWEEN THE RAIDS

1. *Avesbury*, 437. A payment to the master of the *James* of Exmouth 'going back to England on the lord's business' is among the earliest entries in Henxteworth's journal.

2. Exchequer, Various Accounts, 29 Ed. III, E 101/26/32 and E 101/26/34; Pipe Roll, 29 Ed. III, m. 4; Issue Roll, 30 Ed. III, m. 8.

3. *Avesbury*, 437, 439.

4. *Ibid.*, 439, 434.

5. *Ibid.*, 445.

6. *Froissart* (Macaulay) 129, 130. *Lettenhove*, V, 456–7.

7. Henxteworth, 60.

8. *Baker*, 138; *Chandos Herald*, 657–8.

9. *B.P.R.*, IV, 144.

10. *Ibid.*, IV, 156.

11. Henxteworth, 3.

12. *Ibid.*, 21.

13. *Ibid.*, 22.

14. *Ibid.*, 33.

15. *Ibid.*, 28, 31, 36.

16. *Ibid.*, 52, 58.

17. *Ibid.*, 95.

18. *Ibid.*, 62, 68. French currency was widely used. Cf. an order by the seneschal to John de Stretelee to pay '3*l*. 6*s*. 8*d*. sterlingorum vel eorum valorem in alia moneta'. Exchequer (Q.R.) 172/1, No. 47.

19. *The Anonimalle Chronicle*, 35.

20. *Chandos Herald*, lines 657–64.

21. Henxteworth, 13, 14, 15. The sheet containing payments made on Dec. 11th, 12th, 13th is torn.

22. *Ibid.*, 32.

23. *Avesbury*, 445.

24. Henxteworth, 32, 38, 44.

25. *Ibid.*, 46.

26. Sharp, M., 'A Jodrell Deed' in *The Bulletin of the John Rylands Library*, Vol. 7, No. 1 (1922).

27. Henxteworth, 47.

28. *Breuils*, 58–9.

29. *Avesbury*, 445.

30. *Ibid.*, 137–9.

31. *Baker*, 138.

32. *Chandos Herald*, lines 676–94.

33. *Avesbury*, 456. The Prince himself went to Perigueux. B.P.R., III, 337.

34. *Ibid.*, 457.

35. Henxteworth, 68.

36. *Ibid.*, 76, 83, 88, 95, 115.

37. *Avesbury*, 449–50; Moisant, 175–96.

38. Henxteworth, 110.

39. *Archives Historiques du Poitou*, t. XVII, xxxvii.

40. *Rymer*, III, i, 316. Moisant (p. 45) appears to have misunderstood this step. He says that the king viewed the prince's 'incessant hostilities' with uneasiness, but at the date on which the prince's powers were renewed, the king had not received the detailed report on the autumn campaign nor the news that the prince had ordered his captains to resume hostilities after Christmas.

41. *Avesbury*, 449.

42. *Moisant*, 47–8.

43. 'Ratione adherencie sue regi'; 'ratione fidelitatis et adherencie parti regis'; 'ad regiam obedientiam reducendum locum de Alba'; 'ad regiam venit obedientiam'; 'sua spontanea voluntate ad obedientiam Regis revienienti'; 'causa adhesionis ipsius Bertrandi Regi'; 'sua spontanea voluntate ad obedientiam Regis redeunti plures alios nobiles secum ducendo ad obedientiam antedictam'; gratis ad obedientiam Regis rediit, plures magnates secum ducendo ad obedientiam predictam' (Pipe Roll, 36 Ed. III, especially mm. xv and xv dorse). Henxteworth (101 and 109) also records at least two payments 'causa adventus sui ad obedientiam domini Regis Anglie'.

44. '. . . no arrows can be obtained from England because the king has taken for his use all the arrows that can be found anywhere there'. B.P.R., III, 223.

45. *Ibid.*, 224.

46. *Ibid.*, 224.

47. Gascon Roll, 30 Ed. III, mm. 4, 5, 6. The order occurs three times. The first two entries are partly crossed out. The third entry contains the additional words '*qui equos habent*'.

48. B.P.R., III, 223–5.

49. *Ibid.*, 225.

50. *Ibid.*, 225.

51. Gascon Roll, 30 Ed. III, m. 6.

52. B.P.R., II, 94. Gascon Roll, 30 Ed. III, m. 6.

53. *Ibid.*, 94. Gascon Roll, 30 Ed. III, m. 6.

54. Henxteworth, 87. For Adam Kentish see B.P.R., IV, 48, 63, 153.

55. Gascon Roll, 30 Ed. III, m. 6.

56. *Ibid.*, m. 6.

57. C.P.R., 1354–8, 348.

58. *Rymer*, Appendix. E, 19; C 66/68, m. 4.

59. Gascon Roll, 30 Ed. III, m. 6.

60. C.C.R., 1354–60, 244.

61. *Rymer*, Appendix E, 22, 25, 27.

62. *Ibid.*, 26.

63. Henxteworth, 99.

64. C.P.R., 1354–8, 419.

65. B.P.R., II, 98; C.P.R., 1354–8, 468; Gascon Roll, 30 Ed. III, m. 1.

66. Lodge, R., *The Close of the Middle Ages* (London, 1910), 79.

67. Tourneur-Aumont, 120-1, 282-4.

CHAPTER V: THE SECOND RAID AND THE BATTLE OF POITIERS

The purely military aspects of the ground covered in this chapter have been treated at some length in the works of Hilaire Belloc, Colonel A. H. Burne, Sir Charles Oman, R. Delachenal, H. S. Denifle, F. Lot and J. M. Tourneur-Aumont. Of the French writers, Delachenal is scholarly. Tourneur-Aumont (*La Bataille de Poitiers, 1356*) on the other hand is very biased, but his study is so massive and so detailed that it cannot be neglected.

1. *Baker*, 140.
2. The route is given in *Eulogium*, III, 215-17. The maps in Pope and Lodge, *Life of the Black Prince*, p. 191, and Burne, A. H., *The Crécy War*, p. 282, appear to be in error concerning Lussac. The route passes through Lussac les Eglises and not through Lussac les Chateaux.
3. *Eulogium*, III, 219-20; *Baker*, 141; the prince's account is printed in Riley, H. T., *Memorials of London and London Life*, 285-8; Burghersh's account is in Lettenhove's edition of *Froissart*, Vol. XVIII, 385.
4. *Riley, op. cit.*, 286.
5. *B.P.R.*, IV, 145.
6. *Riley, op cit.*, 216.
7. *Baker*, 142.
8. *Jean le Bel*, II, 196.
9. *Eulogium*, III, 222.
10. *Froissart*, V, 403.
11. *Tourneur-Aumont*, 192, 202.
12. *B.P.R.*, IV, 145.
13. *Chandos Herald*, lines 826-56.

> Je ne puis pas ceste matère
> Acomplir sanz le Roy, mon père
>
> .   .   .   .   .
>
> Le ferai à vostre plaisir
> Ou gré de mon père assentir.

14. See Preface.
15. *Tourneur-Aumont*, 239-45, and the aerial view at the end of that work.
16. Belloc, *Poitiers*, 20, 77-9; *Oman*, II, 164; M. Perroy (*The Hundred Years War*, 105-6) puts the Anglo-Gascon force at 5,000-6,000 men in all and the French at 15,000. See also Tait, J., in *Chronicon Johannis de Reading*, 124 and 360.
17. *Froissart*, V, 411-12.
18. Riley, *op. cit.*, 288.
19. Some of the ground is treated in *Oman* and Burne, A. H. See also Galbraith, V. H., in *The Anonimalle Chronicle*, 38, and note 165; and *Tourneur-Aumont*, 250-7.
20. The 'French' view is found in *Delachenal* and *Tourneur-Aumont*. Galbraith, V. H., treated the matter in *E.H.R.*, LIV (1939), 473. Burne, A. H., wrote an anlysis in *E.H.R.*, LIII (1938), 21, and has dealt with the controversy again in his *The Crécy War*, 296 *et seq.*
21. *Baker*, 149.
22. *Baker*, 149; *Froissart*, V, 451; *Chandos Herald*, lines 1249-53.
23. *Baker*, 144.
24. *Froissart*, V, 443-4, 427; Chronique des règnes de Jean II et de Charles V, 72.
25. *Tourneur-Aumont*, 224-9, 467-72.
26. The writer of the Chronique des règnes de Jean II et de Charles V

mentions the flight and proceeds immediately to the causes of the French defeat but does not attempt to explain the flight (*op. cit.*, 72). See *Tourneur-Aumont*, 277–84.

27. *Froissart*, V, 409, 437. *Chandos Herald*, lines 983–7.

28. *Froissart*, V, 442, 126; *Baker*, 149–51; *Chandos Herald*, lines 988–9, 1121–3, 1157, 1390–2.

29. Chronique des règnes de Jean II et de Charles V, 72, *Chandos Herald*, lines 1224–7, 1326–7; *Froissart*, V, 425, 441–2; *Baker*, 148 (Stow's translation), 303.

30. *Baker*, 150, 151.

31. *Froissart*, V, 439, 441; *Baker*, 151.

32. *Baker*, 150 (Stow's translation) 304; *Froissart* (Macaulay), 126, (Lettenhove) V, 447.

33. *Chandos Herald*, lines, 1390–1400; *Froissart* (Macaulay), 125, (Lettenhove) V, 426. For the prisoners *vide infra*.

34. *Froissart*, V, 436, 440, 454. 'Dalés le prince pour lui garder et consillier estoit Messire Jean Chandos,' and see *Froissart*, XVII, 356. *Chandos Herald*, lines 1278–82: Deux chevalers plain de valour La tenoient de deux costees. Moult estoient plain de bontees Ceo feurent Chaundos et Audelee.

35. *Eulogium*, III, 224; *Froissart*, V, 436; *Baker*, 145, 146.

36. *Froissart*, V, 441, 454; *Baker*, 153; Walsingham, 282.

37. *B.P.R.*, IV, 203.

38. *Ibid.*, IV, 206, 209, 262. *Ibid.*, III, 237, 251.

39. *Ibid.*, IV, 178, 196, 207, 210, 215. *Ibid.*, II, 99.

40. *Ibid.*, IV, 191, 193, 209, 219, 234–5; III, 231, 244, 255, 257, 258, 261, 263, 267, 270.

41. *Ibid.*, IV, 193; III, 252, 253.

42. See Preface to *B.P.R.*, III.

43. Pipe Roll, 36 Ed. III (Mich.), E 372/207, m. XVII.

44. These are my own conclusions and the third principle is very rarely found. The subject is treated also in Audinet, *op cit.*, lxxxix *et seq.*

45. Knighton, 89; *Chandos Herald*:

> Et si ny aies point de deport
> Qe toutz ne les mettez a mort (957–8)

> .   .   .   .

> Et gardes bien pur dieu mercy
> Qe naies denglois mercy
> Mais les mettez toutz a mort (1005–7)

> .   .   .   .

> Et gardez si le Prince preignez
> Qe par devers moi lamesnez (1011–12)

46. *B.P.R.*, IV, 338.

47. *Froissart*, V, 449–51; see also *Baker*, 149–50.

48. *Chandos Herald*, lines 1394–7.

49. *Froissart*, V, 452.

50. *B.P.R.*, IV, 339–40.

51. *Froissart*, V, 453.

52. *Ibid.*, 453, 468. *Vide infra*, p. 150. Both claimants died before the dispute was settled.

53. *Froissart*, V, 463–4. The Chronique des règnes de Jean II and Charles V, p. 75, says that the Count of Eu was released on his honour till the feast of All Saints because he was wounded, and that the less important prisoners were put to ransom and released on their honour that they might go and get their ransoms. Froissart says that the Almains, in contrast to the English and Gascons, were very exacting over the sums demanded.

54. *Ibid.*, V, 453; *B.P.R.*, IV, 285, 363, 389.

55. *Froissart*, V, 428, 436, 447, 454. Of Chandos: 'ne oncques le jour ne s'en parti' and 'par lequel conseil il ouvra et persévéra le journée'. Of Chandos and Audley, 'qui de mener et ensseigner le prince fissent ce jour bien leur devoir car il n'y prissent oncques prisonniers'.

56. Of Audley 'oncques . . . ne prist prisonnier le journée, ne n'entendi au prendre, mais toujours à combatre et à aler avant sus ses ennemies'. *Ibid.*, V, 439.

57. *Baker*, 157.

58. *Froissart* (Macaulay), V, 468.

59. (Ship) *B.P.R.*, IV, 254 (crown and star), *ibid.*, 323; British Museum Roy. MS. 19 D. ii; Bibliothèque Nationale 24, 541 des Nouvelles Acquisitions Francaises.

60. *Froissart*, V, 463 (the words are taken from Jean le Bel, II, 237).

61. *Froissart*, V, 456, 457, 459, 466. See Appendix A.

62. *Chandos Herald*, line 1440.

63. *Froissart*, V, 432, 451–2.

64. *Textes et Documents d'Histoire* (ed. Calmette, J.) Paris, 1937, II, 115–16.

65. *Op. cit.*, II, 236.

66. *The Anonimalle Chronicle*, 38; *Knighton*, 92.

67. Issue Roll 30 Ed. III, (Mich.), m. 3.

68. *Ibid.*, m. 1.

69. *C.C.R.* (1354–60), 334.

70. *Froissart*, V, 465.

71. *Baker*, 154. See also the letters of the prince and of Burghersh in Froissart, XVIII, 385, 389, Sir Henry Peverel's letter in Chartulary of Winchester Cathedral (ed. Goodman, A. W., Winchester, 1927), 161, 162, and Knighton, II, 92; *Eulogium*, III, 225; Chronique des Quatre Premiers Valois, 56.

72. *Froissart*, V, 75.

73. *Ibid.*, VII, 219.

74. *Op cit.*, 92. Cf. Chaucer: Knight's Tale (Globe edition), lines 1005–8:
> To ransake in the taas of bodyes dede,
> Hem for to strepe of harneys and of wede,
> The pilours diden bisynesse and cure
> After the bataille and disconfiture.

75. *Baker*, 155. The prince, Burghersh, Knighton, Peverel and the *Eulogium* also supply names or figures (as in note 71 *supra*), and there are lists in *Archives Historiques du Poitou*, t. XLVI, pp. 164–170.

76. Burghersh and Peverel quote these figures.

77. *Eulogium*, 225–6.

78. *C.C.R.*, 1354–60, 334.

79. Devon, F.: *Pell Records*, 165.

80. *Ibid.*, 155, 136, 259. See also *C.C.R.*, 1354–60, 95, 166, 329, where a John Cook is Treasurer of Queen Philippa.

81. *Pell Records*, 166. See Appendix C.

82. *C.C.R.*, 1354–60, 334.

83. *Episcopal Registers, Diocese of Exeter*, John de Grandison, Part II, 1331–60 (Exeter, 1897), 1173, 1190–1.

84. *Froissart*, V, 469. The quotation is from Macaulay's edition, p. 133, but the translator (perhaps using other sources of information) has been more explicit than the text warrants. It runs 'solennities par les eglises si grandes et si nobles que merveilles seroit à penser et à considerer'.

CHAPTER VI: AFTER THE RAIDS

1. Pipe Roll, 36 Ed. III (Account of John de Stretelee), m. 18.

2. *C.P.R.*, 1354–8, 277, 471, 472.

3. *Ibid.*, 1354–8, 467.

4. *B.P.R.*, II, 105, 107.

5. *C.P.R.*, 1354–8, 477; *B.P.R.*, IV, 236.

6. E 101/313/29.

7. *B.P.R.*, IV, 254.

8. Riley, H. T., *Memorials of London*, 285; *Froissart*, XVIII, 389.

9. *B.P.R.*, IV, 193 *et seq.* There are some errors in the dates. That of the grant made to Cusyngton on p. 178 is obviously wrong. Those of October 1st, London, in IV, 190–1, and II, 98–9, are almost certainly wrong.

10. *B.P.R.*, IV, 254.

11. *C. Pap. Lett.*, III, 619–21.

12. *Froissart*, V, 469. *Baker*, 155.

13. *B.P.R.*, IV, 144.

14. *Rymer*, III, i, 333–4.

15. *C.C.R.*, 1354–60, 321.

16. *Rymer*, III, i, 341.

17. He was a D.C.L. (Oxford). Lodge, E. G., *The Constables of Bordeaux in the Reign of Edward III*, 234; Thompson, A. H., *Associated Architectural Societies' Reports*, XXXVI (1921), 1–3.

18. *C.C.R.*, 1354–60, 321.

19. *Breuils*, 61.

20. *Ibid.*, 62.

21. *Rymer*, III, i, 348–9.

22. *Ibid.*, III, i, 348–9.

23. *Cal. Pap. Lett.*, III, 622–3.

24. *Baker*, 155; *Anonimalle Chronicle*, 40; *Froissart*, V, 469.

25. *Rymer*, III, i, 348–9.

26. Charles de Blois, pretender to the duchy of Brittany, had been a prisoner in England since 1347 and Jean de Melun, sire de Tancarville, Chamberlain of France since 1346.

27. *Froissart*, VI, 15–16. There is a briefer account of the episode in *Jean le Bel*, II, 239.

28. *Froissart*, VII, 145–6.

29. *Vide infra*, p. 160–2.

30. *B.P.R.*, IV, 268, 269.

31. *Ibid.*, IV, 269.

32. *Froissart*, VI, 17.

33. *Ibid.*, VI, 17.

34. *B.P.R.*, IV, 269.

35. *Chronique des règnes de Jean II et de Charles V*, 107.

36. French Rolls, 30 Ed. III, mm. 2, 5; Gascon Rolls, 30 Ed. III, m. 2.

37. *C.P.R.*, 1354–8, 514, 515.

38. *B.P.R.*, II, 110; III, 236.

39. *C.P.R.*, 1354–8, 519–531; *C.C.R.* 1354–60, 346–7.

40. Of the sixteen vessels in the first list, the two from Polruan and Fowey are mentioned in *B.P.R.*, II, 141. Payment is recorded to the masters or owners of the remaining fourteen vessels in Issue Roll 403/387, mm. 11, 21, 22. For the *Cog John* see also *B.P.R.*, IV, 283. The *Blaunche, Christofre, Jerusalem* and *Gabriel* were among the nine vessels requisitioned in December 1356, but I have not traced payment for their use. The other five of these nine are included in the fourteen mentioned above.

41. *B.P.R.*, IV, 253.
42. Issue Roll 403/387, m. 11. This vessel had been prepared for the prince in July 1355. *B.P.R.*, IV, 143.
43. *B.P.R.*, III, 237-8. The place and date of arrival of the prince and King John were for long the subject of controversy. See for example *Moisant*, 63; and for a summary of conflicting evidence in the chronicles, see *Chronicon Johannis de Reading*, 267. In view of the evidence given here and in the next two paragraphs, the controversy may be regarded as ended.
44. *B.P.R.*, IV, 253.
45. Pipe Roll, 30 Ed. III, m. 38.
46. *B.P.R.*, IV, 204-5.
47. Issue Roll 403/387, m. 9.
48. John lived at the Savoy, at Berkhamstead, at Hertford, at Somerton (Lincolnshire). The records of the time contain very many references to his guards, his servants, his victuals and wine.
49. *Baker*, 154.
50. *Froissart*, V, 468.
51. *Rymer*, III, 1, 385.
52. *Lavisse*, IV, 150-6; Broome, D. M., *The Ransom of John II. Camden Misc.*, XIV (1926), vii; *Chronicon Johannis de Reading*, 208, 262.
53. *Delachenal*, I, 243.

CHAPTER VII: RANSOMS, REWARDS AND PARDONS

Nys (*op. cit.*, 242, 245-6) and Audinet (*op. cit.*, ci–cv) deal briefly with Ransoms. In his *Vie de Bertrand du Guesclin* (ed. Clairiere, vv. 13,367–13,725) Cuvelier attributes to the Black Prince some comments on the general subject and on a particular instance, viz. the ransoming of Bertrand.

1. *Froissart*, V, 449, 451. In the second 'rédaction' the phrase runs 'vous m'aves loyaument conquis', which may be translated, as in the text 'ye have by law of arms won me'. In the first 'rédaction' the phrase is 'par bel fet d'arme l'avoit-il conquis'. A third little drama of capture (dated 1388) also contains the words 'rescue or no rescue'. *Ibid.*, XIII, 233-4.
2. Broome, D., *The Ransom of John II* in Camden Misc., XIV, inset between pp. 10 and 11. Concerning weight and alloy of coins, see *C.P.R.*, 1358–61, 582.
3. *Delachenal*, II, 325. Broome, *op. cit.*, vii–xxvi.
4. Hay, D., *The Division of the Spoils of War*, 94–9. In 1359, the Earl of Warwick received a licence to put to ransom the Archbishop of Le Mans, his prisoner, 'a fourth part of whose ransom pertains to the king.' *C.P.R.*, 1358–61, 167.
5. *B.P.R.*, II, 129.
6. *Ibid.*, III, 251; IV, 249.
7. *Pell Records*, ed. Devon, F., 174, 177.
8. *C.P.R.*, 1358–61, 167.
9. *B.P.R.*, IV, 379.
10. *Rymer*, III, i, 420.
11. *B.P.R.*, IV, 379.
12. Carte, *Rolles Gascons*, II, 63–70.
13. *Moisant*, 59–60. *Archives Historiques de Poitou*, t. XVII, 241, 244, 255.
14. Leland, *Itinerary in England* (ed. Smith, L. T.), IV, 132, 133.
15. *Froissart*, XI, 108.
16. Riley, H. T., *Memorials of London*, 290.
17. *Archives Historiques du Poitou*, t. XVII, xxvii.

18. *B.P.R.*, IV, 379.

19. *Rymer*, III, i, 415, 420.

20. *Ibid.*, 487. Article XV names Prince Philip and fifteen nobles taken prisoners at the battle of Poitiers together with twenty-five other nobles who are to be hostages. See also Article XVI and the important documents about prisoners, *ibid.*, III, i, 498, 499, 503, 511, 512, 537, 538, 539.

21. The purchase: *Rymer*, III, i, 346; the payment: *Pell Records*, 168; completion of payment: *Rymer*, III, i, 415; and *vide infra* n. 53.

22. *B.P.R.*, II, 199, 208, 209, 214; III, 452; IV, 285, 364, 389, 442, 477.

23. *B.P.R.*, IV, 252.

24. *Ibid.*, IV, 252.

25. *Ibid.*, IV, 207.

26. *Pell Records*, 174.

27. *Ibid*, 174.

28. Issue Roll 403/388, m. 16.

29. *Ibid.*, mm. 16, 27.

30. *C.P.R.*, 1358–61, 300. *Pell Records*, 177, shows a payment of 3333*l*, 6*s*. 8*d*. in 1362.

31. These prisoners were taken over as explained on page 156 above.

32. *Pell Records*, 167. Suffolk's share was 3,000 florins (see *D.N.B.*)

33. Issue Rolls, 31 Ed. III (Easter), m. 28; 32 Ed. III (Mich.), m. 16.

34. *C.P.R.*, 1358–61, 167.

35. *Ibid.*, 1358–61, 63.

36. *C.C.R.*, 1354–60, 384.

37. Issue Rolls, 31 Ed. III (Easter), m. 27, 32 Ed. III (Mich.), m. 22.

38. Carte, *Rolles Gascons*, II, 63–70.

39. *B.P.R.*, IV, 269.

40. Pasture *B.P.R.*, III, 238, 244, 251, 255, 263–5; turbary, *ibid.*, III, 239–42, 254–5, 261.

41. *Ibid.*, III, 264–5, 238, 240, 245, 249, 250, 259, 261.

42. *Ibid.*, III, 238, 245, 253, 258, 282, 318.

43. *Ibid.*, III, 239, 261, 280. Concerning the importance of Middlewich, see Hewitt, *Medieval Cheshire*, 108–22.

44. *Ibid.*, III, 250.

45. *Ibid.*, III, 238–9, 254, 257, 282, 299, 313.

46. *Ibid.*, III, 277.

47. *Ibid.*, III, 244, 246.

48. *Ibid.*, III, 238, 248–9.

49. *Ibid.*, III, 237–75.

50. *C.P.R.*, 1354–8, 478, 487, 490, 559–61 *et passim*; 1358–61, 5, 6, 8, 16, 30–1, 48, 89 *et passim*.

51. And there are a few in 1359. Three had been granted in November-December 1356. Four were granted 'at the asking of the Earl of Warwick'. Two grantees had served in the Earl of Salisbury's company. The last pardon I have found (date September 15th, 1359) contains the words 'killed before 28th March in the thirty-first year'.

52. See the indenture of 1355 in *B.P.R.*, IV, 145, and Prince, A. E. *The Indenture System under Edward III*, p. 295.

53. *Vide supra*, p. 158. The receipt is in Excheq. Accts E 101/28/8.

54. *Vide supra*, p. 158.

55. *B.P.R.*, IV, 251, 252, 333, 351, 388, 391.

56. E. A. 172/3, numbers 19, 37, 38, 40, 42, 44, 45, 47. The payments to these men are recorded in the Account of John de Stretelee in Pipe Roll, 36 Ed. III, m. XV dorse.

57. *Vide supra*, p. 131.

CHAPTER VIII: EPILOGUE

1. *B.P.R.*, IV, 203, 251–3.
2. *Vide supra*, pp. 162–3.
3. *B.P.R.*, III, 277, 307–13.
4. *Ibid.*, IV, 254.
5. *Ibid.*, III, 205; *C.C.A.*, 236.
6. *Ibid.*, 371–2; *C.C.A.*, 272.
7. *Ibid.*, III, 264.
8. *Ibid.*, III, 265.
9. *Ibid.*, III, 251, 294.
10. *B.P.R.* ,III, 331, 349–50, 356, 357.

AUDLEY'S ESQUIRES AT THE BATTLE OF POITIERS

ACCORDING to Froissart (Lettenhove V, 457–66), the prince visited the wounded Audley and promised him a handsome annuity, which annuity Audley promptly transferred to the four esquires who had attended him during the battle. At some date a tradition grew up that the esquires were Delves of Doddington, Fouleshurst of Barthomley, Hawkestone of Wrinehill and Dutton of Dutton. (Dutton is in Little Leigh, north Cheshire; the remaining three places are all near the Cheshire, Shropshire, Staffordshire boundaries as is also Helegh where Audley had lands.)

The earliest mention I have found of the tradition occurs in Ashmole, Elias, *The Institution, Laws and Ceremonies of the most Noble Order of the Garter*, London, 1672, p. 705. Ashmole cites 'Lib MS penes W. Flower nuper Norry King of Arms.' This is followed by Beltz, G. F., *Memorials of the Order of the Garter*, London, 1841, p. 79, n. 1, and Ormerod, G., *History of Cheshire* (2nd edition, ed. Helsby, London, 1882), III, 518, and the Dictionary of National Biography (Article: Audley, Sir James). In less authoritative works, the names have been copied again and again.

It is very doubtful whether the presence of any of these esquires at Poitiers can be proved.

There is a very strong probability that Delves was not there.

(1.) John de Delves held the important office of lieutenant of the Justice of Chester (*B.P.R.*, III, 141, onwards) and, since the Justice, Bartholomew de Burghersh, was accompanying the prince in France, it is unlikely that his lieutenant also would be sent, or allowed to go abroad at the same time.

(2.) Delves' salary as lieutenant was paid for the period Michaelmas, 1356 to June 1357 (*C.C.A.*, 235).

(3.) In the middle of July 1356, orders were issued to him and he was also appointed a commissioner of the peace for the county of Salop (*B.P.R.*, III, 229, 230; *C.P.R.*, 1354–58, 388, 449).

(4.) He was in London on November 12th, 1356 (*B.P.R.*, III, 231).

(5.) A note in the Register, dated 'October 20th, London', states that certain business was done 'by the advice of John de Delves' (*B.P.R.*, II, 101).

(6.) I have not found his name in any of the lists of men to whom letters of protection were issued, nor did he receive any reward for service with the prince in the campaigns of 1355–6, nor—so far as I can trace—does his name occur in Henxteworth's journal.

Even if it be held that Delves' 'advice' (5, above) might have been given some months earlier, it still seems quite improbable that he left England and returned between July and November, 1356.

As regards Thomas de Dutton, he was Sheriff of Chester and, in the period Michaelmas 1356 to Midsummer 1357, he paid over to the chamberlain the estreats of the County Courts as in the preceding and succeeding years (*C.C.A.*, 208, 224, 233, 238).

Concerning Robert de Fouleshurst, the Chamberlain of Chester was directed to make out letters of protection in his favour on June 28th, 1355. He was 'to go with the *king* to the war in parts beyond the sea' (*B.P.R.*, III, 207). Whether 'the king' is an error for 'the prince' I leave undecided, but (*a*) there is at least one other instruction to the chamberlain to make out letters of protection in which 'the king' occurs correctly and (*b*) it was usual in letters of protection for men who were to accompany the prince to add the words 'to the parts of Gascony' (*B.P.R.*, III, 203, 211).

As for Hawkestone, I have found no evidence of his whereabouts at this time.

It may be added that the names of two esquires of Audley are to be found in Henxteworth, viz. Laurence Pecche (section 6, date October 3rd, 1355) and John Welles (section 68, date March 16th, 1356).

This appendix is of course concerned solely with the tradition mentioned above. All four men appear to have rendered valuable service to the prince. Delves and Dutton, as we have seen, were in charge of important work at home in 1356. In 1346, Delves and Hawkestone had served in France in the company of Richard, Earl of Arundel, and Audley was in the same company (Wrottesley, G., *Crécy and Calais*, 33, 34, 114).

APPENDIX B

NEWS OF THE BATTLE OF POITIERS, p. 138.

DELACHENAL's view (*Histoire de Charles V*, 1,243 and 243 n. 1.) that Denis de Morbek was chosen by the Black Prince to take the news to London is at variance with the evidence.

(i) Delachenal himself says that de Morbek was wounded (1,242).

(ii) Delachenal rests his statement on an emendation of the entry in the Pells Issue Rolls, 31 Ed. III (Easter), m. 28, where he substitutes *nuncio* for *servicio*. I believe that the emendation is unnecessary and that the text indicates no more than an interim payment to de Morbek for the good service he gave in connection with the capture of John, not for the good news of John's capture.

(iii) I have shown that Geoffrey Hamelyn, John le Cok and Thomas the Messenger were indisputably bearers of news. Delachenal appears not to have known of their work.

The dates of the payments to these men in the Issue Rolls are not of course reliable indications of the dates of their arrivals. Actually, John le Cok who was the first to bring the news to the king, was the last to receive payment. Geoffrey Hamelyn is the first of whom we can be sure that he *both* came from Gascony *and* bore news of the battle.

The dates of payment are as follows:

To Thomas the Messenger	.	.	. 12th October, 1356.
To Geoffrey Hamelyn	.	.	. 14th December, 1356.
To John le Cok	.	.	. 14th October, 1357.

Payment of expenses in connection with the 'tarrying at Westminster' of members of the Council when news of John's capture was received is recorded on November 25th, 1357, Issue Rolls, 30 Ed. III (Mich.) and 31 Ed. III (Mich.).

Concerning the identity of John le Cok of Cherbourg, I have suggested that he was a clerk in the wardrobe. In view of the words 'of Cherbourg', an alternative hypothesis might be that he was a Norman who gained early news of John's capture, sped *northwards* (possibly through Brittany where Henry of Lancaster could have given him facilities), reached a Channel port and arrived in England before either of the English messengers. He might have been one of Lancaster's 'coureurs'. It may be added that the name "Cok messag." occurs in a muster roll of men serving in the fortresses near Guines in 30 Edward III (E 101/27/6).

A NOMINAL ROLL OF MEN WHO
SERVED IN THE EXPEDITION

THE chief sources of the names in the following list are (1) records of payments, especially payment of wages, (2) letters of protection, (3) grants of pardon, (4) grants of rewards. A few names are derived from records of business in connection with prisoners or ransoms and a few (Gascons) from receipts for payment of pensions.

The evidence is fairly broad-based, but two features must be noted. In the first place, the evidence relates far more to men serving in the prince's own company than to men who served in the companies of the earls, of Cobham and de Lisle. The rewards were made to the prince's staff and the Cheshire archers; the pardons were granted by the king (at the prince's request) mainly to men who served in the prince's company or by the prince to his Cheshire men; the records of wage-payments are those made by Henxteworth for men serving in the prince's company.

Secondly, the enrolment of grants of pardon given as rewards for military service ensured the survival of the names of many criminals—and their inclusion in our list. Broad figures may be mentioned. The English list contains about 890 names of which about 140 are those of Cheshire men. Of the 750 men from other counties, nearly 140 received pardons and the great majority of the pardons were for murder. Of the Cheshire men, 3 received pardons for murder and nearly 40 received general pardons. The figures are in no way surprising but the ratio of criminals to non-criminals is higher in the list than it was in the army.

The treatment of variant spellings of a name needs explanation. In some instances, e.g. Caryngton, Karinton or Steuicle, Styeucle, Stuclee, other evidence points to a single person and the name is shown once only. In others, it is clear that similar spellings refer to different men. William de Apelton was indicted of murder and received a pardon from the king; William de Apulton was a Cheshire man rewarded by the prince. There remain many instances in which though certainty cannot be reached, I have felt the probability to be sufficiently high to warrant the citing of one form only. As for the form of spelling quoted, my choice has had to be arbitrary, but since my list has been compiled from records, I have retained Henxteworth's Daubriggecourt as against Froissart's d'Aubrecicourt and Chandos Herald's d'Abriche-court.

As Henxteworth records payments for goods and services, it is not always clear whether payees are Gascon (dealers or contractors) or English.

Finally, many names occur several times in B.P.R. or Henxteworth or in both. A single reference is quoted as evidence that a man served in Gascony in 1355–57, but for many of the men, a little more information may be found.

Abbreviations used:

H.	Henxteworth's journal.
Ry.	Rymer's Foedera.
Ry.E.	Rymer's Foedera, Appendix E.

This list also serves as an index to those names which are mentioned in this book. Page numbers are given in italic numerals.

ENGLISH

Acton, Adam de	B.P.R. III, 253.
Acton, Henry de	H. 89.
Acton, John de	H. 47.
Acton, Richard de	B.P.R. III, 246.
Acton, Robert de	B.P.R. III, 301
Acton, Thomas de	H. 47.
Acton, William de	B.P.R. III, 253.
Aldrington, Henry de	H. 27. *23, 85.*
Aldingbourne, Thomas de	Ry. III, i, 325
Aliewik, John	H. 43.
Alnewyk, John de	Ry. E. 16.
Amory, Roger	B.P.R. III, 249.
Angst, Thomas	H. 71.
Apelton, William de	C.P.R., 1354–8, 559.
Appleby, Edmund de, Kt.	Ry. III, i, 323.
Appleby, Robert de	Ry. III, 325.
Apulton, William de	B.P.R. III, 238.
Ardene, Thomas de, Kt.	Ry. III, i, 325.
Arderne, Richard de	H. 27.
Argan, Alan	H. 47.
Arkenstalle, Hugh	H. 95.
Arnald, Peter	H. 11.
Arnald, William	H. 52.
As, John, of Dudyngton	C.P.R., 1354–8, 592.
Asshley, Hamo de	H. 33.
Astell, Robert	B.P.R. III, 238.
Aston, Richard de	C.P.R., 1354–8, 490.
Astyn, Adam	C.P.R., 1358–61, 5.
Atherle, William	H. 81.
Audley, James, Kt.	B.P.R. IV, 291. *9, 22–3, 66, 78, 80–1, 83, 87–9, 104, 115, 130, 134, 147, 157–8, 160, 167, 192–3.*
Audley, Roger de	H. 25.
Aungre, Alexander de	Ry.E. 16.
Auteley, Henry	H. 81.
Avenal, Giles	H. 9.

Bache, Peter	H. 38.
Bacton, William de	B.P.R. III, 137. *23*.
Bagley, Hamo de	B.P.R. III, 299.
Bagley, John de	B.P.R. III, 299.
Baien, Richard	H. 6.
Baione, John	H. 45.
Bajous, Robert de	Ry. III, i, 325.
Bakepins, William	Ry.E. 16.
Baker, Richard le	Ry.E. 16.
Baltine, John le	Ry.E. 15.
Bampton, John de	C.P.R., 1354–8, 559.
Barbour, Cok	H. 71.
Bardolf, John, Kt.	H. 6.
Bardolf, Thomas	H. 18.
Baret, Roger	H. 96.
Barwe, Adam del	C.P.R., 1354–8, 559.
Baser, Thomas de	H. 12.
Baskerville, Richard, Kt.	B.P.R. IV, 403. *83, 160*.
Bassett, Ralph	C.P.R., 1358–61, 220. *83*.
Bassingbourne, Warin de, Kt.	B.P.R. IV, 249.
Beauchamp, John, Kt.	Baker, 129. *50*.
Beauchamp, Thomas, Earl of Warwick	B.P.R. IV, 144. *4, 20–2, 24, 36–7, 50, 81, 88–9, 115, 118–19, 133–4, 145, 156, 167*.
Beaupell, Ralph	Ry. III, i, 325.
Beaupre, John, Kt.	H. 37.
Bechynton, William de	B.P.R. III, 251. *131*.
Bekensfeld, Richard de	H. 2.
Belgrave, Thomas de	B.P.R. III, 249.
Bene, Thomas, of Byngham	C.P.R., 1354–8, 592.
Benet, Robert	B.P.R. III, 247.
Benett, John	H. 38.
Beneyt, William	Ry. III, i, 325.
Benstede, John de	H. 5.
Bentone, Richard de	Ry.E. 16.
Berchels, Ralph	H. 47.
Berclei, Walter	H. 20.
Bercley, Thomas de, Kt.	Ry. III, i, 325.
Berebred, John, of Rumnee	C.P.R., 1354–8, 559.
Bereford, Baldwin de	H. 5.
Bereford, John	Ry. III, i, 325.
Bereton, John	H. 77.
Berewyk, Richard de	Ry.E. 17. *159*.
Berkeley, Edward de	H. 6.
Berkeley, John	H. 7.
Berkeley, Maurice, Kt.	H. 33. *52, 124, 130, 132, 157*.
Berkeley, Nicholas de	Ry.E. 16.
Berkhampstead, Henry de	B.P.R. IV, 196. *130, 160*.
Bernard, Arnold	H. 11.

Bernardstone, Thomas de	Ry. III, i, 325.
Berne, Ralph	Ry.E. 16.
Berton, Hugh de	H. 13.
Beuvys, Roger	C.P.R., 1354-8, 544.
Bikebury, William de	Ry. III, i, 325.
Bintre, John, Kt.	H. 27.
Birch, William	H. 5.
Bisshop, William	H. 6.
Bisshopesgate, John	H. 43.
Blacforby, John de	C.P.R., 1354-8, 559.
Blacwood, William, Kt.	H. 107.
Blak, Henry	H. 11.
Blakburn, Henry, Kt.	H. 13.
Blakwater, William	B.P.R. IV, 208. *161*.
Blaunkminster, John, Kt.	Ry.E. 16. *133*.
Blond, John, of Little Hereford	C.P.R., 1354-8, 560.
Blount, Thomas, Kt.	Ry.E. 17.
Boardhewer, Adam	B.P.R. III, 296.
Bodrigan, Oto de	Ry. III, i, 325.
Bodryngan, William de, Kt.	Ry. III, i, 325.
Bolde, Hugh	H. 76.
Bolehead, Adam	C.P.R., 1358-61, 228.
Bolt, Robert	B.P.R. III, 261. *131*.
Bolton, John de	B.P.R. IV, 237.
Bond, Nicholas	B.P.R. IV, 197. *161*.
Bond, Richard	H. 7.
Bonemure, Peter de	H. 38.
Bosedon, Roger de	B.P.R. III, 238.
Bostock, Adam de	B.P.R. III, 241. *131*.
Bostock, Nicholas de	B.P.R. III, 242.
Botetourt, Baldwin de, Kt.	B.P.R. IV, 215. *22, 66, 78, 81, 88, 130, 141, 161*.
Botourt, John	H. 5.
Boudon, Jordan	H. 96.
Boulge, William	H. 21.
Boure, John	H. 96.
Bourchier, John, lord	Baker, 129. *52*.
Bowden, Robert	B.P.R. III, 371.
Bower, John le	B.P.R. III, 261.
Bowyer, Richard	H. 39.
Boyal, John	H. 72.
Boydel, John	H. 91.
Bradestone, Edward, Kt.	H. 47.
Bradestone, Robert, Kt.	H. 8.
Bradgate, Thomas	H. 21. *83*.
Braunche, Richard	Ry.E. 18.
Braybrook, Gerald	H. 4.
Bredbury, Ralph de	B.P.R. III, 258.
Brercle, Thomas de	H. 23.

Brercle, William de	H. 23.
Brerley, Thomas, Kt.	H. 81.
Bret, John	Ry. III, i, 325.
Bretford, Richard	Ry. III, i, 325.
Brewes, Thomas de	Ry.E. 16.
Bridham, Hugh, Kt.	H. 8.
Bridyn, William	B.P.R. III, 250
Broghton, William de	C.P.R., 1354–8, 559.
Brok, William, of Hedersete	C.P.R., 1354–8, 560.
Brokholes, Edmund de	C.P.R., 1354–8, 572.
Brownleye, William	C.P.R., 1358–61, 399.
Bruge, John, Kt.	H. 5.
Brumpton, Peter de	H. 8.
Brun, Maurice le	Ry.E. 16.
Brun, Robert	B.P.R. III, 243. *42, 83.*
Brun, Thomas	H. 45. *159.*
Bruyn, Adam le	B.P.R. III, 249.
Bryn, Robert le, of Stapleford	C.P.R., 1354–8, 592.
Bryn, William le	B.P.R. III, 250.
Bucher, Richard	H. 111.
Bunche, Thomas, of Stokebrewere	C.P.R., 1354–8, 592.
Burghersh, Bartholomew de, Kt.	H. 33. *4, 21, 23, 50, 61, 81, 87–8, 115, 134, 145, 167, 192.*
Burle, Peter de	Ry.E. 17.
Burleigh, Richard	C.P.R., 1354–8, 560.
Burnham, John de	H. 47.
Burnyngham, Fulk	Ry. III, i, 325.
Burton, William de, Kt.	Ry. III, i, 325. *145.*
Bury, John de	H. 7.
Bushell, William	Ry. III, i, 325.
Bynynam, Nandon de	H. 25.
Calday, William	B.P.R. III, 279.
Caldwell, William	C.P.R., 1358–61, 89.
Camel, John	Ry.E. 16.
Candel, Peter	H. 26.
Candelar, Roger	H. 22.
Canon, Walter	H. 47.
Canterbury, Robert de	H. 10.
Canterbury, Thomas	H. 32.
Canterbury, William	H. 65.
Capel, Thomas	Ry. III, i, 325.
Cappe, Henry	C.P.R., 1354–8, 478.
Carpenter, Geoffrey	B.P.R. III, 261.
Carpenter, Richard	H. 43.
Carter, Walter	H. 24.
Caryngton, William de	B.P.R. III, 332; H. 43.
Cauntebrigge, Henry de	C.P.R., 1358–61, 5.
Cauntelough, John	Ry.E. 16.

o

Chamberlain, Ralph — Ry. III, i, 325.
Chandeler, Thomas — H. 3. *159.*
Chandos, John, Kt. — B.P.R. IV, 193. *9, 22–3, 66, 78, 80–1,*
87–9, 90, 104, 115, 128–9, 130, 134,
145, 147, 157–8, 160–1.

Chaumberleyn, Thomas — H. 43.
Chapel, Bartholomew de la — H. 27.
Chaplein, Richard — H. 7.
Charnels, Thomas — Ry. III, i, 325.
Chaumbre, Nicholas de la — C.P.R., 1358–61, 25.
Chaumbre, John de le — Ry.E. 16.
Chester, John — H. 9.
Chevenyng, William de — C.P.R., 1354–8, 569.
Cheyne, Alan — B.P.R. III, 237. *23, 130, 161, 167.*
Chorlegh, William de — B.P.R. III, 238.
Cifrewaz, William — Ry.E. 16.
Cirecieux, John of — Ry. III, i, 325.
Clayne, Hugh — H. 53.
Clifford, Roger de, Kt. — C.P.R., 1354–8, 241. *21, 50.*
Clivedon, Edmond de — Ry.E. 16.
Clonford, John — C.P.R., 1358–61, 31.
Clynton, Robert de — C.P.R., 1358–61, 63. *159.*
Cobham, Reginald, Kt. — B.P.R. IV, 144. *24, 50, 88, 115, 133–*
134, 137, 145, 147, 159, 167, 195.

Coke, Peter — Ry.E. 16.
Coke, Robert — C.P.R., 1354–8, 560.
Cokefeld, John de — C.P.R., 1358–61, 232.
Cokkejacke, John — H. 37.
Colaborn, Richard of — H. 114.
Cole, Adam — Ry. III, i, 325.
Cole, William, of Bikesbury — C.P.R., 1354–8, 626.
Colier, Robert, of Atherstone — C.P.R., 1354–8, 626.
Colkardon, William — H. 6.
Colket, Peter — H. 88.
Collard, John, of — C.P.R., 1354–8, 559.
   Suthkylyngwerth
Colle, Richard — Ry.E. 16.
Colney, John — H. 5.
Colsweynesok, Hugh de — B.P.R. IV, 207. *158.*
Coly, Randolph — C.P.R., 1358–61, 5.
Comyn, Thomas, Kt. — Ry.E. 18.
Cook, Richard le — Ry. III, i, 325.
Cornaw, Bernard — H. 56.
Cornlee, Roger de — Ry.E. 16.
Cornwall, John — H. 7. *92.*
Cornwall, William — H. 29.
Cornyson, William — H. 54.
Corwode, William — Ry.E. 17.
Costantin, Peter — H. 56.

Cotelin, John	H. 63.
Cotesford, Roger, Kt.	B.P.R. IV, 196. *23, 130, 141, 161.*
Cotton, John de	B.P.R. III, 261, *130.*
Cotton, Thomas de	H. 91
Courtney, Edward, Kt.	Ry. III, i, 325.
Cranehow, Thomas de, of Halughton	C.P.R., 1354–8, 626.
Cresway, John	Ry. III, i, 325.
Cretigny, Edmund de	C.P.R., 1358–61, 397.
Cristmasse, John	H. 8.
Crosby, Gilbert of	Ry. III, i, 325.
Crossele, Roger	H. 10.
Crouther, Richard le	B.P.R. III, 241
Crouther, Yevan	B.P.R. III, 272.
Cursoun, Hugh	Ry.E. 17.
Cusyngton, Stephen, Kt.	B.P.R. IV, 178. *23, 130, 161.*
Dagenal, John	Ry. III, i, 325
Dagnet, John	Ry.E. 17.
Dagworth, Nicholas de	Ry.E. 16.
Daldeby, Walter de	Carte, Rolles Gascons, II, 65–6, *159.*
Dalkwyne, Theobald	Ry.E. 17.
Dancastre (an esquire)	H. 90.
Dancastre, Ralph de	C.P.R., 1354–8, 592.
Daneys, Rouland, Kt.	Ry. III, i, 325.
Danyers,[1] John, Kt.	B.P.R. III, 257. *83, 130.*
Dardene, Thomas	B.P.R. III, 212.
Dargentein, John, Kt.	Ry.E. 24.
Dasseles, John, Kt.	Ry.E. 24.
Daubeneye, John	C.P.R., 1358–61, 208.
Daubriggecourt, Eustace (a Hainaulter)	H. 4. *118.*
Dautre, Davy	H. 5.
Daventre, Thomas de	Ry. III, i, 325.
Davy, William	B.P.R. III, 257. *131.*
Dele, Gilbert	Ry.E. 16.
Dene, Robert atte	H. 45.
Derby, William de	C.P.R., 1358–61, 5.
Derlyng, John, of Bukkeby	C.P.R., 1354–8, 592.
Dermington, William	H. 77.
Despenser, Edward le, Kt.	H. 37.
Despenser, Thomas, Kt.	H. 37.
Destafford	See Stafford.
Devel, Henry, of Langeleye	C.P.R., 1354–8, 592.
Dighton, John de	H. 83.
Dighton, Richard	C.P.R., 1358–61, 5.
Ditteworth	H. 3.

---

[1] Often written Danyel.

Dod, William	H. 45.
Doiton, William de	H. 5.
Dokeseye, Richard	C.C.A. 243. *23, 161.*
Domere, Edmund	Ry.E. 16.
Dorchemaud, Simon	Ry.E. 18.
Dosforde, Walter, Kt.	H. 30.
Doun, Thomas	B.P.R. III, 249.
Dounes, Nicholas del	B.P.R. III, 251. *130.*
Dounes, William del	B.P.R. III, 258. *130.*
Dounhed, John	C.P.R., 1354–8, 592
Dover, Thomas de	Ry. III, i, 325
Doyly, John	Ry.E. 16.
Drap, Roger	H. 89.
Draper, John	H. 71.
Drax, Richard	H. 1.
Drayton, Richard	H. 13.
Dufford, Walter	H. 5.
Dure, John	H. 38.
Dyere, John	H. 8.
Dymmok, John	H. 1. *159.*
Ede, Richard	Ry.E. 17.
Edesley, David de	H. 96.
Edmund (a clerk)	H. 7.
Egremont, Robert	H. 28. *23.*
Eign Ony, Ken ap	H. 111.
Elton, John de	C.P.R., 1354–8, 544.
Elwyn, John	C.P.R. 1354–8, 560.
English, John	H. 70.
Estune, Richard	H. 47.
Eton, John de	H. 8.
Etone, John de	Ry.E. 16.
Etton, William de	H. 25.
Eversfelde, William de	Ry.E. 18.
Fairchild, John	B.P.R., III, 258.
Fastolf, Thomas	H. 76.
Felton, Thomas, Kt.	B.P.R. IV, 207. *78, 115, 130, 161.*
Fendik, Hugh de	C.P.R. 1354–8, 626.
Ferrar, Roger	H. 4.
Ferrers, William de	Ry. III, i, 325.
Ferrour, John le (of Edenbrigge)	C.P.R., 1358–61, 31.
Ferour, John (of Bomstede)	Ry., III, i, 325.
Ferour, John del	Ry., III, i, 325.
Ffichet, Thomas, Kt.	H. 5.
Ffish, Gilot,	H. 21.
Fisshere, William	H. 22.

Fitoun, John, Kt.	B.P.R. III, 267.
Fitoun, John (son of Hugh Fitsun)	B.P.R. III, 267.
FitzWilliam, William	C.P.R., 1354–8, 487.
Flecchere, Richard of Wulveton	C.P.R., 1354–8, 592.
Flecchere, William	B.P.R. III, 249.
Flegg, Henry	C.P.R., 1354–8, 30.
Flete, Laurence	Ry. III, i, 323.
Fog, John	B.P.R. III, 251.
Folyot, Peter	C.P.R, 1354–8, 592, 603.
Forest, Walter	Ry.E. 16.
Fouler, Robert	H. 110.
Foulsloe, Richard	C.P.R., 1354–8, 560.
Fouler, William	H. 46.
Frere (an archer)	H. 88.
Frodsham, Thomas	B.P.R. III, 238.
Galard, John	H. 115.
Galei, Alan	H. 14.
Gamage, John	C.P.R., 1354–8, 592.
Gamel, Thomas	B.P.R. III, 251.
Garland, William	H. 83.
Garsyde, Peter	H. 20.
Gate, Henry atte	C.P.R., 1354–8, 560.
Geephay (Gupphey), Walter	Ry.E. 16.
Gentilthorpe	H. 62.
Gentiltois, Nicholas	H. 57.
Gerlesthorpe, Thomas de	H. 4.
Gilbert, Reginald	H. 11.
Gildesburgh, John de	H. 90.
Giles, William	H. 9.
Gille, Roger	B.P.R. III, 308.
Gilliam, William	Ry.E. 18.
Gippeswick, John de, Kt.	H. 43.
Gissing, Thomas de, Kt.	Ry. III, i, 325.
Gistels, John, Kt.	H. 4.
Gloucester, Vincent de	H. 1.
Golbourne, Hugh de	B.P.R. III, 204.
Golbourne, William de	B.P.R. III, 308.
Goldesbourne, William	H. 114.
Goldesworth, Hankyn	H. 40.
Goldsmith, Hankyn	H. 42.
Goker, Richard	H. 4.
Goodman, Hugh	Ry.E. 17.
Gormancester, John	H. 8.
Goton, Baldwin	H. 6.
Gouleshulle, Nicholas de	Ry.E. 16.
Gralbere, William	H. 5.
Gray, Richard	H. 5.

Graye, John	H. 46.
Gregory, Gilbert	H. 7.
Grey, Matthew, Kt.	H. 5.
Griffith, Gronou ap	H. 4. *17*.
Griffith, Howell ap, Kt.	H. 4. *17*.
Griffith, Rees ap	H. 5. *159*.
Griffith, Thomas ap	H. 96
Griffyn, John, Kt.	B.P.R. III, 204. *17*.
Grimsditch, Simon de	B.P.R. IV, 254. *130*.
Grobbare, John	C.P.R., 1354–8, 626.
Grobbare, Robert	C.P.R., 1354–8, 626.
Gurney, Matthew, Kt.	H. 8.
Halday, John	H. 12.
Hale, Robert de	H. 46.
Hales, Stephen de	H. 7.
Halford, Robert	H. 83.
Haliday	H. 8.
Halle, William atte	H. 45.
Hamelyn, Geoffrey	Issue Roll, 30 Ed. III (Mich.), m. 3. *136*, *138*, *141*, *194*.
Hampton, John	H. 8.
Hampton, Reginald	H. 71.
Hampton, Thomas, Kt.	Baker, 129. *50*.
Hamstede, Richard	Ry.E. 16.
Hankyn (goldsmith)	H. 7.
Hankyn (minstrel)	*85*.
Hanville, James de, Kt.	Ry.E. 15.
Hanz (taborer)	H. 8.
Harding, John	B.P.R. III, 239.
Hardres, Thomas de	H. 6.
Hargreve, John	H. 38.
Harpenden, William de	H. 10. *161*.
Harpers, Richard	H. 37.
Haselton, John	H. 53.
Haselyngton, Thomas de	B.P.R. III, 261.
Hassale, Ralph	H. 81.
Hatton, Thomas	H. 96.
Hauberger, Ralph	H. 115.
Haverigg, John de	Ry. III, i, 325.
Haveryngge, John de, Kt.	Ry.R. 15.
Haye, John de la	B.P.R. IV, 209. *83*, *130*, *161*.
Hedene, Peter de	H. 24.
Hele, Thomas	H. 99.
Henxteworth, John	H. 63. *81–2*, *84–5*, *192–3*, *195*.
Henxtman, Nicholas	H. 93.
Herthull, Robert	B.P.R. III, 248.
Hervey, Walter, of Ravenser	C.P.R., 1354–8, 560.
Hethersiud, Edmund de	Ry.E. 16.

Hewe, Hamo	H. 38.
Hewe, Hervey le	H. 23.
Hewissh, Richard, Kt.	H. 5.
Hide, John, Kt.	B.P.R. III, 204. *17, 19, 131.*
Hikedon, Richard	B.P.R. III, 398.
Hikedon, Robert	B.P.R. III, 263.
Hill, John del	C.P.R., 1354–8, 592.
Hinton, Walter	H. 28.
Hobba, Stephen, of Kayrow	C.P.R., 1354–8, 626.
Hoghtone, John de	Ry.E. 15.
Holefold, Roger	Ry.E. 16.
Holewold, Roger de	C.P.R., 1354–8, 560.
Holford, William de	B.P.R. III, 231. *130.*
Holiday, John	Ry. III, i, 325.
Honford, Roger de	B.P.R. III, 241. *131.*
Hoo, John de	Ry.E. 16.
Hore, John le, of Northiam	C.P.R., 1354–8, 560.
Hotoft, Nicholas de	Ry.E. 15.
Hotoft, Robert, Kt.	H. 5, 10.
Hoton, Robert de	B.P.R. III, 241.
Houden, William of Rouclif	C.P.R., 1354–8, 592.
Houel, Richard	H. 50.
Houghton (an esquire)	H. 33.
Hounte, John	H. 5.
Hunte, Nicholas, of Warwick	C.P.R., 1354–8, 569.
Hunte, Peter	H. 46.
Hunte, Walter	H. 5.
Husee, Hugh de, Kt.	Ry.E. 17–18.
Huxley, William de	B.P.R. III, 263.
Hynton, William	H. 22.
Ilegh, Richard, Kt.	H. 91. *161.*
Ipswich, John de	Ry.E. 16.
Isle, Robert del	H. 22.
Jacke, David ap	B.P.R. III, 289.
Jakeyln (minstrel)	H. 8.
James (a valettus)	H. 68.
Jeu, John	Ry.E. 17.
Jodrell, John	B.P.R. IV, 254.
Jodrell, William	B.P.R. III, 238. *86.*
Karneworth (an archer)	H. 88.
Kelsall, Randolph de	B.P.R. III, 246, 270.
Kempe, Oliver	C.P.R., 1354–8, 560.
Kendal, John	H. 42.
Kene, John	C.P.R., 1354–8, 626.
Kent, Walter of	Ry. III, 1, 326.
Kentissh, Adam	H. 87. *93.*

Kenton, Ivo de	Ry. III, i, 326.
Kentwode, John de	B.P.R. IV, 285. *134, 158*.
Kerre, Richard del	C.P.R., 1354–8, 560.
Ketel, John	B.P.R. III, 313
Keyfer (a minstrel)	H. 9.
Kirkeby, John de	Ry.E. 16.
Kirkeby, Peter de	B.P.R. III, 251.
Kirkeby, Robert, of Clenfeld	C.P.R., 1354–8, 560.
Kitlington, Robert de	Ry. III, i, 326.
Knight, Robert, of Estnorton	C.P.R., 1354–8, 626.
Kyngestok, John	H. 7.
Kyngeston, William	C.P.R., 1358–61, 129.
Lacy, Peter de, Kt.	H. 42.
Ladde, John	C.P.R., 1358–61, 31.
Lambard, Andrew	C.P.R., 1358–61, 16.
Lambourne, William de	H. 7.
Lameleye, William, of Calverton	C.P.R., 1354–8, 559.
Lane, William in the	C.P.R., 1358–61, 235.
Langhenhall, Simon	C.P.R., 1354–8, 487.
Larton	H. 55.
Lathum, Roger de	Ry.E. 16.
Laurence, John	H. 7.
Lauton, John	H. 43.
Lauton, William	H. 10.
Lawe, Robert, of Melton	C.P.R., 1354–8, 626.
Laxton, Thomas	H. 63.
Lee, Richard atte	H. 13.
Legeard, William	H. 111.
Legh, Robert de	B.P.R. III, 258. *17, 130*.
Leghton, John de	B.P.R. III, 308.
Lenche, John	H. 26.
Lenche, William	B.P.R. II, 98. *23, 161*.
Leominster, Richard	B.P.R. IV, 255. *64, 161*.
Lewes, John	H. 7.
Leybourne, John[1]	H. 66.
Leybourne, Robert[1]	H. 67.
Lincoln, Simon de	Ry.E. 16.
Lisle, John de, Kt.	B.P.R. IV, 144. *20, 50, 52, 73, 79, 195*.
Llewelyn	(See Thlewelin).
Lodelowe, John de	C.P.R., 1354–8, 559, 599.
Lodelowe, Walter	C.P.R., 1354–8, 599.
Lomere, Nicholas de	Ry.E. 16.
Loring, Nigel, Kt.	B.P.R. IV, 206. *22–3, 83, 130, 141, 145, 161*.
Loring, Roger	Ry.E. 16.

---

[1] As Henxteworth's spelling of Libourne is Leybourne, these men may have been Gascons.

Morant, Thomas, Kt.	Ry. III, i, 325.
Moraunt, Thomas	Ry.E. 16.
Morbek, Denis de (an artesian)	C.P.R., 1358–61, 100. *133, 147, 150, 159, 194.*
Morlee, William de, Kt.	Ry. III, i, 325.
Morriers, William	H. 4, 11.
Mottrum, Adam de	B.P.R. III, 254.
Mottrum, Hugh de	B.P.R. III, 254.
Mou, Philip le	B.P.R. III, 242.
Mounte, Edmund	H. 82.
Mountviron, John	H. 40.
Mulyngton, Hugh de	B.P.R. III, 240.
Munden, Edmund de	C.P.R., 1358–61, 258.
Murens, William de	Ry.E. 16.
Murimuth, William	H. 37.
Musseldene, Robert de	Ry.E. 16.
Musshonte (a herald)	H. 7.
Mutsshale, Roger	H. 71.
Neston, Henry	B.P.R. III, 237.
Neufee, John (a Burgundian)	B.P.R. IV, 269. *147.*
Neuse, John	H. 68.
Neville, Robert, Kt.	B.P.R. III, 306. *158, 161.*
Newbold, Robert de	B.P.R. III, 240.
Newton, William de	B.P.R. III, 241. *131.*
Norwich, John	H. 5.
Northley, John de	B.P.R. III, 258.
Northley, Peter de	B.P.R. III, 309.
Northwelle, William de	Ry.E. 16.
Norton, Simon de	B.P.R. II, 124.
Nortone, William	H. 92.
Notehowe, John de	C.P.R., 1358–61, 94.
Notingham, Simon de	H. 81.
Offord, Walter, Kt.	H. 28.
Okeston, Randolph de	B.P.R. IV, 207. *158.*
Ottewell, John de	Ry. III, i, 325.
Overton, John de	B.P.R. III, 237.
Oxencombe, Roger de	Ry. III, i, 325.
Oxford (Earl of)	See Vere, John de.
Pachet, Ralph, of Oversheyle	C.P.R., 1354–8, 559.
Page, Richard	H. 96.
Palington, John	B.P.R. IV, 193. *23, 131, 161.*
Panes, Nicholas	Ry.E. 16.
Pannachardon, Roger	H. 8.
Parker, Wm.	H. 31.
Parkyn, Robert	B.P.R. III, 276.
Passager, William	C.P.R., 1354–8, 559.

Paveley, Walter, Kt.	Ry.E. 17.
Paver, Hugh le	B.P.R. III, 24.
Pecche, Laurence	H. 6. *193.*
Penbrigge, John	H. 8.
Penreth, William de	Ry.E. 16.
Penyngton, Robert de	C.P.R., 1358-61, 127.
Percy, Roger, Kt.	H. 5.
Perkin, Robert	H. 96
Pesyndenne, William de	Ry.E. 16.
Petrestree, Robert de	Ry.E. 16.
Pey, Roger	H. 22.
Peykirke, William	H. 29.
Peytevin, Thomas	H. 6.
Philip (a chaplain)	H. 7.
Pidyngton, William	H. 45.
Pinkilchirche, Walter	H. 47.
Piper (Hankin the)	H. 7.
Pipot, Robert	H. 8. *92.*
Pirie, Adam atte, of Patyngham	C.P.R., 1354-8, 592.
Pitteworthe, Richard	H. 85.
Plays, Richard de, Kt.	B.P.R. IV, 289. *83, 162.*
Platemaker, Richard	H. 97.
Plessaunt, Oswald	H. 7.
Pogeau, Peter	H. 39.
Pointz, Nicholas de	Ry.E. 16.
Pole, Thomas de la	Ry. III, i, 325.
Polyley, John de	C.P.R., 1354-8, 559.
Pomeray, William de	Ry.E. 16.
Portour, Richard	H. 40.
Poudram, Matthew	H. 81.
Poudreham, Matthew de	Ry.E. 16.
Pountfreyt, William de	Ry.E. 16.
Power, Otuel le	C.P.R., 1354-8, 586.
Preston, John, Kt.	H. 58.
Proyn, William	H. 53.
Pullet, Walter	H. 7.
Punchardon, Richard	B.P.R. IV, 307. *162.*
Pygot, Bartholomew	Ry.E. 16.
Pynk, David	B.P.R. III, 272.
Queynterel, John	H. 37.
Raby, Thomas de	B.P.R. III, 248.
Radefforde, Thomas de	H. 8.
Ragaz, Roger	H. 40. *93.*
Raggele, Richard	H. 1.
Ramage, John	C.P.R., 1354-8, 582.
Rasen, Thomas	H. 28.

Saltere, John	Ry.E. 15.
Sandwich, Thomas de	B.P.R. IV, 197–8. *162.*
Sarazin, Francis	H. 11.
Sarnesfeld, John de	B.P.R. III, 251. *130, 162.*
Sauter, John (crier)	H. 35.
Savage, John, of Yevele	C.P.R., 1354–8, 559.
Savage, Richard	B.P.R. III, 255.
Scot, William	B.P.R. III, 261
Seggeswyk, John	C.P.R., 1354–8, 587.
Selby (chamberlain of R. Daneys)	H. 48.
Sellator, Thomas	H. 70.
Semton, Thomas de, Kt.	H. 79.
Semton, William de	H. 79.
Sergeant, Richard le	B.P.R. III, 249.
Shank, William	B.P.R. IV, 203. *130, 162.*
Shareshull, John	H. 4.
Sharp, Thomas	B.P.R. III, 248.
Shelton, Ralph de, Kt.	C.C.R., 1354–60, 334. *159.*
Sherewynd, Nicholas	C.P.R., 1354–8, 592.
Shilynghilde, Nicholas de	C.P.R., 1354–8, 576.
Shippeley, Richard de	C.P.R., 1354–8, 524.
Shirebourne, Thomas	H. 28.
Shupton, Thomas	H. 19.
Sich, William	H. 93.
Siggeswyk, Adam de	C.P.R., 1354–8, 544.
Sigyn, Reginald	H. 9.
Simon the clerk	H. 64.
Simondsone, Roger	B.P.R. III, 253. *131.*
Skauseby, John, of Wamwel	C.P.R., 1354–8, 560.
Skelton, John	H. 88.
Skot, John	H. 43, 115.
Skrop, William, Kt.	H. 4.
Smyth, John	C.P.R., 1358–61, 28.
Smyth, Roger le	B.P.R. III, 313.
Sneyth, John	H. 38.
Solers, John	H. 79.
Somertone, William	H. 7.
Spark, William	B.P.R., III 263.
Sparry, Richard, Kt.	H. 3.
Spencer, John	C.P.R., 1358–61, 6.
Spicer, John le	H. 6.
Stafford, Nicholas	H. 5.
Stafford, Richard de, Kt.	B.P.R. IV, 210. *22–3, 79, 80–1, 83, 85, 91–4, 137, 145, 162, 167.*
Stafford, Simon	H. 47.
Stafford, William de	H. 86.
Stalynburgh, John	C.P.R., 1358–61, 102.
Stanes, Richard	H. 27, 64.

Stanford, Gilbert de	Ry. III, i, 326.
Stapleton, Brian de	Ry.E. 16.
Starkey, Hugh	B.P.R. III, 247.
Starkey, John	B.P.R. III, 244.
Starkey, Nicholas, of Preston	C.P.R., 1354–8, 559.
Starkey, Richard	C.C.R., 1354–60, 371.
Statham, Thomas de	H. 1, 7, 22.
Statone, William de	H. 4.
Steel, William, Kt.	H. 37.
Stewehalle, William de	B.P.R. III, 337.
Stockport, William de	B.P.R. III, 258. *131*.
Stoke, Randolph de	B.P.R. III, 255. *130*.
Stokes, Alan de	H. 18.
Stokton, John de	B.P.R. III, 239.
Stokton, Davy de	H. 47.
Stone, John	Ry.E, 16.
Stonham, Richard	H. 21.
Stormy, Bonaldus	Ry.E. 16.
Stratton, Gilot de	Baker, 129.
Stretford, John de	C.P.R., 1354–8, 522.
Stretton, William de	Ry. III, i, 325.
Styuecle, Thomas de, Kt.	Ry.E. 15.
Suffolk (Earl of)	See Ufford, Robert.
Sully, John, Kt.	B.P.R. II, 99. *19, 130, 162*.
Sunningworth, William, Kt.	H. 6.
Sutton, Thomas	H. 4.
Sutton, William de	H. 23.
Swafham, Robert de	C.P.R., 1354–8, 592.
Swan, Robert	H. 53.
Swettenham, Richard de	B.P.R. III, 299.
Swettenham, Roger de	B.P.R. III, 254.
Swynburn, Robert of	Ry. III, i, 326.
Synthwaite, William de	Ry.E. 15.
Taillour, John le	B.P.R. III, 265.
Talbot, Gilbert, Kt.	H. 21.
Talbot, Richard, Kt.	B.P.R. IV, 214.
Tamerdre, John	H. 37.
Teukesbury, Thomas de	H. 37.
Thecchere, John le, of Herleston	C.P.R., 1354–8, 561.
Thenewall, William de	B.P.R. III, 255. *130*.
Thlewelin, William ap	H. 71.
Thomas (a messenger)	H. 50. *130, 138, 194*.
Thoralby, William de	C.P.R., 1358–61, 375.
Thornley, David de	B.P.R. III, 255. *130*.
Thornton, John, of Burton in Lonsdale.	C.P.R., 1354–8, 560
Thorp, William	H. 10.
Tildesle, Thorstande	H. 53.

Tilewale	H. 9.
Tilly, John, Kt.	H. 5.
Tounneshed, John, of Bodyham	C.P.R., 1354–8, 560.
Trailly, John	B.P.R. IV, 339. *133*.
Tregate, William	H. 26.
Tregatou, Gilbert	H. 28, 46.
Treveignon, John, Kt.	H. 5.
Treveignon, Robert	Ry.E. 17.
Tright, John de	C.P.R., 1354–8, 634.
Trykingham, Lambert	H. 52.
Trumper, Ralph	H. 7.
Trussell, Wm., Kt.	B.P.R. IV, 261. *23, 132, 162*.
Tryvet, John	Ry.E. 17.
Tuwe, John de	B.P.R. III, 249.
Tuwe (Tuey), William	H. 37.
Twenbrook, John de	B.P.R. III, 251.
Twenbrook, Thomas de	B.P.R. III, 251.
Twisden, Walter, of Gouderst	C.P.R., 1354–8, 626.
Tynewelle, Simon de	H. 47.
Ufford, Robert, Earl of Suffolk	B.P.R. IV, 144. *20, 22, 24, 37, 52, 81, 88, 93, 115, 132, 134, 145, 159*.
Underwode, Robert, of Belton	C.P.R., 1354–8, 592.
Valle, Bernard de	H. 49.
Vaughan, David ap Blethin	*83*.
Veel, Peter de, Kt.	Ry.E. 16.
Veel, Peter de, Kt. (son)	Ry.E. 17.
Veer, Alfred, Kt.	H. 31, 47, 90.
Veer, Aubrey	H. 22.
Vegge, John, of Wachet	C.P.R., 1354–8, 559.
Vere, John de, Earl of Oxford	B.P.R. IV, 144. *20, 22, 24, 50, 88, 115, 128, 134*.
Vernon, William	H. 37.
Wade, William, of Qualynpoul	C.P.R., 1354–8, 559.
Waffrer, John	H. 7.
Wakefeld, William de	H. 9, 59.
Walisman, Clement le	B.P.R. III, 318.
Walk	H. 55.
Walkere, William	H. 88.
Walkfare, Thomas, Kt.	H. 36. *159, 162*.
Walsham, Robert	H. 8.
Walsingham, William, Kt.	H. 8.
Walssh, Geoffrey	Ry.E. 16.
Walssh, Thomas, of Halstede	Ry.E. 15.
Waltare, Stephen, of Walshale	C.P.R., 1354–8, 630.
Waltham, William de	C.P.R., 1354–8, 626.
Warde, Robert	B.P.R. III, 240.

Ware, John	H. 47.
Warn, Henry	H. 5.
Warnburgh, John de	H. 5.
Warre, Roger de la, Kt.	H. 4. *50, 159.*
Warremund, Arnold de	H. 76.
Warwick, Earl of	See Beauchamp, Thomas.
Watre, Thomas atte	B.P.R. III, 248.
Wauncy, Edward, Kt.	H. 60. *130, 134, 158, 162.*
Weaverham, Thomas de	B.P.R. III, 264–5.
Webbe, Simon le, of Wandlesworth	H. 46.
Wegt, Richard atte	H. 79.
Welesby, William of	See Chapter VIII, n. 16. *157.*
Welles, John	H. 68. *193.*
Wendesworth, Simon de	H. 8.
Wengfeld, John, Kt.	Avesbury, 437. *22–3, 53–4, 73, 75, 78–9, 81, 85, 88, 91, 159.*
Werde, John	H. 46.
Werselee, John de	Ry.E. 16.
Wesenham, Hugh de	Ry.E. 15.
Weternot, William	H. 47.
Whalesbrewe, John	H. 4.
Whirle, Geoffrey	H. 28, 56, 70.
Whyte, Geoffrey	H. 7.
Widweel, John	C.P.R., 1358–61, 263.
Wight, William de	B.P.R. III, 240.
Wikes, John de	H. 71.
Wiking, John	H. 36.
Wikwane, William	H. 49, 110.
William (valettus of B. de Burghersh)	H. 16.
Willoughby, John de, Kt.	H. 6. *19, 50.*
Wisman, Stacy	H. 43.
Wode, John atte	C.P.R., 1354–8, 560.
Wode, Benet del	B.P.R. III, 258.
Wode, Stephen atte	C.P.R., 1354–8, 592.
Wodeham, Reginald de	H. 24.
Wodehous, Thomas de	B.P.R. III, 268.
Wodehull, David de	B.P.R. III, 239.
Wodehull, William de	H. 79.
Wodeland, Walter de, Kt.	H. 6. *130.*
Wodhull, Walter de	H. 79.
Woodford, William de	B.P.R. III, 251.
Wright, Nicholas le, of Bleseworth	C.P.R., 1354–8, 559.
Writhok, Henry	C.P.R., 1354–8, 626.
Wrotham, William de	H. 5.
Wyclif, Robert	H. 4, 71.
Wyght, William	H. 64.

Wyght, Walter, of Gainsborough	Ry.E. 16.
Wyghton, John de	C.P.R., 1354–8, 560.
Wynington, Robert de	B.P.R. IV, 205.
Wynington, William de	B.P.R. IV, 242.
Zouche, William la, of Lobesthorpe	Ry.E. 16.

Froissart adds Peter Audley, the lord Warin and the lord Richard of Pembroke.

GASCONS

Albret (Lebret), Bernard Ezi, lord of	Baker, 140. *28, 36, 44, 88, 101–2.*
Albret, sons of the above	Baker, 132.
Buch, John de Grailly, Captal de	Ry. III, i, 346. *10, 28, 44, 53, 88–9, 115, 121–3, 145, 147, 157–9, 164.*
Capene, lord of	Pell Records, 174. *158.*
Caumont, lord of	H. 83.
Curton, Petiton de	H. 25. *165.*
Fossade, Aymeric de	H. 83.
Frank, Bertrand	H. 30.
Lebret	See Albret.
Lesparre, Guillaume Sans, lord of	B.P.R. IV, 391. *44, 165.*
Mauleon, Bascot de	Froissart, XI, 108. *157.*
Monte Pesato, lord of	E.A. 172/3, No. 19. *165.*
Montbaden, Reymond de	H. 30.
Montferrand, Aymery de Biron, lord of	H. 49. *44, 52, 88, 145, 159.*
Mussidan, Auger de Montaut, lord of	H. 83. *44, 89, 147, 164.*
Pelagria, Raymond de[1]	E.A. 172/3, No. 42. *165.*
Pommiers, Amanieu de	H. 25. *165.*
Pommiers, Elie de	Issue Roll, 31 Ed. III, Easter, m 27. *88, 159.*
Pommiers, Eustace de	H. 25.
Pommiers, Guillaume	Baker, 129. *44, 52, 145.*
Pommiers, Jean de	E.A. 172/3, No. 49. *165.*
Raymond, Arnold	H. 86. *158.*
Sonynyak, Emericus	H. 48.
Tartas, Gerard de	H. 30. *165.*
Tastes, Aymeric de	H. 30. *165, 147.*
Trau, Soldan de	Excheq. Q. R., E.A. 172/3, No. 51. *165.*
Troyes, Bernard de	C.P.R., 1358–61, 320. *133, 147.*
Urtria, Vicomte de	C.C.R., 1358–61, 384. *159.*

[1] Pellegrue. See Boutruche, 353, n.3.

P

ALMAINS

Dale, Tiderick van	B.P.R. IV, 207. *39, 130, 161*.
Fromaldo (esquire of Zedeles)	H. 79.
Gransekyn, Seyner (esquire of Zedeles)	H. 79.
Landestrene, John de (esquire of Zedeles)	H. 79.
Pesse, Daniel van	H. 3. *44, 130, 101*.
Pipard, Gotherin	H. 80.
Qwad, William	H. 3. *44, 82*.
Rode, John	B.P.R. IV, 252.
Strenckin, John	H. 65.
Trouer, Hans	B.P.R. IV, 234. *130, 162*.
Zedeles, Bernard van	B.P.R. IV, 234. *44, 130, 159, 162, 166*.
Zobbe, Ingelbrith	H. 3. *44, 82*.

SPANIARDS

Deossent, of Spain	B.P.R. IV, 252. *147*.
Gunsals, John	B.P.R. IV, 269. *147*.
Lopes, Benedict	B.P.R. IV, 269.
Martyn, Ferrand	B.P.R. IV, 269.
Rays, John	H. 61.

Note: Not all the names found in Henxteworth are included in the above lists. There remain some which I cannot classify under nationality and some which seem more likely to be dealers or messengers than members of the expeditionary force.

INDEX OF PERSONS AND PLACES

Names of members of the expeditionary force are in the Nominal Roll (Appendix C)

INDEX OF SUBJECTS